Genesis

of the Nation *of*

"WE THE PEOPLE"

A comprehensive view of ancient and current history regarding the formation of our nation and the Rule of Law development through the ages.

James Robert Boynton

Acknowledgments

I would like to express my heartfelt gratitude to those who have supported me throughout the journey of writing this book. My deepest thanks go to my wife of 42 years, Linda D. Boynton, for her unwavering support and encouragement. I also extend my appreciation to my daughter, Kimberly Anne Boynton, for her invaluable assistance with technical computer issues. Lastly, I am grateful to my sister, Susan Boynton, for her guidance and support.

Dedication

This book incorporates materials from notable figures of ancient times and includes contributions from individuals and organizations whose critical information shaped these pages. I dedicate the success of this manuscript to these sources, my personal reviewers, and the publishing team's efforts that made this work possible.

About the Author:
Hon. James (Jim) Boynton

Jim Boynton holds dual majors in Business and Accounting, with a minor in Computer Science. He pursued a Direct Masters/Doctoral program for a Doctor of Philosophy in Operations Management. An accomplished author and speaker, Jim has been published in conference journals, periodicals, and editorials, and is known for his work, The New Green Deal; Back to the Stone Age (under the pseudonym Shane Roberts).

With 55 years of industry, consulting, and farming experience, Jim has held significant roles, including President and CEO of Focus NH Institute, and leadership positions in international organizations such as APICS and ASQ. He has contributed to educational reforms, including curriculum development at the University of New Hampshire and New Hampshire Community Technical College.

Jim's political career includes serving as a New Hampshire State Representative and County Commissioner. He was also a candidate for the State Senate and an active participant in various community and state initiatives, including water resources and economic development.

His military service spanned over two decades, including active and reserve duty in the Navy and Massachusetts National Guard, where he held various leadership and operational roles.

Retiring in 2004, Jim moved to Tennessee, where he bred rare Desert Arabian horses until an injury ended his career in 2014. He now resides in a secluded community, enjoying a peaceful life amidst nature.

Contents

An Opening Prayer

Dear lord, please energize my mind and heart to research and deliver a manuscript worthy of Your grace. In our time of growing civic and political division, a clear view of the principles that guided our founders in establishing the Rules of Law is sorely needed. Open the hearts of the many to clearly understand our ancient and cherished Rule of Law principles and guiding documents to assist in healing the unholy divisions plaguing our country.

Chapter 1

Why Is History Important and How Can It Benefit Your Future?

History is a topic that many find boring to study or a waste of time. But there is more to studying history than meets the eye. Let's answer the age-old question: "Why is history important?"

History is the knowledge of and study of the past. It is the story of the past and a form of collective memory. History is the story of who we are, where we come from, and can potentially reveal where we are headed.

Place yourself in the role of the ancients. When someone invented something, and it got passed on to others, let's say a spear was invented with this nifty spear point. You watched it being made, and the other inventor moved on, and you did, too. Years later, you lost your spear or spear point in a Mastodon hunt and needed another. You said to yourself, "Self, how did that person do this?" And you figured it out.

Now, you just experienced knowledge learned from what we can simply define as reaching back in history, so you wouldn't need to reinvent the wheel again, as they say. Yup, it's a simple thing, but since you bought this book, after reading it, you will now understand the meaning of the word "Genesis." It really does mean moving forward.

Why not borrow the good things you find and apply them to your situation? That, my reader, is what our founders did, and I will try to show you how they did it by applying ancient thought processes for our benefit throughout the ages.

History is important to study because it is essential for all of us to understand ourselves and the world around us. There is a history for every field and topic, from medicine to music to art, and it started eons ago. To know and understand history is absolutely necessary, even though the results of historical study are not readily visible, and less immediate unless you search for them, but they are there in some useable form. I know, I researched history to produce this book.

Along with History comes responsibility and concerns such as personal attributes one should possess, Civic pride, Ethics, and Morality and how to apply them to advance the goals of a free society.

A Very Special and Deeply Rooted Thought Before You Read This Manuscript

Genesis: Its Literal Meaning Defined

What does the word Genesis literally mean?

The first book of the Old Testament; its first words are "In the beginning" (Genesis is a Greek word for "beginning") Dictionary.com.

genesis. noun. gen·e·sis ˈjen-ə-səs. plural geneses -ˌsēz. : the origin or coming into being of something: the process or mode of origin.

When researching materials for this book, many sources came to light, some very profound and revealing, having an effect on me. One very thought – it actually woke me up very early this morning. It was what I can loosely call a miracle of creation, an epiphany, if you will. I write about people coming together to create a nation to free themselves from being a colony of states under oppressive rule. The thought-epiphany was how it did. We know about Washington, Jefferson, Franklin, Locke, and others, but what drove them? Were there guiding lights to direct their thoughts? I found my answer in what these powerful personages were guided by. The mystery was their belief in the people. They believed in and were guided by ancient secret organizations, which are revealed in this writing. The wonderment, as if guided by an overreaching hand, is that each of them melded their ancient secret teachings to bring us a nation of Rule of Law. I speak of Freemasons, Illuminati, Rosicrucian, Templars, the Decoding of the Great Seal, Indigenous Natives' spirit, and the unfailing guiding hand of God.

Travel with me on this journey to discover how this miracle evolves.

The Meaning of the Great Seal of The United States

What is the Great Seal?

The Great Seal of the United States is the official emblem and heraldic device of the United States of America. It was adopted by the Continental Congress on June 20, 1782, to represent the nation and to demonstrate to other nations of the world the ideas and values of its Founders and people. Great Seals have their origins in the royal seals of the 7th, 8th, and 9th centuries.

The Great Seal is used to authenticate important official U. S. documents such as treaties, presidential proclamations, appointments of government officials, congressional resolutions, executive orders, and presidential communications to heads of foreign nations. It is even featured on some currency notes and coins, including the U. S. $1 bill, providing U. S. citizens with a ready reference to the nation's foundational ideas. It is used 2,000-3,000 times per year to seal documents. The custody of the Great Seal is assigned to the U.S. Department of State. The seal can be affixed by an officer of the Secretary of State.

The Great Seal was first used officially on September 16, 1782, to guarantee the authenticity of a document that granted full power to General George Washington "to negotiate and sign with the British an agreement for the exchange, subsistence, and better treatment of prisoners of war." Thomas Jefferson was the first Secretary of State to have custody of the Great Seal.

What Does the Great Seal Represent?

"Symbolically, the Seal reflects the beliefs and values that the Founding Fathers attached to the new nation and wished to pass on to their descendants."

– *U.S. Department of State, Bureau of Public Affairs*

The Great Seal Design

The Great Seal has two sides and displays several important symbols. The front (obverse) side of the seal shows the coat of arms of the United States. The U.S. coat of arms is officially used for coins, postage stamps, stationary, publications, flags, military uniforms, public monuments, public buildings, embassies and consulates, passports, and items owned by the U.S. government.

OBVERSE

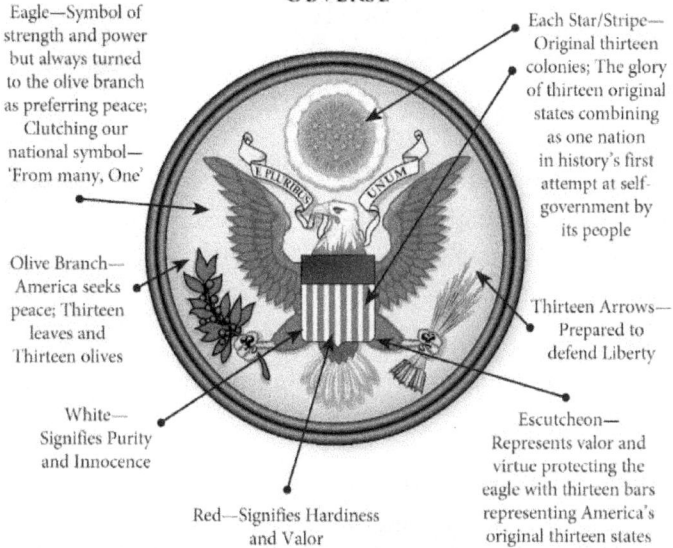

Eagle—Symbol of strength and power but always turned to the olive branch as preferring peace; Clutching our national symbol—'From many, One'

Each Star/Stripe—Original thirteen colonies; The glory of thirteen original states combining as one nation in history's first attempt at self-government by its people

Olive Branch—America seeks peace; Thirteen leaves and Thirteen olives

Thirteen Arrows—Prepared to defend Liberty

White—Signifies Purity and Innocence

Escutcheon—Represents valor and virtue protecting the eagle with thirteen bars representing America's original thirteen states

Red—Signifies Hardiness and Valor

REVERSE

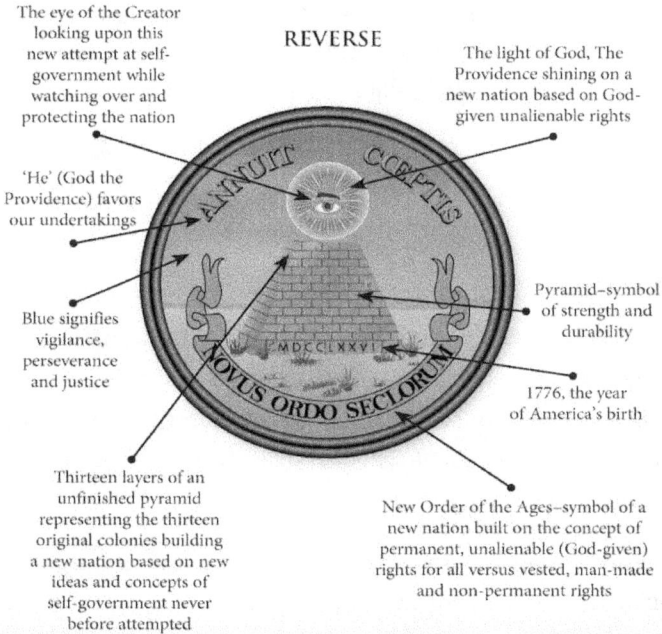

The eye of the Creator looking upon this new attempt at self-government while watching over and protecting the nation

The light of God, The Providence shining on a new nation based on God-given unalienable rights

'He' (God the Providence) favors our undertakings

Pyramid—symbol of strength and durability

Blue signifies vigilance, perseverance and justice

1776, the year of America's birth

Thirteen layers of an unfinished pyramid representing the thirteen original colonies building a new nation based on new ideas and concepts of self-government never before attempted

New Order of the Ages—symbol of a new nation built on the concept of permanent, unalienable (God-given) rights for all versus vested, man-made and non-permanent rights

Attribute to American Heritage Education Foundation Inc. for the Seal to include the original wording and the arrows.

Chapter 2

Forward

Have you ever stood in front of the Lincoln Memorial? Or our Capitol on 900 Pennsylvania Avenue? Did you wonder how something so impressive, so emotionally moving, and wonderful could even exist? Likewise, did you ever wonder about your own government? The one who is responsible for creating those monuments and all the other treasures we cherish representing and heralding your freedoms.

How could these even exist? Who or what might be responsible? How old is this government? How and when did it start? Who or what is in charge? What really holds its structure together? Is it alive? Will it last? So many questions and answers that need to be presented for your review. What this writing will bring forward will astound you and, I believe, will make you thirst for much more, as it did for me!

Some say history is in the past, so let's scrap it and move on, but is this wise?

I think not; wise men and women learn and build on history so as not to make the same mistake again. Learned individuals learn and grow by studying history, but our educators have decided that history is bunk and removed it from our educational institutions. However, thanks to the independent school systems, we are back to teaching traditional subject matter.

Obviously, I disagree with our government and teachers' unions, and as much as I dislike reporting this, our educational institutions prepare teachers for all levels of education who teach our public-school students. Now, the sad news is that this drastic change started in the late 1980's. Want proof? How were, or are, your children today? Are they prepared for current times and the future the way you were prior to the Department of Education changes? A study I prepared for my doctoral dissertation regarding students entering college was startling evidence of our lack of preparedness in higher education and support for the workplaces of our nation.

All good questions and advise, you know, I am talking about the United States of America, your and my home, the *"Land of the Free and Brave."* Just ask someone who has fought for our freedom and lifestyle. This manuscript will address all these questions with historical accuracy and facts in detail that will astound you that most books would not cover. I am sure you will be drawn to the riveting and exciting events of our country's formation, hopefully enticing you to get involved in this wonderful continuing story that has turned the world on its head in just 400 years.

Have you really looked closely at a dollar bill or our coinage? Why is there a pyramid and an eye on our dollar bill and the striking images on our coinage? How did Washington, DC, evolve in its construction? Did the design of the dollar and the layout of Washington, D.C., by others, cause major influences on the formation of our nation today? Can we relate to the involvement of the Free Masons, Templars, Rosicrucian, American Indigenous Natives, and others rumored, or proven, to be influencers in our country's formation? You will discover how the Revolutionary War was fought and who represented secretive assistance in our involvement with the British Crown.

Chapter 3

Preface

There are many very important reasons for me to pen this manuscript, all of which are very serious. Our nation and its Rule of Law are suffering. There are many pressing issues stemming from our declining educational system that have eliminated the knowledge of what this nation is and how it works. My overriding hope for this manuscript is to research and then report to all, in these pages, what it took the founders to create a durable set of documents and a Rule of Law that has governed our nation for 400-plus years using history lessons to develop rights common to societies going back millions of years. Yes, I said millions. Let me explain.

History is the knowledge of and study of the past. It is the story of the past and a form of collective memory. History is the story of who we are and where we come from, and it can potentially reveal where we are headed.

Place yourself in the role of the ancients. When someone invented something, and it got passed on to others, let's say a spear was invented with this nifty spear point. You watched it being made, and the other inventor moved on, and you did, too. Years later, you lost your spear or spear point in a Mastodon hunt and needed another, and you said to yourself, self, how did that person do this, and you figured it out.

Now, you just experienced knowledge learned from what we can simply define as reaching back in history, so you wouldn't need to reinvent the wheel again, as they say. Yup, it's a simple thing, but since you bought this book and after reading it, you too will now understand the meaning of the word Genesis. It really does mean moving forward.

Why not borrow the good things you find and apply them to your situation? That, my reader, is what our founders did, and I will try to show you how they did it by applying ancient thought processes for our benefit throughout the ages.

History is important to study because it is essential for all of us to understand ourselves and the world around us. There is a history of every field and topic, from medicine to music to art, and it started eons ago. To know and understand history,[1] is absolutely necessary, even though the results of historical study are not readily visible and less immediate unless you search for them, but they are there in some useable form. I know, I researched history to produce this book.

Along with History it comes with responsibility and concerns such as personal attributes one should possess, Civic pride, Ethics and Morality and to apply them to advance the goals of a free society.

This book reveals factual knowledge to live by, focusing on the ancient Rule of Law practiced throughout 4,520 years. My research has revealed that there are patently basic human rights. Our freedoms are represented as Articles in our original first Ten Articles of the Bill of Rights, which are inviolable, by the way, and cannot be changed. These Articles are what protect you and me in our daily lives and are enforced all the way up to our protectors of our Rule of Law, The Supreme Court of the United States.

Let's define what we call the Rule of Law simply.

I attribute this definition to WikiLeaks:

> "a principle of governance in which all persons, institutions
> and entities, public and private, including the State itself,
> are accountable to laws that are publicly promulgated,
> equally enforced and independently adjudicated, and

---

[1] The Top 8 Jobs For History Majors | University of the People | (uopeople.edu)

which are consistent with international human rights norms and standards."

Before putting pen to paper for this work, I had written another book which was published under a pseudonym, Shane Roberts, titled *The New Green Deal: Back to the Stone Age*. This book was an answer to what could, and very well did, upset our society in innumerable ways. Little did I know that an ultra-progressive admin, driven by people intent on destroying our foundational government, would bring to life this very bad plan. On the very first day, a very large number of executive orders began to unravel and actually undid the work of functional governments before it. They even suggested denying and removing our Bill of Rights tenants designed to protect us.

Folks, this was the start of the unraveling of our Rule of Law in 2020.

This administration, without foresight, canceled projects that had been started because our country needed them, placing tens of thousands of workers in unemployed roles in construction, the oil and gas industries, and others. It even violated international treaties with Canada and Mexico. What I can now call a factual handle, a very weak administration that is obvious to many, did not plan for the destructive consequences that would evolve; I predicted this in my previous book almost to the letter when it was first proposed and failed. It promised to ensure financial and social security for our citizens. It even condoned paying people to stay out of work and does so under the guise of a pandemic where fabricated case numbers are keeping our citizens at home and our vulnerable children out of schools, placing burdens on parents and jeopardizing our children's education. Yes, it has even set our educational measurements of children's education back years, and I fault our department of education and using teachers' unions for allowing this travesty for the last years (November 2020 to May of 2024 so far), blocking historic education and societal norms. They are even using or rewriting and indoctrinating our children and parents, with children locked down at home and parents muted if they disagree with what education is being pushed by the unions and teachers.

The following applies to us all, and I quote the venerable Ben Franklin with his wisdom:

> *"Tell me and I forget. Teach me and I remember. Involve me and I learn."*

All of our freedoms are being attacked by most forms of media and online organizations who censor our thoughts with so-called "fact checkers," and I freely state, "blatant misinformation or lies," and lock us down, or deny, if we want to share opinions. Without delving into what this socialist administration seems to be doing, or is being driven to do, through weak leadership and seemingly captured lower and upper houses of government, that is reacting to ultra-socialist drivers, it is obvious that it is causing our country to slip in respect around the world and does not seem to be getting better.

Sadly, it's obvious that we are now a government divided along partisan lines. We have a Democratic party being torn apart by left-leaning members in a socialist green movement. What, how, and why did this happen? Furthermore, political dissension between the three branches of government has now occurred, and the rejection of a duly elected President, and alarmingly, the constitutionally incorrect activities of the Intelligence and Judicial committees that took place in an impeachment process leading to a largely ineffective House of Representatives for the past eight years in what has been called a coup attempt. Our government has failed us for eight whole years, from 2016 to 2024, due to major blocking efforts that disrupted all efforts of sitting parties.

Can we assume that our government is effectively "hamstrung" without remedy?

Further, the House was taken over by a socialist gang of four driving a green movement, and surprisingly, many other House Representatives, Senators, and presidential contenders from both parties. That list includes some **70** U.S. **Representatives**, 10 or more Senators, and nearly all announced Democratic Presidential contenders who **signed** onto the Green New Deal in HR-109,

That agreed association suggests insane societal changes. It highly suggests a mandate and radical rewrite or even elimination of our standing Declaration of Independence, Constitution, and The Bill of Rights to suit their social purposes. I see no cohesive document other than a failed New Green Deal, HR-109, that spells out far-left incomplete initiatives for a formed government. It appears all the power will go to the left to rule and, I might add, destroy 400 years of steadily evolving government designed for "All the People," and I'm pretty sure all the people do not want this brand of government. I pray for a reasonable "silent majority" with common sense that will affect their stabilizing will on the nation as elections come about.

If change wasn't enough, in the FBI, CIA, and compromised FISA Court, left-leaning federal courts who block executive orders, a possible leveraged buyout of the Democrat presidential election by an oligarch, and even disruptive people inside the White House working against the legal administration.

Well, that was the Trump administration under attack. We now have an extremely liberal administration with a President who has thrown all caution to the winds, removing all checkmate policies that were seeming to stabilize our economy and kowtowing to radical factions.

Who else or what will rise up to potentially overthrow our government in what I, and others, have called a continuous and blatantly obvious coup attempt and a restructuring of our government? Here is a current factual example proffered on 7/7/2020 that will stun you!

I have extreme condemnation of so-called Congressional persons in the "gang of four Middle East rabble-rousers" who are not just far left-leaning. They border on treason in my mind. These people came to the United States and became citizens, swearing to serve the US but holding terrorist ties to their homelands that are clearly proven. They got elected to Congress, and as I write this, they brassily are submitting legislation to disassemble our country by defunding all police, tearing up our economic system, redoing the criminal justice system, and literally condoning the overhaul of all of America. My question is, why is this destabilization of our Congress allowed? Where is the Speaker of the House who should have removed them? Attempts to destroy our country are only part of what they desire, like Sharia law; I'll keep my head, thank you. These people need to be stripped of their offices, have their citizenship revoked, and returned to their countries to continue their terrorist ways, but not here.

It's disgusting! Our founding fathers are probably rolling over in their graves. I ask you who the heck is really in charge. What is happening to our government?

Chapter 4

Introducing Lady Columbia

What if I told you our American history had a real goddess, not one you read about in ancient anthologies, but our very own? It's very true, a wonderful gift to a developing nation it was.

We read about ancient goddesses throughout history, but who would imagine that a struggling gathering of colonies would anoint a figurehead to the status of a goddess who would guide us through the formation of the 13 colonies, a revolution, the generation of the foundational documents of our government, the War of 1812,

For those of you who have never met her, she was the symbol and longest figurehead of our country before it became a country. She came to life in the early 17th century when Samuel Seaward, in a 1697 essay, wrote that she was the emblem of the "New Heaven" of the American Colonies. Draped in a neoclassical gown, she held a sword, an olive branch, and a Laurel wreath as symbols of justice, peace, and victory as a Goddess. She epitomized a burdening nation's aspirations and ambitions of the colonists as a mother figure and, to some, an avenging angel.

She reigned for two centuries as our cherished emblem for the development of a young democracy. During the Revolutionary War in 1775, African American poet Phillis Wheatley actually sent General George Washington an ode to Columbia: "Columbia's arm prevails… proceed great chief with virtue on thy side, /thy every action let the Goddess guide.

During the Revolution, she was seen as a source of strength, a rallying cry. By the end of the war, the victorious colonists celebrated their triumph by invoking her: "Hail Columbia, happy land. Hail, ye heroes, heav'n-born band, / /Who fought and bled in freedoms cause, "the lawyer and poet Joseph Hopkinson wrote in 1798. The verses were set to music, and "Hail Columbia" became our unofficial national anthem in the 19th century. In the War of 1812, she and a new figure, Uncle Sam, brought forward fierce independence. "Hail Columbia" Was replaced with the "Star Spangled Banner". She greeted immigrants in 1881 to embrace an American identity. In 1893, she headlined posters for the World's Columbian Exposition. Her reign ended in 1886 when a usurper, "The Statue of Liberty," became our national symbol.

There is much more to this wonderful symbol of liberty all the way from 1697 to 1931 when "Hail Columbia" was replaced, and Columbia slipped into obscurity. But not really, she has been the figurehead for Columbia Pictures since 1924 until today. I encourage all who read this to call up a wonderful article from the Smithsonian where a wooden six-foot figure resides. I also encourage you to call up and review Cari Shanes' work as foundational and enlightening.

Credits for the work belong to:

Cari Shane, the history correspondent article, was written and excerpted from a published document with this author's abbreviated comments. Sept/Oct 2023. An article also excerpted was from the Smithsonian Magazine issue of Sept/October 2023

The face of the Statue of Liberty.

Isabella Boyer's life is like an exciting novel. She was born in Paris, the daughter of an African pastry chef and an English mother. Isabella had a special beauty, and at age 20, she married Isaac Singer, the sewing machine maker, who was 50 years old. After Singer's death, Isabella became the richest woman in the country. It is not surprising that she was chosen as the model for the Statue of Liberty, as she embodied the American dream. Widowed, Isabella traveled the world and married the Dutch violinist Victor Robstett, becoming a countess. He became a prominent figure in America and Europe and met the French sculptor Frédéric Bartholdi at a world event. Bartholdi, impressed by her beauty and history, used her face as a model for the Statue of Liberty. Isabella married a third time and died in Paris in 1904 at age 62, but her face lives on in the iconic statue in New York, symbolizing freedom and American pride.

Credits to the rightful owner.

Chapter 5

An Energized Reader

My fondest hope is that you, my reader, will be energized, embrace, and perhaps personally become involved in the many ways that exist to assist in the preservation of our heritage and, most importantly, the forward protection of our freedoms that many, relatively unknown peoples and our ancestors "hard won" so we could live in freedoms, sunshine and be examples for others as a leader of world nations, as a beacon of success. In fact, as a politician, I personally observed this transfer of our guiding principles, our constitutional documents, and our formed government, which were sought by the island nation of Madagascar. This has been the case in many other instances I am aware of.

I will state that the U.S. Constitution in and of itself is not the only accepted form of government. Some governments actually use a mix of democratic Republic Rule of Law and Parliamentary forms, which are defined elsewhere in this book. Others may extract what they find suits their people and develop their own Constitutions. The colonies used a number of sources to develop our guiding Rule of Law documents in a wide search for what they wanted our government to be.

Pluto, a statement:

> *If you do not take an interest in the affairs of your government, then you are doomed to live under the Rule of Fools.*

Chapter 6

We the People Loses Appeal to People Around the World

Is our Constitution behind the times around the world?

New York Times Adam Liptak Feb.26, 2012

WASHINGTON — The Constitution has seen better days.

Sure, it is the nation's founding document and sacred text. It is the oldest written national constitution that is still in force anywhere in the world, but its influence is waning.

In 1987, on the Constitution's bicentennial, Time magazine calculated that "of the 170 countries that exist today, more than 160 have written charters modeled directly or indirectly on the U.S. version."

A quarter-century later, the picture looks very different. "The U.S. Constitution appears to be losing its appeal as a model for constitutional drafters elsewhere," according to a new study by David S. Law of Washington University in St. Louis and Mila Versteeg of the University of Virginia.[2]

The study, to be published in June in The New York University Law Review, bristles with data. Its authors coded and analyzed the provisions of 729 constitutions adopted by 188 countries from 1946 to

---

[2] Law, David S. and Versteeg, Mila, The Declining Influence of the United States Constitution (May 26, 2012). New York University Law Review, Vol. 87, No. 3, pp. 762-858, June 2012, Washington University in St. Louis Legal Studies Research Paper No. 11-09-01, Virginia Public Law and Legal Theory Research Paper No. 2011-39, Available at SSRN: https://ssrn.com/abstract=1923556

2006, and they considered 237 variables regarding various rights and ways to enforce them.

"Among the world's democracies," Professors Law and Versteeg concluded, "constitutional similarity to the United States has clearly gone into free fall. Over the 1960s and 1970s, democratic constitutions as a whole became more similar to the U.S. Constitution, only to reverse course in the 1980s and 1990s."

"The turn of the twenty-first century, however, saw the beginning of a steep plunge that continues through the most recent years for which we have data, to the point that the constitutions of the world's democracies are, on average, less similar to the U.S. Constitution now than they were at the end of World War II."

There are many possible reasons. The United States Constitution is terse and old and guarantees relatively few rights. The commitment of some members of the Supreme Court to interpreting the Constitution according to its original meaning in the 18th century may send the signal that it is of little current use to, say, a new African nation. The Constitution's waning influence may be part of a general decline in American power and prestige.

In an interview, Professor Law identified a central reason for the trend: the availability of newer, sexier, and more powerful operating systems in the constitutional marketplace. "Nobody wants to copy Windows 3.1," he said.

In a television interview during a visit to Egypt last week, Justice Ruth Bader Ginsburg of the Supreme Court seemed to agree. "I would not look to the United States Constitution if I were drafting a constitution in the year 2012," she said. She recommended, instead, the South African Constitution, the Canadian Charter of Rights and Freedoms, or the European Convention on Human Rights.

The rights guaranteed by the American Constitution are parsimonious by international standards, and they are frozen in amber. As Sanford Levinson wrote in 2006 in "Our Undemocratic Constitution,"[3] "the U.S. Constitution is the most difficult to amend of any constitution currently existing in the world today." (Yugoslavia used to hold that title, but Yugoslavia did not work out.)

Image

Occupy activists tested a float made with a copy of the Constitution in California. Credit: Jae C. Hong/Associated Press

Other nations routinely trade in their constitutions wholesale, replacing them on average every 19 years. By odd coincidence, Thomas Jefferson, in a 1789 letter to James Madison, once said that every constitution "naturally expires at the end of 19 years" because "the earth belongs always to the living generation." These days, the overlap between the rights guaranteed by the Constitution and those most popular around the world is spotty.

Americans recognize rights are not widely protected, including ones to a speedy and public trial, and are outliers in prohibiting the

---

[3] Our Undemocratic Constitution | Faculty - Sanford V. Levinson | Texas Law | Texas Law (utexas.edu)

government establishment of religion. But the Constitution is out of step with the rest of the world in failing to protect, at least in so many words, a right to travel, the presumption of innocence, and entitlement to food, education, and health care.

Adam Liptak

Supreme Court reporter

"I try to make the Supreme Court accessible to readers. I strive to distill and translate complex legal materials into accessible prose while presenting fairly the arguments of both sides and remaining alert to the political context and practical consequences of the court's work."

It has its idiosyncrasies. Only 2 percent of the world's constitutions protect the right to bear arms, as does the Second Amendment (Its brothers in arms are Guatemala and Mexico.)

The Constitution's waning global stature is consistent with the diminished influence of the Supreme Court[4] which "is losing the central role it once had among courts in modern democracies," Aharon Barak, then the president of the Supreme Court of Israel, wrote in The Harvard Law Review in 2002.

---

[4] U.S. Court Is Now Guiding Fewer Nations - The New York Times (nytimes.com)

Many foreign judges say they have become less likely to cite decisions of the United States Supreme Court, in part because of what they consider its parochialism.

"America is in danger, I think, of becoming something of a legal backwater," Justice Michael Kirby of the High Court of Australia said in a 2001 interview. He said that he looked to India, South Africa, and New Zealand instead.

Mr. Barak, for his part, identified a new constitutional superpower: "Canadian law," he wrote, "serves as a source of inspiration for many countries around the world." The new study also suggests that the Canadian Charter of Rights and Freedoms, adopted in 1982, may now be more influential than its American counterpart.

The Canadian Charter is both more expansive and less absolute. It guarantees equal rights for women and disabled people, allows affirmative action, and requires that those arrested be informed of their rights. On the other hand, it balances those rights against "such reasonable limits" as "can be demonstrably justified in a free and democratic society."

There are, of course, limits to empirical research based on coding and counting, and there is more to a constitution than its words, as Justice Antonin Scalia told the Senate Judiciary Committee in October. "Every banana republic in the world has a bill of rights," he said.

"The bill of rights of the former evil empire, the Union of Soviet Socialist Republics, was much better than ours," he said, adding, "We guarantee freedom of speech and of the press. Big deal. They guaranteed freedom of speech, of the press, of street demonstrations and protests, and anyone who is caught trying to suppress criticism of the government will be called to account. Whoa, that is wonderful stuff!" Or is it?

"Of course," Justice Scalia continued, "It's just words on paper, what our framers would have called a 'parchment guarantee.'"

Does this make you sit upright? Thought it might.

Chapter 7

The United States Constitution

From Wikipedia, the free encyclopedia U.S. Department of State

The US Constitution had an international influence on later constitutions and legal thinking. Its influence appears in similarities of phrasing and borrowed passages in other constitutions, as well as in the principles of the rule of law, separation of powers, and recognition of individual rights. The American experience of constitutional amendment and judicial review motivated constitutionalists at times when they were considering the possibilities for their nation's future. Examples include Abraham Lincoln during the American Civil War, his contemporary and ally Benito Juárez of Mexico, the second generation of 19th-century constitutional nationalists José Rizal of the Philippines, and Sun Yat-sen of China, and the framers of the Australian constitution.

The historian William H. McNeill argued that the United States saw itself as "one of a family of peoples and nations," making a history apart from the European civilization of their colonization. According to this viewpoint, the United States Constitution is an expression of Americans diverging from colonial rule. Its effect is reflected in the ideals of limiting the rulers of a state apart and above sitting lawgivers in a parliament. The concepts of governance influencing others internationally are not only found among similarities in phrasing and entire passages from the U.S. Constitution. They are in the principles of the rule of law and recognition of American historian George Athan Billias, who wrote, "The influence of American constitutionalism abroad was profound in the past and remains a remarkable contribution to humankind's search for freedom under a system of laws." Billias describes six waves of influence:

From 1776 to 1811, after the American Revolution began, it influenced northwestern Europe and its colonial connections.

1811–1848, after the decline of Napoleon's reputation, it was referenced by Latin American, Caribbean, and European nationalists.

1898–1918, after the Spanish–American War, nationalist movements borrowed from the U.S. Constitution in Asia and Latin America.

1918–1945, after World War I, its influence spread with movements for decolonization of Africa, Mid-east and Asia.

1945–1974, after World War II, independence movements consulted it.

1974–1989, after the United Nations expansion, once nondemocratic regimes, including European ones, transitioned towards constitutional democracies incorporating elements of the U.S. Constitution.

Hold the presses. There has been a New Discovery about the Constitution's Declaration of Independence's real authorship.

Author's Note:

During my research for factual information regarding our founding, I have come across many articles that I believe the whole story has not been told to people for a long time, in this case, actually 200 years, and is historically misleading. For instance, I, by chance, came across an article in a publication of the Sons of the American Revolution, dated in the Fall of 2021, Vol – 116 No. of page 18, an organization of which I am a member, it postulated, the reveal actually, that the actual events refuted the theory that Thomas Jefferson, alone, penned the official Declaration of Independence! In fact, he eventually did, but his actions caused huge embarrassment to the Colonial Congress and the 13 states. There is much more to this historical series of events that the reader should know and give credit to, according to the historical record, the individuals who deserve it, albeit late.

Author's Note:

We thought that Jefferson was the main author involved in the writing of the Declaration of Independence. A king brought us up short as a result! The discovery of the rejected Jefferson-authored Declaration of Independence, albeit 200 years later, permits us to better comprehend the full story of the authorship of this document. Our comprehension of actual written and archived history and what it can tell us to set the historical record straight is paramount to what we stand for. We founded our government primarily on empirical history and have lived by it ethically as a model for other entities, as well as our people. I personally see no reason why we should not reveal our historical missteps.

This reveal was too important for my readers not to know about it.

It is a fact that Thomas Jefferson did write an unauthorized Declaration of Independence paper that was carried by a special courier, Silas Deane, who was to go to France for Revolutionary War supplies of gunpowder and other articles needed for the Revolution and was charged to bring the document supposedly representing what Jefferson declared was the Declaration of Independence to the court of King Louis XV1.

Author's Note:

It seems to me that Jefferson actually "jumped the gun" without the full authority of the Continental Congress and the full participation of the American United Colonial Colonies, which would be officially corrected by the 13 Colonies and President Hamilton.

Author's Note:

I am going to include the fact that Silas Deane did present Jefferson with what he called the official Declaration of Independence to the King. The actual document follows:

American United Colonies' A Transcribed Copy of the Jefferson Declaration of Independence. It has not been altered since it is an original correspondence.

American United Colonies'

'In Congress May 15, 1776. Whereas his Britannic Majesty, in conjunction with the lords and commons of Great Britain, has, by a late Act of Parliament, excluded the Inhabitants of these United Colonies from the protection of his Crown, and Whereas, no answer, whatever, to the humble petition of the Colonies for redress of grievances and reconciliation with Great Britain, has been or is likely to be given; but the whole force of the Kingdom, aided by foreign Mercenaries, is to be exerted for the Destruction of the good People of these Colonies; And whereas, it appears absolutely irreconcilable to Reason and good conscience, for the people of these Colonies to take the Oaths and Affirmations necessary for the support of any government of Great Britain, and it is necessary for the Exercise of every kind of Authority of under said Crown should be totally suppressed, and all in the power of the Government exerted, under the Authority of the People of these colonies, for the preservation of internal Peace, Virtue, and good order, as well as for the defense of ourselves, Liberties and properties, against the hostile invasion and cruel depredations of our Enemies Therefore Resolve that it be recommended to the respective assembles and Conventions of the United Colonies, where no Government sufficient to the exigencies of their Affairs has been hither to established, to adopt such Government as shall in the opinion of the Representatives of the People best conduce to the happiness and Safety of their Constituents, in particular and America in general. By Order of Congress Signed – John Hancock, President

Author's Note:

Of course, after deliberation by the British court of King Louis XV1, the Jefferson Declaration of Independence was rejected. I have included the British Courts' answer to the Continental Congress in its historical text unaltered:

"From the Court of King Louis XVI. Without intelligence from April to this time, leaves me quite uncertain and extremely anxious about the line of conduct now pursuing by Congress, and consequently I cannot, without further intelligence and instructions proceed in my negotiations either with safety or honor. The resolution of Congress of the 15th May, is not considered by the ministry as a declaration of independence, but only a previous step, and until this decisive step is taken, I can do little more too any purpose. This taken, I dare pledge myself, the United Colonies may obtain all the countenance and assistance they wish for, in the most open and public manner, and the most unlimited credit with the merchants of this kingdom; I must therefore urge this measure, if not already taken, and that this declaration be in the most full and explicit term."

Author's Note:

It was obvious to me that the Court and King were not pleased that the colonies jumped the gun, and it lacked key elements that were expected in a Declaration of Independence and could not react to the declaration.

This was further revealed after the French received news of the Declaration of Independence being received in England and rushed to France. Hancock was not aware of the rejected document until the French, in a secret correspondence dated August 18, 1776, was sent to the Committee of Secret Correspondence of the Continental Congress.

The response to Hancock by the British only identified Hancock by referring to him in the following passage: "The resolution of Congress of May 15th is not considered by the ministry to be as a declaration of independence, but only a previous step, and until that step is taken, I can do little more too any purpose."

Here, Deane explains that the extension of credit by America has been halted by a need for their Declaration of Independence from Great Britain. Deane notes: "This taken, I dare pledge myself, the United Colonies may obtain all the countenance and assistance they wish for, in the most open and public manner, and the most unlimited credit with the merchants of this kingdom." Then Deane explains "that this declaration be in the most full and explicit term." There were existing expectations for this document.

This advice will not be sent in time to aid Thomas Jefferson, but it does provide that the Declaration of Independence was to serve some special objectives that have been made known to Deane. Silas Deane tells him it is not "credit" but a Declaration of Independence that will produce the shipment of gunpowder and armaments.

The presentation of the rejected Declaration of Independence would become a hidden event from known history. In fact, this rejected document was part of the personal effects of Deane when he was murdered aboard a ship that would return him to America.

Author's Note:

President of Congress John Hancock wrote the following in response on May 15, 1776, after John Adams and Richard Henry Lee authored the May 15, 1776 Resolution of Independence. It is a historical document and has not been altered.

American United Colonies' 'In Congress May 15, 1776' Whereas his Britannic Majesty in conjunction with the lords and commons of Great Britain, has, by a late Act of Parliament, excluded the

Inhabitants of these United Colonies from the protection of his Crown, and Whereas, no answer, whatever, to the humble petition of the Colonies for redress of grievances and reconciliation with Great Britain, has been or is likely to be given; but the whole force of the Kingdom, aided by foreign Mercenaries, is to be exerted for the Destruction of the good People of these Colonies; And whereas, it appears absolutely irreconcilable to Reason and good conscience, for the people of these Colonies to take the Oaths and Affirmations necessary for the support of any government of Great Britain, and it is necessary for the Exercise of every kind of Authority of under said Crown should be totally suppressed, and all in the power of the Government exerted, under the Authority of the People of these colonies, for the preservation of internal Peace, Virtue, and good order, as well as for the defense of ourselves, Liberties and properties, against the hostile invasion and cruel depredations of our Enemies Therefore Resolve that it be recommended to the respective assembles and Conventions of the United Colonies, where no Government sufficient to the exigencies of their Affairs has been hither to established, to adopt such Government as shall in the opinion of the Representatives of the People best conduce to the happiness and Safety of their Constituents, in particular and America in general. By Order of Congress Signed – John Hancock, President[5]

The 13 Colonial legislatures would provide the authority to break their bond to Great Britain and the authority for each delegate to sign a treaty with a foreign power. The Resolution passed on June 11, 1776. RESOLVE. A Committee is appointed to prepare a treaty plan to be proposed to foreign powers. After permission to sign had been granted by all 13 Colonial legislatures, and after it was

---

[5] "[Wednesday May 15. 1776] ," *Founders Online,* National Archives, https://founders.archives.gov/documents/Adams/01-03-02-0016-0120. [Original source: *The Adams Papers*, Diary and Autobiography of John Adams, vol. 3, *Diary, 1782–1804; Autobiography, Part One to October 1776*, ed. L. H. Butterfield. Cambridge, MA: Harvard University Press, 1961, pp. 385–386.]

comprehended that gunpowder, brass cannons, and armaments for an army are not produced in America, the necessity of a foreign power was obvious. Deane was sent to be our agent in France. How do we know a foreign agent signed a treaty that ensured gold, gunpowder, and armaments? We received these funds and war supplies, and the army fought, eventually, with France's assistance.

On June 19, 1776, Congress passed a resolution to produce a Velum Declaration of Independence on June 19, 1776, which was signed by all the delegates and was a signed secret.

The name of the treaty was Secret Treaty Number One. That treaty was signed by all the delegates to the Continental Congress with the foreign agent on July 4, 1776. Keeping this signing secret was a top priority. Even rumors of the signing had to be quelled after they were accidentally leaked. The British Court and King Louis XV1 finally got the combined weight of the 13 Colonies in a Declaration of Independence, of which the full context of that document will be displayed later on in this book.

Author's Note:

What an amazing reveal; it dives deeply into the secret, intriguing dealings of our fledgling Democratic Republic.

Chapter 8

Education: Critical knowledge of Civics, Morality, Ethics and History

Before I get started on the main purpose of this manuscript, I am going to detail to you what I feel is a very critical and necessary knowledge that all students, citizens, and those who wish to become citizens of our country need. It should be taught formally, brought to us through early education, or in mandatory special classes for immigrants. We have been robbed, ironically, by our very own Department of Education in the 1980s to 2024. This omission is so important that I feel it is basic to our understanding of the systems we have in place to survive in our society now, as well as mandatory knowledge moving forward into the future. I find that this lack of basic education has affected our very foundation of understanding about who we really are. These basic foundational skills are CIVICS, MORALITY, and ETHICS, and I will add another I find critically important, HISTORY. These are hopefully learned from our parents and expanded upon by our educational system if, and I mean if included, in the educational curriculum in our formative years K-12 and beyond. I am going to examine each and relate to you their effects on our very lives in the chapters below relating to our Democratic Republic.

Perhaps we could even fund all effective school systems to better educate our children, bringing them on par with other countries. See chart below.

The Program for International Student Assessment is administered by the Organization for Economic Cooperation and Development (OECD), and it tests 15-year-old students around the world. The

U.S. placed 11th out of 79 countries in science when the test was last administered in 2018. It did much worse in math, ranking 30th.[1]

The U.S. scored 478 in math, below the OECD average of 489. That's well below the scores of the top five, all of which were in Asia:

- Singapore: 569, Macao: 555, Hong Kong: 551, Taiwan: 531, Japan: 527

Need more educational facts? Here is a major study that discovered some really interesting facts.

Note: Average math scores of students in grades three through eight. Source: The Educational Opportunity Project, Stanford University and the Center for Education Policy Research, Harvard University

As part of a team of researchers from Harvard, Stanford, Dartmouth, Johns Hopkins, and the testing company NWEA — the Education Recovery Scorecard project — we have been sifting through data from 7,800 communities in 41 states to understand where test scores declined the most, what caused these patterns and whether they are likely to endure. The school districts in these communities enroll 26 million elementary and middle school students in more than 53,000 public schools, roughly 80 percent of the public K-8 students in the country.

We've looked at test scores, the duration of school closures, broadband availability, COVID death rates, employment data, patterns of social activity, voting patterns, measures of how connected people are to others in their communities, and Facebook survey data on both family activities and mental health during the pandemic.

To get a sense of how probable it is that students will make up the ground they lost over the next few years, we looked at earlier test scores to see how students recovered from various disruptions in the decade before the pandemic.

Our detailed geographic data reveals what national tests do not: The pandemic exacerbated economic and racial educational inequality.

In 2019, the typical student in the poorest 10 percent of districts scored one and a half years behind the national average for his or her year – and almost four years behind students in the richest 10 percent of districts – in both math and reading.

By 2022, the typical student in the poorest districts had lost three-quarters of a year in math, more than double the decline of students in the richest districts. The declines in reading scores were half as large as in math and were similarly much larger in poor districts than in rich districts. The pandemic left students in low-income and predominantly minority communities even further behind their peers in richer, whiter districts than they were.

However, while the effects of the pandemic on learning were quite different *across* communities, they were, surprisingly, evenly distributed among different types of students *within* each community. You might expect that the more affluent children in a district would be better protected from the educational consequences of the pandemic than their lower-income classmates. But that's not what we found.

Looks like we need to wake up to some startling facts concerning education

As you can see, I added HISTORY. I am a student of history from the distant past to current events today that, like it or not, shape or mold our very environment. Here is a statement by the Department of History UW-Michigan that reinforces my point. Thank you, UW-Michigan.

"Studying history helps us understand and grapple with complex questions and dilemmas by examining how the past has shaped (and continues to shape) global, national, and local relationships between societies and people."

Chapter 9

How <u>not</u> to run an airline, or for that matter a country: Stop spending. DEBT is BAD!

Perhaps this statement, made by a well-known individual leader, will shed some light on this issue:

FOX News, September 20, 2019, Mr. Panetta, of the Panetta Institute stated, "Our government is dysfunctional and if not corrected our democracy is in trouble". I am afraid this is not a statement that I hear just in Washington or on the news; associate acquaintances of mine share this feeling and are troubled by the future of our government and way of life. Folks, our government today is in a state of upheaval because of our split government, and many do not see a turnaround. We need leadership that possesses, at minimum, those I speak of above, along with other people-savvy traits that serve constituents and the primary needs of the public.

Now, let me discuss the current affairs of our nation that greatly concern me – something that is totally inconceivable and unconstitutional to me. The current administration has done the unthinkable; they have embraced the concept of hyper-socialism in the form of The New Green Deal, spending money that we today cannot afford, leaving huge burdens to our progeny, and if I might be so bold to suggest, their progeny and way beyond. They continue to propose spending trillions more on top of our $21 and now a 27 trillion-dollar debt as of September 2021, and actually 34 trillion in March of 2024.

Author: A nation cannot exist in debt, especially the amounts we owe. As a homeowner, I know how much I make and how much I can spend. If I borrow, I am actually spending money I do not currently have and need to budget for its payback within my calculated earnings from the future. Why am I stating this? We as a nation have gross earnings from taxes, imports, and sales of things such as military hardware and the like. We pay a horrendous interest payment to the nations we borrow from; I really do not want to reveal these numbers in fear you will not buy my book because you owe at the current per-person figure over $100,000.00 (not exactly since this fluctuates daily as the government spends your money) In reality, the government has no money, it uses yours. Oh wait, I forgot that they have none. They just print another trillion) as your share of this debt. That's right, EACH PERSON!

To you, my reader, the breakdown of who owns our debt and what our debt and borrowing pays is frightening. I suggest you sit down before you look at the below chart. Let your children know this and tell them they will need to inform them of this debt they have, and also let them know their kids will also need to ante up as well – it's that bad.

SHOCKING TRUTH!

As of May 2024, it cost taxpayers $728 billion to maintain the debt, which is 16% of the total federal spending in fiscal year 2024.[6]

Author's Note: what I am about to reveal is eye-opening:

Just think, if this number was halved and our debt profile reduced, the government could pay back the social security funds they borrowed, making the system more solvent. You do know, of course, that the SS system will only be solvent until 2035. Perhaps we could even fund all effective school systems to better educate our children, bringing them on par with other countries. See chart below.

Not to insult sailors, but "Hey, fellas in Washington, stop spending money 'like a drunken sailor.'" You give to every Tom, Dick, and

---

[6] Federal Spending | U.S. Treasury Fiscal Data

Harry in the world, but why can't you look over your shoulder and see us 'ins out there who need the money. Just why are we giving money to people who hate us and want us to die or cease being a country?

Enough pontificating, "Government, get with the program, doggone it!"

The National Debt defined

The national debt has increased every year over the past ten years. Interest expenses during this period have remained fairly stable due to low interest rates and investors' judgment that the U.S. Government has a very low risk of default. However, recent increases in interest rates and inflation are now resulting in an increase in interest expense.

Types of Debt

U.S. national debt is categorized as intragovernmental debt and public debt. Intragovernmental debt is debt held within the U.S. by federal agencies and entities. It makes up about a fifth of the total outstanding U.S. debt. This debt includes money owed to Social Security, Military Retirement Funds, Medicare, and other retirement funds.

The remainder is public debt. Foreign governments hold a large portion of the public debt, while the rest is owned by U.S. banks and individual investors, the Federal Reserve, state and local governments, mutual funds, pensions funds, insurance companies, and holders of savings bonds.4

Attribution: TreasuryDirect. "Frequently Asked Questions about the Public Debt."

As of **May 31, 2024, $27.60 trillion** of the national debt is public debt. Oh no! I peeked again today; as of June 14, 2024, the U.S. national debt is **$34.68 trillion!**

US foreign-owned debt (January 2023 fiscal yr.)	US foreign-owned debt (January 2023)
Japan	$1,104,400,000,000
China	$859,400,000,000
United Kingdom	$668,300,000,000
Belgium	$331,100,000,000
Luxembourg	$318,200,000,000
Switzerland	$290,500,000,000
The Cayman Islands	$285,300,000,000
Canada	$254,100,000,000
Ireland	$253,400,000,000
Taiwan	$234,600,000,000

As of January 2023, the five countries owning the most US debt are Japan ($1.1 trillion), China ($859 billion), the United Kingdom ($668 billion), Belgium ($331 billion), and Luxembourg ($318 billion).

Investors from Russia, China, and Indonesia had sharp drops in US Treasurys over the last several years due to sanctions and short-term capital needs, among other reasons.

Despite a few alarming headlines, nobody really seems to care. In fact, NPR did a story highlighting the supposed "benefits" of a massive national debt. REALLY? Bring it on, we say, NOT![7]

The debt continues to increase at a dizzying pace. When Congress effectively eliminated the debt ceiling on June 5, the national debt stood at $31.46 trillion. Since that time, the Biden administration has added $2.54 trillion to the national debt.

The government is running up the debt at roughly $1 trillion every three months. It eclipsed $32 trillion on June 15 and $33 trillion on September 15.

Since the beginning of 2016, the total debt has spiked by $15 trillion. That's an 80 percent increase.

It's hard to wrap one's head around $34 trillion. To put things into perspective, every U.S. citizen would have to write a $101,234 check to pay off the debt. Every American taxpayer is on the hook for $264,090.00.

---

[7] The national debt tops $34 trillion — a record high. How worried should we be? : NPR

Or to look at it another way, $34 trillion is more than the total economies of China, Japan, Germany, and the UK combined.

Our current administration is seeking to recoup this massive debt through a major revision of the taxation system, taxing the rich and literally anything they can think of. Their driving issue is to control vaccinations for COVID-19 when their own CDC says the shots do not work and simply states the shots they insist on are actually killing a large number of people and expire in a short time with boosters in the future for all who have taken the duo of shots. Many have chosen not to take the shots, postulating that this is a fraudulent vaccine that has suspicious ingredients and that people getting the shots are dying.

Chapter 10

Invading Illegals-Stop Them – Send Them Back! CRITICAL!

Something I thought I would never need to expound upon.

I strongly demand, as of this writing, that we immediately reverse the inflow of illegal invaders, costing each of us personally in the taxes we pay to support "the invaders." We are aware that we give them credit cards, free phones, lodging, and transportation to anywhere they want by vouchers, and why didn't they ask me if this was what I wanted? How about you? Your money and your taxes, and they are coming for both, in creative ways to get both.

In a former writing, I interviewed the Department of Agriculture about our food supply. I was stunned at our current population growth. That agency projected that with "normal growth," our food supply would be stressed by 2060. Now, here is the kicker: an estimated illegal invasion of 20-25 million on top of our own population will bring that number down to approximately 2045 if the illegal population influx is not reversed. This shortage was also addressed as critical, the Chinese buying up our companies, farmland, and crops at an alarming rate and shipping it to China. Never mind the fact that the farmland and companies they buy are next to the U.S. military bases of sensitive manufacturers.

My questions are now turned to "fearful" if these trends continue. How would we feed ourselves? Our money is grossly undervalued, and our costs are extreme for all commodities. If they don't like the Consumer Price List, they change it to suit themselves, not you. I want them to pick commodities we depend on in our daily lives, such as fuels, bread products, milk, and others we use to live, and do not change them at a whim to show false indicators of how their administration is operating "for the New York bridge they want to sell you at a bargain."

Chapter 11

The End of our Democratic Republic?

Could this be the end of our Democratic Republic? I can say with certainty that this is largely because of the lack of CIVIC knowledge, ETHICAL behavior, a lack of MORAL judgments, and, most importantly, disrespect for our Rule of Law. That we are a Democratic Republic should be taught throughout all the foundation years of our student populations, but these supposedly are not critical issues with a large sector of our home situations and definitely not being supported in our educational institutions. I cannot understand fully why these are being blocked by educational unions, and "get this" they have actually stated that they know better than the parents and demand that the parents have no rights. I beg your veracity; this isn't even your right. You are not the child's parent!

Are you aware that almost three generations of our young population are our future leaders, and will they not be fully prepared to guide our nation into the future? There is one salvation: a good number of responsible parents and educators are either home-schooling or admitting their children into schools that do not have a progressive agenda, but funding spent on the public systems needs to follow the student.

All people who enter our country attend classes before being sworn in as citizens. No free entry without education, and if they do not want it or default on their oath of allegiance to the United States, "back on the boat." Are there Knights in White Shining Armor to repel these socialist invaders? At this point in 2023/4, with a wide-open border and free entry into our country, our knights have been slain with faulty, bordering treasonous thoughts and actions. Today, in 2024, cities advertise that they are open states, and cities are crying wolf because they cannot stand the influx of illegal aliens. It's insane they have to support literally an estimated 8 to 12 million illegals with food, medical, lodging, transportation, phones, and money, replenished monthly by guess who? YOU AND I. There is no sight to the end of this self-imposed invasion. Please be aware I have no issue with legal entry into the U.S. Everything else is labeled by me as an invasion, and they need to go home and try the legal route. I feel bad for those who did come legally. What is happening to them is abject injustice.

Chapter 12

Democratic Republic or a Representative Democracy

Let me define the difference between Anti-Federalists and Federalists. These are two wholly different ways to run a government and are critical to its optimal operation to define and address before constructing a formal government. Who, after the Revolution, was against Federalism and wanted the power to be in the hands of states and local governments? If you think this was an easy decision, think again. We had 13 colonies with four divisions regarding the colonies and dramatically, clearly defined thought processes on how to form a cohesive coalition. A prime example of what we have today is the farm belts and Southern states, contrasted by the industrial and massive population states and cities, which are clearly overpowering. Let me give the definitions of both Anti and Federalists so we can better understand what they mean and then look at what they did to coalesce.

Anti-Federalists: People after the Revolution were strongly against Federalism and wanted the power to be in the hands of states and local government bodies. In effect, losing control of their states' freedoms for centralized control.

Federalists: People who supported the ratification of the Constitution and advocated for the centralization of power in a federal government that managed all the states. Contending that all states and local governments needed to be managed from a common center

The conceptions of each are ironically co-entwined in our formal Constitutional documents today, and these salient points below individually will show the divergent points that need to be ironed out for a formal, workable government.

Subject	Federalist	Anti-Federalist
Prominent Personality	James Monroe T Jefferson	G Washington John Jay
Population	Sam Adams, Patrick Henery	John Adams A. Hamilton
Basic cause	Rural areas, villages, small states	Urban areas, most educated
Economical Approach	States responsible, manage	
Fiscal Policy	Individually	Centralized government
	Farmers mostly, ruled by	Control of debts, tensions
	Rural communities	Managed businessmen
	Power to states,	Stable economy
	Manage revenue spend	Central financing
	accordingly	Central banking

The above was provided by Harlon Moss on February 27, 2019, with thanks.

Author's Note: I excerpted key information from an article, The Formation of the Constitution, by Matthew Spaulding, Vice President of American Studies, the Heritage Foundation, with respect and thanks.

Roger Sherman proffered what is often called "the Great Compromise" (or the Connecticut Compromise, after Sherman's home state) that the House of Representatives would be apportioned based on population, and each state would have an equal vote in the Senate. A special Committee of Eleven (one delegate from each state) elaborated upon the proposal, and then the Convention adopted it. As a precaution against having to assume the financial burdens of the smaller states, the larger states exacted an agreement that revenue bills could originate only in the House, where the more populous states would have greater representation

Author's Note: Complicated? Let me give an example of how complicated it really was. Articles of Confederation, proposed in 1777 and ratified in 1781, built in a weakness, making the whole process very convoluted and almost unworkable. Each state governed itself with elected representatives who, in turn, elected a weak national government to cover national debts. Furthermore, there was no independent executive, and Congress had no authority to impose and collect taxes to pay national debts. Anything the central government did had to be ratified by each state. Actually, it needed nine of the states to approve, which meant five did not (**The author,** in my mind suggested unbalance and a federal viewpoint of non-representative government.) This is rich; the government could negotiate treaties with foreign governments, but all treaties had to be approved by the states.

The defects of the Articles became more and more apparent during the "critical period" of 1781-1787. By the end of the war in 1783, it was clear that the new system was, as George Washington observed, "a shadow without substance."

From May 25 to September 17, 1787, state delegates met in Independence Hall in Philadelphia, Pennsylvania, as it says in the Constitution's Preamble to "form a more perfect Union."

The Constitutional Convention

There were three basic rules of the Convention: voting was to be by state, with each state, regardless of size or population, having one vote; proper decorum was to be maintained at all times; and the proceedings were to be strictly secret.

Author's Note: This gave the attendees equal weight in decision-making, undoing the Federalist premise of superior positioning to get their way. This was later improved with the following. Roger Sherman proffered what is often called "the Great Compromise" (or the Connecticut Compromise, after Sherman's home state) that the House of Representatives would be apportioned based on population, and each state would have an equal vote in the Senate. A special Committee of Eleven (one delegate from each state) elaborated upon the proposal, and then the Convention adopted it. As a precaution against having to assume the financial burdens of the smaller states, the larger states exacted an agreement that revenue bills could originate only in the House, where the more populous states would have greater representation.

George Washington thought it was "little short of a miracle" that the delegates had agreed on a new Constitution. Thomas Jefferson, who was also concerned about the lack of a bill of rights, nevertheless wrote that the Constitution "is unquestionably the wisest ever yet presented to men."

On September 28, Congress sent the Constitution to the states to be ratified by popular conventions. *See* Article VII (Ratification). Delaware was the first state to ratify the Constitution on December 7, 1787; the last of the thirteen original colonies to ratify was Rhode Island on May 29, 1790, two-and-a-half years later. It was during the ratification debate in the state of New York that Hamilton, Madison, and John Jay wrote a series of newspaper essays under the pen name of Publius, later collected in book form as The Federalist, to refute the arguments of the Anti-Federalist opponents of the proposed Constitution. With the ratification by the ninth state, New Hampshire, on June 21, 1788, Congress passed a resolution to make the new Constitution operative and set dates for choosing presidential electors and the opening session of the new Congress.

There are many forms of definition for the Democratic Republic, but this one is one of the best: https://www.thoughtco.com/republic-vs-democracy-4169936

Oct 04, 2019: The United States, while basically a republic, is best described as a "Representative Democracy." In a republic, an official set of fundamental laws, like the U.S. Constitution and Bill of Rights, prohibits the government from limiting or taking away **certain "inalienable" rights of the people**, even if that government was freely chosen by a majority of the people.

Author's Note: I disagree; there is nothing basic about what our Founding Fathers set up as a Democratic Republic. I do agree that our government has Representatives and Senators who are supposed to represent our states when they aren't biased, or wrongfully governing along party lines or having their votes bought, and that is blatantly clear in our governing documents we are forced to adhere to and pay the pipers bill to support them and their "special interests."

Many ask and even dispute the fact that we are a Republic and not a Democracy. In fact, the 2016 election was heavily disputed because of this very question, even to the suggestion that some believe that the Electoral College is the most dangerous constitutional institution dreamed up by the founders and placed into our Rule of Laws governing elections. The opposition to this practice claims simply that it distorts the one person, one vote principle. In fact, they say it is totally undemocratic. The amusing thing is that they are right but forget that the Founding Fathers set up conventions to ensure we would be a Republic. In fact, the word democracy does not, and I repeat for those of you who think we are a democracy, the mention of the word does not appear in the Declaration of Independence, the Constitution, or any documents that formed our government.

Let's shed some light on the subject of democracy by the very people who gave us our Republic and observed its rule.

The article partially excerpts from a Walter Williams article dated January 19, 2018, in the Daily Signal.

➤ Federalist Paper #10: James Madison wanted to prevent rule by the majority, and he said, "Measures are too often decided, not according to the rules of justice and rights of the minority party, but by the superior force of an interested and overbearing majority."

➤ John Adams warned in a letter, "Remember democracy never lasts long, it soon wastes, exhausts and murders itself. There was never a democracy yet that did not commit suicide."

➤ Chief Justice John Marshall is quoted as saying, "Between a balanced republic and a democracy, the difference is like that between order and chaos."

➤ The founders actually expressed contempt for the tyranny of majority rule throughout our Constitution as impediments to tyranny.

EXAMPLES

• The most prominent are the two Houses of Congress, exampled by 51 senators, which can block the bill of 435 representatives and 49 senators.

- The President can veto the bill of 535 congressional members, but the veto can be overridden by two-thirds of both houses of Congress.

- To change the Constitution, it requires the states to call a Constitutional convention, then submit it to both Congressional houses and a 2/3's vote of approval then to the states who need 3/4's of the states to ratify the change.

- The next to last and, in my mind, the most important is one that belays majority rule. There are 12 states with massive populations, and if we did not have the electoral college all of us (I live in Tennessee) would effectively not have a vote in national elections due to overpowering populations in those 12 states. Most of these states are run by democratic principles, and frankly, I do not want ultra-liberal states to decide my fate; yes, I am talking about New York, New Jersey, and California for a few who cannot govern themselves let alone insist on a popular vote to elect persons to our highest levels of government.

- LASTLY, AND I OPENLY ADMONISH OUR SITTING GOVERNMENT. IF YOU ALLOW ILLEGAL ALIENS WHO INVADED OUR COUNTRY TO TAKE OUR JOBS, CONTINUE TO FUND THEM, GIVE THEM PHONES AND FREE TRAVEL, RUN RAMPANT DOING HARM TO OUR POPULATION, DESTROY OUR CITIES, THROW OUR VETERANS OUT ON THE STREET TO GIVE THEM LODGING, OR VOTE WHICH IS NOT THEIR RIGHT, YOU ARE VERY WRONG.

YOU ARE TRAMPLING ON OUR RIGHTS. WE WILL REACT AS OUR CONSTITUTION ALLOWS US TO DO. THE NOISE LEVEL IS RISING; PAY ATTENTION!

On a personal note, all one needs to do is look at these large population states; most are broke and constantly need government assistance (Take a look at the COVID-19 situation.) These states were totally unprepared to handle themselves; they had no monetary reserves, and the hands went out immediately while other states were self-sustaining. Here is the big question: do you want these 12 states to take care of our government issues? Be honest with yourself when answering this question; it could affect your future if you give a wrong answer.

I believe the New Green Deal being presented by the socialist move to the far left in 2016-2020 actually wants to throw out our Republic, and folks, if it happens (this book may not ever be printed if they get their way) be prepared for devastation.

I believe the Founders and all those who labored on our behalf were psychic and saw what was to come, and personally, I am very glad they were.

Don't know about you, but I want my government back and all the political and socialist chicanery stopped! If the citizens want change, do it the way it is ordained in the Constitutional documents, in the ballot box, and respect and support the results we can all agree to. Appear in person with a valid ID declaring a viable address and vote. Magic votes appear out of the blue with unverified persons (are they real or fabricated or manufactured?), You tell me.

There is a constitutionally correct manner in which they can petition the 34 states in the republic to pass legislation to meet the Convention of the States' requirements to present changes to the convention. 15 states have already signed on by their legislative bodies, 8 have passed one chamber, and 11 have active legislation. Work with the balance of the states to get the requisite 34 progressing. There are also 1,647,397 signers who want to have this Convention of States happen as of 7/8/2020.

Here is the abbreviated text of Article Five of the Constitution that contains all the requirements and remedies:

Article V of the U.S. Constitution gives states the power to call a Convention of States to propose amendments. It takes 34 states to call the convention and 38 to ratify any amendments that are proposed.

The full text of the Constitution's Article V reads:

The Congress, whenever two thirds of both houses shall deem it necessary, shall propose amendments to this Constitution, or, on the application of the legislatures of two thirds of the several states, shall call a convention for proposing amendments, which, in either case, shall be valid to all intents and purposes, as part of this Constitution, when ratified by the legislatures of three fourths of the several states, or by conventions in three fourths thereof, as the one or the other mode of ratification may be proposed by the Congress; provided that no amendment which may be made prior to the year one thousand eight hundred and eight shall in any manner affect the first and fourth clauses in the ninth section of the first article; and that no state, without its consent, shall be deprived of its equal suffrage in the Senate.

The **Convention of States Action resolution** allows the states to discuss amendment proposals that "limit the power and jurisdiction of the federal government, impose fiscal restraints on the federal government, and place term limits on federal officials." This is truly a solution as big as the problem but is a Constitutional remedy to make changes rather than tear the government apart through tyranny and start new.

Should we do this? There are a number of states already signed up.

Which states are in the convention of states?

Fifteen states have already passed the Convention of States Project's application (Florida, Georgia, Alaska, Alabama, Tennessee, Indiana, Oklahoma, Louisiana, Arizona, North Dakota, Texas, Missouri, Arkansas, Utah, and Mississippi).

How many states are required in order for a convention to meet?

Under Article V of the U.S. Constitution, Congress is required to hold a constitutional convention if two-thirds of state legislatures (34 states) call for one.

Convention to propose amendments to the United States Constitution

From Wikipedia, the free encyclopedia:

This article is about amending the U.S. Constitution. For the proposal to reform and rewrite the Constitution, see the Second Constitutional Convention of the United States.

A **convention to propose amendments to the United States Constitution**, also referred to as an **Article V Convention, state convention,** or **amendatory convention,** is one of two methods authorized by Article Five of the United States Constitution whereby amendments to the United States Constitution may be proposed: on the Application of two-thirds of the State legislatures (that is, 34 of the 50) the Congress shall call a convention for proposing amendments, which become law only after ratification by three-fourths of the states (38 of the 50). The Article V convention method has never been used, but 33 amendments have been proposed by the other method, a two-thirds vote in both houses of Congress, and 27 of these have been ratified by three-fourths of the States. Although there has never been a federal constitutional convention since the original one, at the state level more than 230 constitutional conventions have assembled in the United States.

While there have been calls for an Article V Convention based on a single issue, such as the balanced budget amendment, it is not clear whether a convention summoned in this way would be legally bound to limit discussion to a single issue; law professor Michael Stokes Paulsen has suggested that such a convention would have the "power to propose anything it sees fit," whereas law professor Michael Rappaport and attorney-at-law Robert Kelly believe that a limited convention is possible.

In recent years, some have argued that state governments should call for such a convention. They include Michael Farris, Lawrence Lessig, Sanford Levinson, Larry Sabato, Jonathan Turley, Mark Levin, Ben Shapiro, and Greg Abbott. In 2015, Citizens for Self-Governance launched a nationwide effort to require Congress to call an Article V Convention through a project called Convention of the States in a bid to "rein in the federal government." As of 2024, CSG's resolution has passed in 19 states. Similarly, the group Wolf-PAC chose this method to promote its cause, which is to overturn the U.S. Supreme Court's decision in *Citizens United v. FEC*. Their resolution has passed in five states.

In late 2023, The Heritage Foundation issued a report titled *Reconsidering the Wisdom of an Article V Convention of the States.*

Organizations opposed to an Article V convention include the John Birch Society, the Center on Budget and Policy Priorities, Eagle Forum, Common Cause, Cato Institute, and the Ron Paul Institute for Peace and Prosperity. Law Professor emeritus William A. Woodruff has pointed out that James Madison, the Father of the Constitution, a member of the Virginia legislature, a delegate to the Philadelphia Convention, and a delegate to the Annapolis Convention that recommended what became the Philadelphia Convention was opposed to an Article V convention to consider adding a bill of rights to the Constitution. When asked whether a convention should be called to consider a bill of rights, Madison said, "Having witnessed the difficulties and dangers experienced by the first Convention which assembled under every propitious circumstance, I should tremble for the result of a second . . . . " Woodruff urges state legislators who are asked to vote in favor of an application to Congress to call an Article V convention to carefully consider the knowns and unknowns of the convention method before opening Constitutions to a series of unintended consequences.[8]

---

[8]   https://en.wikipedia.org/wiki/Convention_to_propose_amendments_to_the_United_States_Constitution#:~:text=A%20convention%20to%20propose%20amendments,may%20be%20proposed%3A%20on%20the

Chapter 13

A Personal Note Concerning My Ambition to Pen This Manuscript

The Magna Carta Full Text

As a child, my parents always took us to historic sites such as Fort Ticonderoga, Concord, Boston, and all its famous sites, the historic USS Constitution, Plymouth, and many others representing the founding of our nation. They thought that even young minds would absorb what they saw. It worked; we are all very well based on our societal roles.

As a researcher, an extension of my early years, into our family history, it was discovered that a relative, **Ingram De Boynton,** Yorkshire, England, actually rebelled against King John from the years of 1216 to 1220. The people of England needed relief. A. Magna Carta Libertatum (Medieval Latin for "Great Charter of Freedoms"), commonly called Magna Carta or sometimes Magna Charta ("Great Charter"), is a royal charter of rights agreed to and affixed his seal by King John of England at Runnymede, near Windsor, on 15 June 1215. On this day, Ingram De Boynton, a knight, returned home, married into money and estate, and lived as a country gentleman.

The Magna Carta was and is the first document to put into writing the principle that the king and his government were not above the law. I am including the full content of the Magna Carta since the points in the document closely resemble to points the framers of our Constitution used.

The Magna Carta with translations by the British Library

The king and the rebel barons negotiated a peace settlement in June 1215. The king agreed to accept the terms of the Magna Carta, which is dated 15 June 1215.

Note by British Library: Clauses marked (+) were repeated in the charter of 1225, but with minor changes. Clauses marked (*) were omitted in all later reissues of the charter. In the charter itself the clauses are not numbered, and the text reads continuously.

JOHN, by the grace of God, King of England, Lord of Ireland, Duke of Normandy and Aquitaine, and Count of Anjou, to his archbishops, bishops, abbots, earls, barons, justices, foresters, sheriffs, stewards, servants, and to all his officials and loyal subjects, Greeting.

KNOW THAT BEFORE GOD, for the health of our soul and those of our ancestors and heirs, to the honour of God, the exaltation of the holy Church, and the better ordering of our kingdom, at the advice of our reverend fathers Stephen, archbishop of Canterbury, primate of all England, and cardinal of the holy Roman Church, Henry archbishop of Dublin, William bishop of London, Peter bishop of Winchester, Jocelin bishop of Bath and Glastonbury, Hugh bishop of Lincoln, Walter bishop of Worcester, William bishop of Coventry, Benedict bishop of Rochester, Master Pandulf subdeacon and member of the papal household, Brother Aymeric master of the knighthood of the Temple in England, William Marshal earl of Pembroke, William earl of Salisbury, William earl of Warren, William earl of Arundel, Alan of Galloway constable of Scotland, Warin fitz Gerald, Peter fitz Herbert, Hubert de Burgh seneschal of Poitou, Hugh de Neville, Matthew fitz Herbert, Thomas Basset, Alan Basset, Philip Daubeny, Robert de Roppeley, John Marshal, John fitz Hugh, and other loyal subjects:

+ (1) FIRST, THAT WE HAVE GRANTED TO GOD, and by this present charter have confirmed for us and our heirs in perpetuity, that the English Church shall be free, and shall have its rights undiminished, and its liberties unimpaired. That we wish this so to be observed, appears from the fact that of our own free will, before the outbreak of the present dispute between us and our barons, we granted and confirmed by charter the freedom of the Church's elections – a right reckoned to be of the greatest necessity and importance to it – and caused this to be confirmed by Pope Innocent III. This freedom we shall observe ourselves, and desire to be observed in good faith by our heirs in perpetuity. TO ALL FREE MEN OF OUR KINGDOM we have also granted, for us and our heirs for ever, all the liberties written out below, to have and to keep for them and their heirs, of us and our heirs:

(2) If any earl, baron, or other person that holds lands directly of the Crown, for military service, shall die, and at his death his heir shall be of full age and owe a 'relief', the heir shall have his inheritance on payment of the ancient scale of 'relief'. That is to say, the heir or heirs of an earl shall pay £100 for the entire earl's barony, the heir or heirs of a knight 100s. at most for the entire knight's 'fee', and any man that owes less shall pay less, in accordance with the ancient usage of 'fees'.

(3) But if the heir of such a person is under age and a ward, when he comes of age he shall have his inheritance without 'relief' or fine.

(4) The guardian of the land of an heir who is under age shall take from it only reasonable revenues, customary dues, and feudal services. He shall do this without destruction or damage to men or property. If we have given the guardianship of the land to a sheriff, or to any person answerable to us for the revenues, and he commits destruction or damage, we will exact compensation from him, and the land shall be entrusted to two worthy and prudent men of the same 'fee', who shall be answerable to us for the revenues, or to the person to whom we have assigned them. If we have given or sold to anyone the guardianship of such land, and he causes destruction or

damage, he shall lose the guardianship of it, and it shall be handed over to two worthy and prudent men of the same 'fee', who shall be similarly answerable to us.

(5) For so long as a guardian has guardianship of such land, he shall maintain the houses, parks, fish preserves, ponds, mills, and everything else pertaining to it, from the revenues of the land itself. When the heir comes of age, he shall restore the whole land to him, stocked with plough teams and such implements of husbandry as the season demands and the revenues from the land can reasonably bear.

(6) Heirs may be given in marriage, but not to someone of lower social standing. Before a marriage takes place, it shall be made known to the heir's next-of-kin.

(7) At her husband's death, a widow may have her marriage portion and inheritance at once and without trouble. She shall pay nothing for her dower, marriage portion, or any inheritance that she and her husband held jointly on the day of his death. She may remain in her husband's house for forty days after his death, and within this period her dower shall be assigned to her.

(8) No widow shall be compelled to marry, so long as she wishes to remain without a husband. But she must give security that she will not marry without royal consent, if she holds her lands of the Crown, or without the consent of whatever other lord she may hold them of.

(9) Neither we nor our officials will seize any land or rent in payment of a debt, so long as the debtor has movable goods sufficient to discharge the debt. A debtor's sureties shall not be distrained upon so long as the debtor himself can discharge his debt. If, for lack of means, the debtor is unable to discharge his debt, his sureties shall be answerable for it. If they so desire, they may have the debtor's lands and rents until they have received satisfaction for the debt that

they paid for him, unless the debtor can show that he has settled his obligations to them.

* (10) If anyone who has borrowed a sum of money from Jews dies before the debt has been repaid, his heir shall pay no interest on the debt for so long as he remains under age, irrespective of whom he holds his lands. If such a debt falls into the hands of the Crown, it will take nothing except the principal sum specified in the bond.

* (11) If a man dies owing money to Jews, his wife may have her dower and pay nothing towards the debt from it. If he leaves children that are under age, their needs may also be provided for on a scale appropriate to the size of his holding of lands. The debt is to be paid out of the residue, reserving the service due to his feudal lords. Debts owed to persons other than Jews are to be dealt with similarly.

* (12) No 'scutage' or 'aid' may be levied in our kingdom without its general consent, unless it is for the ransom of our person, to make our eldest son a knight, and (once) to marry our eldest daughter. For these purposes only a reasonable 'aid' may be levied. 'Aids' from the city of London are to be treated similarly.

+ (13) The city of London shall enjoy all its ancient liberties and free customs, both by land and by water. We also will and grant that all other cities, boroughs, towns, and ports shall enjoy all their liberties and free customs.

* (14) To obtain the general consent of the realm for the assessment of an 'aid' – except in the three cases specified above – or a 'scutage', we will cause the archbishops, bishops, abbots, earls, and greater barons to be summoned individually by letter. To those who hold lands directly of us we will cause a general summons to be issued, through the sheriffs and other officials, to come together on a fixed day (of which at least forty days notice shall be given) and at a fixed place. In all letters of summons, the cause of the summons will be stated.

When a summons has been issued, the business appointed for the day shall go forward in accordance with the resolution of those present, even if not all those who were summoned have appeared.

* (15) In future we will allow no one to levy an 'aid' from his free men, except to ransom his person, to make his eldest son a knight, and (once) to marry his eldest daughter. For these purposes only a reasonable 'aid' may be levied.

(16) No man shall be forced to perform more service for a knight's 'fee', or other free holding of land, than is due from it.

(17) Ordinary lawsuits shall not follow the royal court around, but shall be held in a fixed place.

(18) Inquests of novel disseisin, mort d'ancestor, and darrein presentment shall be taken only in their proper county court. We ourselves, or in our absence abroad our chief justice, will send two justices to each county four times a year, and these justices, with four knights of the county elected by the county itself, shall hold the assizes in the county court, on the day and in the place where the court meets.

(19) If any assizes cannot be taken on the day of the county court, as many knights and freeholders shall afterwards remain behind, of those who have attended the court, as will suffice for the administration of justice, having regard to the volume of business to be done.

(20) For a trivial offence, a free man shall be fined only in proportion to the degree of his offence, and for a serious offence correspondingly, but not so heavily as to deprive him of his livelihood. In the same way, a merchant shall be spared his merchandise, and a villein the implements of his husbandry, if they fall upon the mercy of a royal court. None of these fines shall be imposed except by the assessment on oath of reputable men of the neighbourhood.

(21) Earls and barons shall be fined only by their equals, and in proportion to the gravity of their offence.

(22) A fine imposed upon the lay property of a clerk in holy orders shall be assessed upon the same principles, without reference to the value of his ecclesiastical benefice.

(23) No town or person shall be forced to build bridges over rivers except those with an ancient obligation to do so.

(24) No sheriff, constable, coroners, or other royal officials are to hold lawsuits that should be held by the royal justices.

* (25) Every county, hundred, wapentake, and tithing shall remain at its ancient rent, without increase, except the royal demesne manors.

(26) If at the death of a man who holds a lay 'fee' of the Crown, a sheriff or royal official produces royal letters patent of summons for a debt due to the Crown, it shall be lawful for them to seize and list movable goods found in the lay 'fee' of the dead man to the value of the debt, as assessed by worthy men. Nothing shall be removed until the whole debt is paid, when the residue shall be given over to the executors to carry out the dead man's will. If no debt is due to the Crown, all the movable goods shall be regarded as the property of the dead man, except the reasonable shares of his wife and children.

* (27) If a free man dies intestate, his movable goods are to be distributed by his next-of-kin and friends, under the supervision of the Church. The rights of his debtors are to be preserved.

(28) No constable or other royal official shall take corn or other movable goods from any man without immediate payment, unless the seller voluntarily offers postponement of this.

(29) No constable may compel a knight to pay money for castle-guard if the knight is willing to undertake the guard in person, or

with reasonable excuse to supply some other fit man to do it. A knight taken or sent on military service shall be excused from castle-guard for the period of this service.

(30) No sheriff, royal official, or other person shall take horses or carts for transport from any free man, without his consent.

(31) Neither we nor any royal official will take wood for our castle, or for any other purpose, without the consent of the owner.

(32) We will not keep the lands of people convicted of felony in our hand for longer than a year and a day, after which they shall be returned to the lords of the 'fees' concerned.

(33) All fish-weirs shall be removed from the Thames, the Medway, and throughout the whole of England, except on the sea coast.

(34) The writ called precipe shall not in future be issued to anyone in respect of any holding of land, if a free man could thereby be deprived of the right of trial in his own lord's court.

(35) There shall be standard measures of wine, ale, and corn (the London quarter), throughout the kingdom. There shall also be a standard width of dyed cloth, russet, and haberject, namely two ells within the selvedges. Weights are to be standardised similarly.

(36) In future nothing shall be paid or accepted for the issue of a writ of inquisition of life or limbs. It shall be given gratis, and not refused.

(37) If a man holds land of the Crown by 'fee-farm', 'socage', or 'burgage', and also holds land of someone else for knight's service, we will not have guardianship of his heir, nor of the land that belongs to the other person's 'fee', by virtue of the 'fee-farm', 'socage', or 'burgage', unless the 'fee-farm' owes knight's service. We will not have the guardianship of a man's heir, or of land that he holds of someone else, by reason of any small property that he may hold of the Crown for a service of knives, arrows, or the like.

(38) In future no official shall place a man on trial upon his own unsupported statement, without producing credible witnesses to the truth of it.

+ (39) No free man shall be seized or imprisoned, or stripped of his rights or possessions, or outlawed or exiled, or deprived of his standing in any way, nor will we proceed with force against him, or send others to do so, except by the lawful judgment of his equals or by the law of the land.

+ (40) To no one will we sell, to no one deny or delay right or justice.

(41) All merchants may enter or leave England unharmed and without fear, and may stay or travel within it, by land or water, for purposes of trade, free from all illegal exactions, in accordance with ancient and lawful customs. This, however, does not apply in time of war to merchants from a country that is at war with us. Any such merchants found in our country at the outbreak of war shall be detained without injury to their persons or property, until we or our chief justice have discovered how our own merchants are being treated in the country at war with us. If our own merchants are safe they shall be safe too.

* (42) In future it shall be lawful for any man to leave and return to our kingdom unharmed and without fear, by land or water, preserving his allegiance to us, except in time of war, for some short period, for the common benefit of the realm. People that have been imprisoned or outlawed in accordance with the law of the land, people from a country that is at war with us, and merchants – who shall be dealt with as stated above – are excepted from this provision.

(43) If a man holds lands of any 'escheat' such as the 'honour' of Wallingford, Nottingham, Boulogne, Lancaster, or of other 'escheats' in our hand that are baronies, at his death his heir shall give us only the 'relief' and service that he would have made to the baron, had

66

the barony been in the baron's hand. We will hold the 'escheat' in the same manner as the baron held it.

(44) People who live outside the forest need not in future appear before the royal justices of the forest in answer to general summonses, unless they are actually involved in proceedings or are sureties for someone who has been seized for a forest offence.

* (45) We will appoint as justices, constables, sheriffs, or other officials, only men that know the law of the realm and are minded to keep it well.

(46) All barons who have founded abbeys, and have charters of English kings or ancient tenure as evidence of this, may have guardianship of them when there is no abbot, as is their due.

(47) All forests that have been created in our reign shall at once be disafforested. River-banks that have been enclosed in our reign shall be treated similarly.

*(48) All evil customs relating to forests and warrens, foresters, warreners, sheriffs and their servants, or river-banks and their wardens, are at once to be investigated in every county by twelve sworn knights of the county, and within forty days of their enquiry the evil customs are to be abolished completely and irrevocably. But we, or our chief justice if we are not in England, are first to be informed.

* (49) We will at once return all hostages and charters delivered up to us by Englishmen as security for peace or for loyal service.

* (50) We will remove completely from their offices the kinsmen of Gerard de Athée, and in future they shall hold no offices in England. The people in question are Engelard de Cigogné, Peter, Guy, and Andrew de Chanceaux, Guy de Cigogné, Geoffrey de Martigny and his brothers, Philip Marc and his brothers, with Geoffrey his nephew, and all their followers.

* (51) As soon as peace is restored, we will remove from the kingdom all the foreign knights, bowmen, their attendants, and the mercenaries that have come to it, to its harm, with horses and arms.

* (52) To any man whom we have deprived or dispossessed of lands, castles, liberties, or rights, without the lawful judgment of his equals, we will at once restore these. In cases of dispute the matter shall be resolved by the judgment of the twenty-five barons referred to below in the clause for securing the peace (§61). In cases, however, where a man was deprived or dispossessed of something without the lawful judgment of his equals by our father King Henry or our brother King Richard, and it remains in our hands or is held by others under our warranty, we shall have respite for the period commonly allowed to Crusaders, unless a lawsuit had been begun, or an enquiry had been made at our order, before we took the Cross as a Crusader. On our return from the Crusade, or if we abandon it, we will at once render justice in full.

* (53) We shall have similar respite in rendering justice in connexion with forests that are to be disafforested, or to remain forests, when these were first afforested by our father Henry or our brother Richard; with the guardianship of lands in another person's 'fee', when we have hitherto had this by virtue of a 'fee' held of us for knight's service by a third party; and with abbeys founded in another person's 'fee', in which the lord of the 'fee' claims to own a right. On our return from the Crusade, or if we abandon it, we will at once do full justice to complaints about these matters.

(54) No one shall be arrested or imprisoned on the appeal of a woman for the death of any person except her husband.

* (55) All fines that have been given to us unjustly and against the law of the land, and all fines that we have exacted unjustly, shall be entirely remitted or the matter decided by a majority judgment of the twenty-five barons referred to below in the clause for securing the

peace (§61) together with Stephen, archbishop of Canterbury, if he can be present, and such others as he wishes to bring with him. If the archbishop cannot be present, proceedings shall continue without him, provided that if any of the twenty-five barons has been involved in a similar suit himself, his judgment shall be set aside, and someone else chosen and sworn in his place, as a substitute for the single occasion, by the rest of the twenty-five.

(56) If we have deprived or dispossessed any Welshmen of land, liberties, or anything else in England or in Wales, without the lawful judgment of their equals, these are at once to be returned to them. A dispute on this point shall be determined in the Marches by the judgment of equals. English law shall apply to holdings of land in England, Welsh law to those in Wales, and the law of the Marches to those in the Marches. The Welsh shall treat us and ours in the same way.

* (57) In cases where a Welshman was deprived or dispossessed of anything, without the lawful judgment of his equals, by our father King Henry or our brother King Richard, and it remains in our hands or is held by others under our warranty, we shall have respite for the period commonly allowed to Crusaders, unless a lawsuit had been begun, or an enquiry had been made at our order, before we took the Cross as a Crusader. But on our return from the Crusade, or if we abandon it, we will at once do full justice according to the laws of Wales and the said regions.

* (58) We will at once return the son of Llywelyn, all Welsh hostages, and the charters delivered to us as security for the peace.

* (59) With regard to the return of the sisters and hostages of Alexander, king of Scotland, his liberties and his rights, we will treat him in the same way as our other barons of England, unless it appears from the charters that we hold from his father William, formerly king

of Scotland, that he should be treated otherwise. This matter shall be resolved by the judgment of his equals in our court.

(60) All these customs and liberties that we have granted shall be observed in our kingdom in so far as concerns our own relations with our subjects. Let all men of our kingdom, whether clergy or laymen, observe them similarly in their relations with their own men.

* (61) SINCE WE HAVE GRANTED ALL THESE THINGS for God, for the better ordering of our kingdom, and to allay the discord that has arisen between us and our barons, and since we desire that they shall be enjoyed in their entirety, with lasting strength, for ever, we give and grant to the barons the following security:

The barons shall elect twenty-five of their number to keep, and cause to be observed with all their might, the peace and liberties granted and confirmed to them by this charter.

If we, our chief justice, our officials, or any of our servants offend in any respect against any man, or transgress any of the articles of the peace or of this security, and the offence is made known to four of the said twenty-five barons, they shall come to us – or in our absence from the kingdom to the chief justice – to declare it and claim immediate redress. If we, or in our absence abroad the chief justice, make no redress within forty days, reckoning from the day on which the offence was declared to us or to him, the four barons shall refer the matter to the rest of the twenty-five barons, who may distrain upon and assail us in every way possible, with the support of the whole community of the land, by seizing our castles, lands, possessions, or anything else saving only our own person and those of the queen and our children, until they have secured such redress as they have determined upon. Having secured the redress, they may then resume their normal obedience to us.

Any man who so desires may take an oath to obey the commands of the twenty-five barons for the achievement of these ends, and to join with them in assailing us to the utmost of his power. We give public and free permission to take this oath to any man who so desires, and at no time will we prohibit any man from taking it. Indeed, we will compel any of our subjects who are unwilling to take it to swear it at our command.

If one of the twenty-five barons dies or leaves the country or is prevented in any other way from discharging his duties, the rest of them shall choose another baron in his place, at their discretion, who shall be duly sworn in as they were.

In the event of disagreement among the twenty-five barons on any matter referred to them for decision, the verdict of the majority present shall have the same validity as a unanimous verdict of the whole twenty-five, whether these were all present or some of those summoned were unwilling or unable to appear.

The twenty-five barons shall swear to obey all the above articles faithfully and shall cause them to be obeyed by others to the best of their power.

We will not seek to procure from anyone, either by our own efforts or those of a third party, anything by which any part of these concessions or liberties might be revoked or diminished. Should such a thing be procured, it shall be null, and void and we will at no time make use of it, either ourselves or through a third party.

* (62) We have remitted and pardoned fully to all men any ill-will, hurt, or grudges that have arisen between us and our subjects, whether clergy or laymen, since the beginning of the dispute. We have in addition remitted fully, and for our own part have also pardoned, to all clergy and laymen any offences committed as a result

of the said dispute between Easter in the sixteenth year of our reign (i.e. 1215) and the restoration of peace.

In addition we have caused letters patent to be made for the barons, bearing witness to this security and to the concessions set out above, over the seals of Stephen archbishop of Canterbury, Henry archbishop of Dublin, the other bishops named above, and Master Pandulf.

* (63) IT IS ACCORDINGLY OUR WISH AND COMMAND that the English Church shall be free, and that men in our kingdom shall have and keep all these liberties, rights, and concessions, well and peaceably in their fullness and entirety for them and their heirs, of us and our heirs, in all things and all places for ever.

Both we and the barons have sworn that all this shall be observed in good faith and without deceit. Witness the abovementioned people and many others.

Given by our hand in the meadow that is called Runnymede, between Windsor and Staines, on the fifteenth day of June in the seventeenth year of our reign (i.e. 1215: the new regnal year began on 28 May).

Translation by the British Library.

Chapter 14

Secret Societies and the Founding of a Nation

Founding fathers, secret societies: Freemasons, Illuminati, Rosicrucian's, and the decoding of the Great Seal / Robert Hieronimus, with Laura Cortner.

Bibliographic records and links to related information are available from the Library of Congress catalog.[9]

Author special note: There is one organization Laura Cortner did not mention in her article and it involved 7 Inner and Middle Templers. I have found evidence of their involvement that have been included in this chapter.

American Declaration of Independence

Templars

Seven members of Inner or Middle Temple were among the signatories to the Declaration of Independence in 1776: Thomas Hayward, Jun., from 1778 Judge of the High Court of South Carolina; Thomas Lynch; Thomas McKean, President of Delaware and Chief Justice of Pennsylvania in 1777; Arthur Middleton; William Paca, later Governor of Maryland; and Edward Rutledge, later Governor of South Carolina. John Dickinson of Middle Temple, who drafted the Articles of Federation and became President of Delaware in 1781,

---

[9] https://lccn.loc.gov/2005028215
Hieronimus, Robert. Founding fathers, secret societies : Freemasons, Illuminati, Rosicrucians, and the decoding of the Great Seal / Robert Hieronimus, with Laura Cortner. Rev. ed. Rochester, Vt. : Destiny Books, c2006.

famously refused to sign since he was still seeking reconciliation with Britain as well as liberty.

Seven Middle Templars signed the American Constitution in 1787: John Blair, Chief Justice of Virginia; John Dickinson; Jared Ingersoll, first Attorney-General of Pennsylvania; William Livingston, Governor of New Jersey; John Rutledge, chairman of the drafting committee and the second Chief Justice of the United States; Charles Pinckney and Charles Cotesworth Pinckney.

The American Declaration of Independence, 4 July 1776. The Preamble declares:

We hold these truths to be self-evident: that all men are created equal, that they are endowed by their Creator with certain unalienable Rights, and that among these are Life, Liberty, and the pursuit of Happiness. That to secure these rights, Governments are instituted among Men, deriving their just powers from the consent of the governed, that whenever any form of Government becomes destructive of these ends, it is the Right of the People to alter or to abolish it, and to institute new Government, laying its foundation on such principles and organizing its powers in such form, as to them shall seem most likely to effect their Safety and Happiness.

On 31 August 1858, at Carlinville, Illinois, Abraham Lincoln, arguing against slavery, described that first sentence as 'the gem of the magna charta of human liberty.' 'We must never cease to proclaim in fearless tones the great principles of freedom and the rights of man which are the joint inheritance of the English-speaking world and which through Magna Carta, the Bill of Rights, the Habeas Corpus, trial by jury, and the English common law find their most famous expression in the American Declaration of Independence.'

John Trumbull, The Declaration of Independence: the Drafting Committee presenting its Work (painted in 1818). From Inner or Middle Temple: 1. Thomas Lynch, at the right-hand end of the seated group. 2. William Paca, standing on the left. 3. Arthur Middleton, standing at the right-hand end of the group. 4. Thomas Heyward, sitting in front of and slightly to the left of Middleton. 5. John Dickinson (not a signatory), standing between two others. 6. Edward Rutledge. 7. Thomas McKean, sitting to their right.

Back to Timeline[10]

American Constitution

1787

Above: Howard Chandler Christy, The Constitutional Convention signing the Constitution of the United States (painted in 1940). From Inner or Middle Temple: 1. John Rutledge. 2. Charles Pinkney. 3. Charles Cotesworth. 4. Jared Ingersoll. 5. William Livingstone. 6. John Blair. 7. John Dickinson.

From the outset, the great clauses of the Magna Carta informed the constitutional life of the New World:

The General Assembly of Maryland, 1639. The inhabitants of this Province shall have all their rights and liberties according to the Great Charter in England.

---

[10] American Independence to the American Constitution – 1776–87 - Temple Church

The Body of Liberties, Massachusetts, 1641. No man's life shall be taken away, no man's honor or good name shall be stained, no man's person shall be arrested, restrained, banished, dismembered, nor any ways punished... unless it is by virtue or equity of some express law of the Country warranting the same.

In 1761, 63 merchants expanded this body of liberties by bringing suit against British Law that allowed the search of homes and businesses without written or prior warning. James Otis lost the case (Paxton and Gray) when the British invoked that an "act against the constitution is void." Otis stated that Britain had no constitution and that case law should have taken precedence.

The question at hand was, "Should we accept tyranny" administered by the British, a global power? At this time, we can say that **"WE THE PEOPLE"** was established.

"We need not feel inadequate for being in the minority. God has designed us to live in freedom."

The Massachusetts Circular Letter of Colonial Defiance of 1767 was a full twenty years before the signing of the Constitution.

Document authored by Andrew Tylock September 13, 2018, as Categories American Revolution; this was eight years before Lexington/Concord. This document was the second notice that the colonists were not going to stand by silently as the British overstepped its constitutional authority. In 1765, the British passed the Stamp Act, but it was quickly repealed due to the uproar as the colonists refused to pay it. Not having learned their lesson, the British passed the Decarity Act or American Colonies Act that laid heavy taxes, and to add insult, they sent over the Townsend Acts that levied duties on imported goods. The final straw, it seems, was the Revenue Act of 1767, which used funds for judges, governors, and tax collectors for the crown, in actions implemented by Samuel Adams and James Otis in 1768, which called for a boycott of British goods. In essence, they did not want "taxation without representation, and they did not care where the taxes came from by the colonists or from Parliament but were abused as the end result.

The British repealed most of the Townsend Act, and this led to the Boston Tea Party.

Acts and Orders for the Colony... of Providence, 1647. That no person in this Colony shall be taken or imprisoned or be seized of his lands or liberties, or be exiled, or any otherwise molested or destroyed, but by the lawful judgment of his peers, or by some known law, and according to the letter of it, ratified and confirmed by the major part of the General Assembly lawfully met and orderly managed.

Constitution of the United States of America, from the Fifth and Sixth Amendments, 15 December 1791. No person shall be deprived of life, liberty, or property without due process of law... The accused shall enjoy the right to a speedy and public trial by an impartial jury of the State and district wherein the crime shall have been committed.

Seven Middle Templars signed the American Constitution in 1787: John Blair, Chief Justice of Virginia; John Dickinson, 'Penman of the Revolution' and President of Delaware and of Pennsylvania; Jared Ingersoll, first Attorney-General of Pennsylvania; William Livingstone, Governor of New Jersey; John Rutledge, chairman of the drafting committee and second Chief Justice of the United States; Charles Pinckney, Governor of South Carolina; and Charles Cotesworth Pinckney, Minister to France and twice Presidential candidate.

Freemasons

Historians have offered many reasons for the fact that a rag-tag American army, led by a general who had to go to the library to brush up on battle tactics, could defeat the strongest military power in the world. Many valid factors have been cited- the barrier of the Atlantic Ocean, the weakness of King George and his problems at home, the guerrilla tactics of the American army, etc. - but what has been overlooked is the influence of secret societies, especially Freemasonry, on America's leaders. Some esoteric historians (Hall, 1951; Case, 1935) cite that of the 56 signers of the Declaration of Independence, at least 50 were Freemasons.

Whether this is a fact or not cannot be presently corroborated, but substantial information supports that many of the officers and enlisted men in the American military were Freemasons, and many practiced the craft in the military lodges. According to General Lafayette (a Freemason himself), Washington "never willingly gave independent command to officers who were not Freemasons. Nearly all the members of his official family, as well as most other officers who shared his inmost confidence, were his brethren of the mystic tie" (Morse, 1924, ix). Freemasonry allowed Washington greater control of and influence on his army. Those who breached military and Masonic secrets faced the penalty of death. Manly Hall (1951) and Paul F. Case (1935) report that 12 of Washington's generals were Freemasons and that this, in part, accounted for their strong allegiance during America's darkest hours. The underlying philosophy of Freemasonry ("The Brotherhood of Man and the Fatherhood of God") was the foundation of political, religious, social, and educational reform, which was opposed by the monarchies of Europe and ecclesiastical authorities as well.

Washington's leadership and involvement with the craft gave him the confidence that America's military secrets were safe. His involvement in Freemasonry, as Master of the Lodge, provided him with more than confidence because the lodge ritual's function was to elevate the participant's consciousness. A group of Freemasons experiencing the rituals and initiations in an altered state of awareness provided the internal strength and fortitude for them to grasp the importance of the American revolutionary experience and its meaning for humanity as a whole. Thus, the Atlantic Ocean, guerrilla tactics, and King George's conflicts contributed to the defeat of the English army, but so did the Freemasonic experience. It provided Washington with the will and capacity to defeat King George when the world expected America's defeat.

Thomas Jefferson

Was Thomas Jefferson a member of any secret societies? Masonic sources say he was, but no one has turned up documentary evidence of his initiation. The Masonic *Bible* (1960), however, has "unmistakable evidence that he was an active mason." These include records of his name as a visitor in a cornerstone-laying ceremony and references in twenty-nine issues of Masonic journals to his status as a Mason. Jefferson's humanitarian beliefs were harmonious with eighteenth-century Masonry. It has been suggested that Jefferson may have been initiated in France. if so, an American initiation record would not exist.

The Rosicrucians

From Wikipedia, the free encyclopedia

It's claimed that Washington and Franklin were members, but these sources do not provide irrefutable evidence. In Jefferson's case, however, Dr. H. Spencer Lewis, former Imperator of the Rosicrucian order, introduces a piece of substantial evidence. Lewis found among Jefferson's papers some "strange-looking characters" that previous researcher had assumed were a code Jefferson had invented. "I recognized it as one of the old Rosicrucian codes used for many years before Thomas Jefferson became a Rosicrucian, and still to be found in many of the ancient Rosicrucian secret manuscripts" (Heindon, 1961, 126). I have submitted this code to several cryptographers and none have yet been successful in identifying it. Mr. Rex Daniels of Concord, Massachusetts, commented (March 14, 1974), "I have taken several tries at the code with no success for the standard ones... you have hit upon something nobody else seems to know about." Jefferson's visions of America can be translated as expansionist. His Louisiana Purchase was not only a landmark in the development of the American nation but an expression of an "Empire for Liberty" that would manifest in the annexing of Canada and Cuba. From this vantage, the Monroe Doctrine, which Jefferson strongly urged upon President James Monroe, was not as much a separation of America from Europe as a natural expansion of America's destiny to include the South American continent. In Jefferson's words: *America, North, and South, has a set of interests distinct from those of Europe . . . while the last is laboring to become the domicile of despotism, our endeavor should surely be to make our hemisphere that of freedom. What a colossus shall we be when the southern continent comes up to our mark! What a stand will it secure as a ralliance for the reason and freedom of the globe!* (Boorstin, 1963, 232) Jefferson's most prized accomplishment, founding the University of Virginia, was based on the traditions of the schools of Athens and Florence and the Alexandrian Library: he wanted to ensure freedom from all theological restraint.

Jennings C. Wise theorized that within Jefferson's architectural design of the university are hidden the teachings of the mystery schools and secret societies. Realizing that curricula could be altered, Wise suggests, Jefferson embedded the philosophy of the mystical tradition in the bricks and mortar of the university, so that its design would convey a philosophy free from dogma and superstition. Jefferson unites the ancient architectural elements of the rotunda and the rectangular academic hall, which symbolize heaven (the rotunda as used in the Chaldean Planet Tower called the House of the Seven Spheres) and earth (the four-cornered rectangle). They are used together in one structure.

Illuminati

Thomas Jefferson | Library of Congress

Robison's warnings of the **Illuminati** reached the United States at a vulnerable time. Still forming their more perfect union, Americans felt acutely vulnerable to foreign interference. But by the late 1790s, this anxiety had broken along partisan lines. Federalists feared that France's revolutionaries were bent on turning Americans against their nascent government, whereas Jeffersonian Republicans worried instead that Great Britain was scheming to reclaim its former colonies.

The New England of Federalists like Dwight was, in particular, primed to receive news of a godless network of spies and invaders. Calvinist remnants of the original Puritans (including Congregationalists and Presbyterians) still dominated New England politics, and they were wary of any attempt to separate church and state. They supported their man John Adams for reelection against the Republican Thomas Jefferson, a Deist who at times seemed to verge into atheism. (While Jefferson believed Jesus Christ to be an enlightened prophet, he famously dismissed both the Resurrection and the miracles of the Gospels as mythology.) This, combined with his generally positive attitude toward post-Revolution France, made him a likely candidate for Illuminati subversion. That July Fourth, Dwight's brother, Theodore, proclaimed, "I know not who belonged to that Society in this country, but if I were about to make proselytes to illuminism in the United States, I should in the first place apply to

Thomas Jefferson, Albert Gallatin [a U.S. House Representative from Pennsylvania and future Treasury secretary under Jefferson], and their political associates."

But having worked to stoke the public's fear of the Illuminati's infiltration of the United States, the Federalists were perhaps not prepared for how quickly this paranoia would be turned against them. Had they known, they would have perhaps been kinder to a man named John C. Ogden. A little-known and long-forgotten preacher, Ogden, had tried for years to establish himself in New England but repeatedly spoke out against what he saw as the entrenched power structure of the Congregationalist clergy, and in 1793, he left New England for New York and Philadelphia. Embittered, he began publishing a series of anonymous articles in the anti-Federalist Philadelphia paper, the *Aurora,* published by William Duane, who would go on to become a powerful lawmaker in Pennsylvania and secretary of the Treasury under President Andrew Jackson.

Ogden's series was about a conspiracy he claimed to have uncovered. The New England of Morse and the Dwight brothers may have publicly opposed Illumatism, Ogden argued, but this was all a front: They were, in fact, secret Illuminati, and it was *they*—not Thomas Jefferson—who were bent on destroying America's young democracy.

Chapter 15

A Civic leader, Lt. Commander Claire Bloom – U.S.S. Constitution

Author note: I have a woman friend, U.S. Navy Lt. Commander Claire Bloom, Retired. She is an extraordinary woman, to say the least, and I am proud to know her. She served as Deputy Director for Women's Policy in the Navy and was the very first woman to serve as the Second in Command (Executive Officer) of a historic ship, The USS Constitution. I attended the ceremonies when she retired from that command at the famous naval shipyard in Charlestown, Massachusetts. She honored her nation by serving in positions of CIVIC duty, setting standards for many other women who serve our nation today. Her 1812-era uniform is on display in the USS Constitution Museum in the Boston/Charleston shipyard. It was my honor to be friends with her. She advocated and paved the way for the inclusion of women in many roles in the military. A true leader and CIVIC pathfinder opening up growth in a formally closed system.

Retired Lt. Cmdr. Claire Bloom, USS Constitution's first female executive officer from April 1996 to October 1998, said she remembers the challenges she faced when the USS Constitution prepared for sailing of the ship for the first time in 116 years and the celebration of the ship's 200th birthday in 1997. "Serving on board the USS Constitution was one of the most exciting times of my life," said Bloom. "As times change, the command is now 30 percent women. From my experience, these Sailors look for guidance from senior enlisted personnel and having a female leader to identify which is crucial to success."

I look at Lt. Commander as a person who continued the women in combat in the Revolutionary War. The U.S. Constitution was an 1812 Revolutionary War ship we all cherish.

Lt. Cmdr. Claire Bloom

The passage above was edited and approved by Lt. Cmdr. Claire Bloom Retired.

Chapter 16

Breeds Hill, Boston – 101Field Artillery
1636 Plymouth

My parents always explained why these events occurred and how they formed our country, and to a young, wide-eyed boy who drew it all in, it was hugely formative. While we were in Boston, we visited Breeds Hill (Bunker Hill). We were told of our many ancestors fighting for our independence against the oppressive British forces, with Thomas Boynton prominently displayed on a monument. Little did I know that this would later play an important role in my own life. I actually spent a year in the Massachusetts National Guard. While attached to the National Guard with the 101st Field Artillery towed in Danvers, Massachusetts (an artillery unit formally formed in 1636 in the then Plymouth Colonies, the third largest in the world at that time.) I was summoned to visit with an Army colonel at the Armory in Boston for reasons unknown. Our meeting was a very important one for me; I found out that he was the commanding officer of the Massachusetts Ancient and Honorable Guard. He offered me a position as a sergeant in the ancient unit in honor of my ancestor, who died on Breeds Hill facing the British troops, a true honor indeed. Today, I am also a member of the Sons of the American Revolution; my sponsor was an ancestor, Captain Joshua Boynton, of Washington's army.

Here is a detail concerning this ancient unit, the 101st Field Artillery.

The Ancient and Honorable Artillery Company of Massachusetts is the oldest chartered military organization in North America and the third oldest chartered military organization in the world. Its charter was granted in March of 1638 by the Great and General Court of Massachusetts Bay and signed by Governor John Winthrop as a volunteer militia company to train officers enrolled in the local militia companies across Massachusetts.

For those of you who still wonder why I would want to pen a comprehensive book concerning our country's origin and all documents, historical parties, and roles leading to the formation of our Constitutional Republic. Frankly I look upon it as a labor of love and pride that I exist in such a wonderful nation, free of oppression, and able to write this manuscript freely without fear. I also saw a nation craftily designed and brought forward with the wisdom of individuals who wished to do it right, using the examples of the wisdom of successful world governments from ancient times (BCE) Before the Christian Era to the early 1800s.[11]

---

[11]   https://en.wikipedia.org/wiki/Ancient_and_Honorable_Artillery_Company_of_Massachusetts

Chapter 17

A Critical Primer About Civics and Deficits

In fact, all successful nations and leaders everywhere come with civic leadership skills acquired through involvement in the political process or learned through study or involvement in the civic process. Not all today have this experience or education, and it has shown up for us in 2020, in a massive way. Studies show why we just did not pay full attention, or we just did not want to because of changing demographics and social challenges. Wake up, folks! I don't care if our demographics of this-or-that is changing; we need to be able to be flexible and respond positively to change with reasoned logic and effective programs. One problem, our growing indifference is showing, and if not dealt with, our demise could be imminent. Should we take a step back, study the issue, read the tea leaves, or whatever, and then take reasoned and proper necessary actions immediately to resolve the issue? I think so.

I wish to make comments here. I am going to delve into our failing education system in this chapter. I am not taking away from the overall intent of this book's formation of our government but something that is so baseline, and I can say something cherished for eons of time, that has steered governments needs its light of day to understand our current plight relating to CIVICS, ETHICS. MORALS and HISTORY that affect everything we encounter in our daily lives. Education and our all-important resource, our children, need to receive the very best we can give them, not watered-down fantasies of a liberal manipulation of a socialist society's needs and the reconstruction of our cherished government. It may not be perfect, but it's better than a liberal, free-will progressive society that largely ignores our Constitution and the Rule of Law.

Another really important basic point needs to be remade. Our personal education starts at home. The all-important role of our parents is to instill pride in us at young ages. Many think that their support, by taking us and attending trips to ballgames, yeah ballgames, where our national game starts out with our anthem, or some other civic pride display, such as a Fourth of July parade or Memorial Day event, doesn't count, it does. This develops into a feeling of belonging to something we grow to love our country. I am afraid the family unit today is no longer, by-in-large, the one I grew up in, and what I stated above is not the norm. Why have we allowed this indifference to take control of generations? A tragedy.

Perhaps we can hope that the trips our parents made to our national parks and monuments further instilled growing pride in our country. Maybe we would serve in the military, signing our lives to the defense of the freedoms we protect for our republic's endurance. CIVICS is not just learning about history; it is the broad-based knowledge we need to be aware of and grow into productive individuals in a prospering society, in our daily lives, and in any number of life events we might encounter. It also helps to know the structure of our government and its guiding Constitutional documents and how they protect you personally and your family.

The facts are indisputable: the lack of civic education remains indelibly etched into our past, and the history of public education in the U.S. is inseparable from the history of our nation. The development of our country and its movement into the future should interest and involve everyone.

I don't care if you were here through your ancestors in 1620, our formation of the colonies, our fight to become free from England, or the ages leading up to today. We are history-rich, with many who want to form a nation, and they say, "Learn history so you do not repeat the mistakes others made moving forward." Our job is to know what drove it and why. I firmly believe that our futures were, then and now, inseparably intertwined.

I recently viewed a three-day series about George Washington, and intertwined throughout the series was a mini view of the trials and tribulations endured to bring our nation to fruition, the penning of the Constitution and the Rule of Law, the 10 articles of the Bill of Rights and the issues to keep the nation together even after we became a nation. It was too brief but enough to show those who watched the series to get a flavor of what former patriots sacrificed to give us what we enjoy as freedom today. Around the fourth of July, this is often recast in historical accuracy. I encourage each of you to watch this production.

Ancient history and our early ancestors defined the and "wrote the book" on CIVICS involvement. Many toiled throughout the startup colonies and, when called to secure their freedom from England, paid with their lives, British troops who would hang them as traitors. We should cherish their actions, remember them fondly, and continually thank them for the Rule of Law freedoms that we have today. I think it wouldn't be a bad idea to try to emulate their actions and involve yourselves in something that would support your country. Many do now, join them. I bet you will feel good about yourself.

Chapter 18

CIVICS Knowledge and Education

My belief is that the lack of generations of students not exposed to proper civics, ethics, morals, and history conditioning education might very well be the primary reason for all that is stated in the Preface.

Years ago, our National Board of Education wrongly removed the need for CIVICS education from our educational system, wishing to "update children's educations." Not surprisingly, with the predicted negative result, the all-important CIVICS knowledge regarding our country's historical background and its guiding foundational documents is appallingly low. More on this later.

Sufficient facts thoroughly support this allegation, with well-documented educational results over more than two generations. Evidence proves it really has resulted in the predicted "dumbing down" of our educational system and the loss of critical CIVICS knowledge, along with other major watered-down educational offerings proving harmful to our nation.

Many years ago, prior to 1965, our citizens were properly prepared to be future leaders of our nation, to have in-depth knowledge of our functioning government, its foundation documents, the reasons for their development, and actually the reasons why many historic sources were referenced in developing our Rule of Law documents for their and our future guidance.

I believe that the left-leaning liberal factions in our nation are seeking to eliminate our constitutional government and replace it with what they call a democratic social government that I simply label a socialist party or communist. A book that will wake you up to actions concerning this destruction of our current government is George Orwell's 1984. This book should be required reading in CIVICS classes with to class instructor comparing it to a functioning, and I might suggest a legally assembled form of government as our constitutional documents provide for us. The Democratic party has seemingly been taken over by what they call a squad of radical socialists. It has become apparent by their platform that it is calling for total government control and the Democratic party. For that matter, the whole House of Representatives has been upset by their disruptive actions. The House does not know how to control the radical left faction, which seems to be growing, and how to take their party back. Could this be the end of the Democratic party? I cannot believe that some of our Representatives and Senators, elected by us to serve us, have violated their oath of service and the Rule of Law of the Constitution. What really makes me wonder is that "the squad seems to be growing, and the people who voted the members into office, many thousands, are continuing to vote them into continuing two-year terms. Really, are we coming apart at the seams? It makes me wonder. I question… is our 400-year-old form of government that broken?

"We, the People, elect leaders not to rule but to serve."

Dwight D. Eisenhower

Chapter 19

Is Our Middle and Higher Education Failing the United States Needs?

As a former educator, I have always believed in a well-rounded education, not one that would prepare everyone for college but just to rake in the government bucks for showing college prep proficiency in graduating students who would only fail in programs they were not prepared for. I worked at a two-year college where inner-city students were given the funds to get an advanced education. The big issue here —inner-city students (New York, Chicago, Philadelphia, and others) actually had to be educated in the basics of Reading, arithmetic, writing, and, well, pretty much all subject matter starting at the 7/8 grade.

A good percentage of our first-year college students personally drove me nuts, having to reeducate them in the 101 classes by teaching remedial classes in history, rhetoric, government, English, literacy, and arithmetic—oh yes, and how to think constructively—because they were not properly prepared in high school for college, let alone life.

Not all, but most predominantly came from inner city education exposure, a sad commentary for the systems. Still, I had very high regard for the students for trying to make a go of their lives moving forward. Our administration went the further mile to make sure they graduated from our institution. I have many beautiful student success stories relating to changed lives and memories of the sincere thanks expressed by these students. All of our instructors considered this as one of the most beautiful experiences, of students crying and literally shaking in disbelief that they have clawed their way to graduation and preparedness for a good job and life in general. I tried to help my students get jobs they would not be able to get otherwise. Money could not buy me and my associates. What we fostered in these students alone was our payday and the cherished memories we will share for life!

Be aware I am emotional now as I write this, and there is a tear in my eyes.

My doctoral dissertation work was based on the mid-1980s recorded results of collegiate starting and ending statistics. Colleges generally lost fifty percent of the starting classes, with successive years of progressive losses, down to an appallingly startling end result of just five to ten percent actually graduating in year four and slightly less in year five.

I always shed a tear for each when I shook their hand at graduation.

The Decline and Fall of American Education

American education is in serious trouble. Why aren't we more concerned? By **Paul E. Peterson**.[12]

Thursday, January 30, 2003, Paul E. Peterson

The Decline and Fall of American Education

By: Paul E. Peterson

---

[12] Paul E. Peterson | Hoover Institution

Perhaps this is "just" math and science, something American schools have never been good at. Besides, apologists say, Asian students (who score at the top on the TIMSS) are inexplicable math and science geniuses.

Yet low performance is not limited to these more challenging subjects. Americans barely reach the international literacy average set by advanced democracies, according to a report issued by the Educational Testing Service after looking at the International Adult Literacy Survey (IALS). Unlike the math and science surveys, the IALS was given to a cross-section of adults aged 16 to 65. Despite the high expenditures on education in the United States—and the large numbers of students enrolled in colleges and universities—the United States ranked 12th on the test.

The United States is living on its past. Among the oldest group in the study (those aged 56–65), U.S. prose skills rose to second place. For those attending school in the 1950s, SAT scores reached an all-time high.

As the years go by, the United States slips down the list. Americans educated in the sixties captured a Bronze Medal in literacy; those schooled in the seventies got 5th place in the race. But those schooled in the nineties ranked 14th.

Have Americans sacrificed quality for equity? One could hope for such egalitarian bliss; unfortunately, the opposite is true. Among the 20 highest-income countries participating in the test, the United States won the inequality Gold Medal.

This is not true for the oldest group, however. For those educated in the fifties, the United States not only managed to achieve the second-highest literacy scores but also scored no worse than average on the inequality index. Equity was not sacrificed for quality or vice versa.

Apologists will find excuses for these outcomes. Immigrants pull down U.S. scores, it will be said, overlooking the fact that other countries have immigrants too. Lifelong learning opportunities are greater in the United States than elsewhere, it will be claimed, so young folks will eventually reach the levels of the oldest group.

But such excuses don't ring true. All signs point to a deterioration in the quality of American schools. Europeans and Asians alike have rapidly expanded their educational systems over the last 50 years. In the United States, stagnation, if not decline, has been apparent at least since the 1970s. Even our high school graduation rates are lower today than they were a decade ago.

Do we care? Economists tell us that human capital is more important than physical capital for long-term economic development. Weak educational systems won't ruin the country overnight, but prolonged incompetence will eventually prove consequential.

Hoover Institution Weekly essay, November 11, 2002. Available from the Hoover Press is *Our Schools and Our Future: Are We Still at Risk?* Edited by Paul E. Peterson.

In my humble opinion, and with critical emphasis, we need to reevaluate our complete spectrum of educational offerings at all levels from K-16 minimally to support the future needs of our complete and complex society within all the occupational divisions and prepare ourselves for even unique future needs to support society's growth. There are 23 occupational groups, a large educational task to tackle. Can our educational system handle this task at our current mindset and delivery levels? I am guardedly skeptical. Let's take a look at what we need to service as a country.

As a wise but, I could say we could all stay home; we would pay them as good socialists and let China or other countries take our meat off the table and turn the US into a third-world country.

I wrote in another book about the possibility of this scenario on bookshelves in August 2020. Its title is: Is It Back to the Stone Age with the Green New Deal? Are You Really Ready for Life-Altering Changes?

Courtesy of the U.S. Bureau of Labor Statistics website

2018 Standard Occupational Classification System

NOTE: The information on this page relates to the 2018 SOC; please see the 2010 SOC System for information on the previous version of the SOC.

Each occupation in the 2018 SOC is placed within one of these 23 major groups:

- 11-0000 Management Occupations

- 13-0000 Business and Financial Operations Occupations

- 15-0000 Computer and Mathematical Occupations

- 17-0000 Architecture and Engineering Occupations

- 19-0000 Life, Physical, and Social Science Occupations

- 21-0000 Community and Social Service Occupations

- 23-0000 Legal Occupations

- 25-0000 Educational Instruction and Library Occupations

- 27-0000 Arts, Design, Entertainment, Sports, and Media Occupations

- 29-0000 Healthcare Practitioners and Technical Occupations

- 31-0000 Healthcare Support Occupations

- 33-0000 <u>Protective Service Occupations</u>

- 35-0000 <u>Food Preparation and Serving Related Occupations</u>

- 37-0000 <u>Building and Grounds Cleaning and Maintenance Occupations</u>

- 39-0000 <u>Personal Care and Service Occupations</u>

- 41-0000 <u>Sales and Related Occupations</u>

- 43-0000 <u>Office and Administrative Support Occupations</u>

- 45-0000 <u>Farming, Fishing, and Forestry Occupations</u>

- 47-0000 <u>Construction and Extraction Occupations</u>

- 49-0000 <u>Installation, Maintenance, and Repair Occupations</u>

- 51-0000 <u>Production Occupations</u>

- 53-0000 <u>Transportation and Material Moving Occupations</u>

- 55-0000 <u>Military Specific Occupations</u>[13]

The educational proposals today are not a solution to the much larger problem of the decline in history and civics being taught in elementary and secondary education. History, civics, social studies, and, in fact, all humanities subjects have been given short shrift. The Obama administration was overly in favor of *STEM* (the acronym *STEM* stands for the disciplines of science, technology, engineering, and mathematics) funding. Unfortunately, in my former research, I discovered the students were not prepared to shoulder these new concepts; not all students have these proficiencies. A well-rounded education for all learning abilities is sorely required to cover all

---

[13] https://www.bls.gov/soc/2018/major_groups.htm

occupational possibilities. In fact, I am strongly in favor of two-year technical colleges discontinued in favor of college prep a serious mistake.

I do understand that our societal need for education is evolving, and it should change to keep up with technology. Unfortunately, not everyone will end up in a white-collar job or a rocket scientist's position. Many will work in blue-collar jobs, home engineers, the medical industry, farmers, in the military or civil service, to name a few. What is common to all these economic sustaining fields is a working knowledge in CIVICS and I will add in ETHICS and MORAL steadfastness. These should be the basic primary focus on tools where I find their immediate classroom application would remedy a critically serious deficit in most all of today's so-called educational programs and then our roles in our lives and government administration to support advanced and worker class education.

As you are now already aware if I have done my job, and before delving further into this chapter, there is something that critically needs to be thoroughly discussed, divulged, or just laid out in plain sight - the matter of *CIVICS EDUCATION* or in this case the lack of it, yes the lack of it, if you can believe it in a way that will awaken you perhaps to a new vision of a governmental support system, put into place by incredible minds, that literally supports you today in what some might call, prophetic endurance.

This following fact astounds me and is very hard to believe. The *U.S. Department of Education (DoE)*, in its infinite wisdom, or the lack of it, actually withdrew $35 million dollars of support from the civics education community, causing additional diminishing support from private grant sources as well in 2011. That action was a radical and not-so-positive reinforcement for the future of our country's interests. To me, for a department not even authorized in the guiding documents and not even elected by the people, this seems to be sort of an off-hand action that needed more scrutiny by *"We the People"* before this action was taken. I view this as being destructive to our educational system, and I fault the (NEA) National Education Association and the union of teachers who allowed it to happen. Let's blame our lawmakers who did not stop the Department of Education from doing it!

I cite a paper in the Civics Constitution vs Propaganda (1) in a Nox and Friends paper written by Uriel on April 29, 2017.

This paper states that there has been an ill-devised insertion into the educational breech, the elimination of the civics curriculum. This effectively cleansed the civics curriculum of foundations, morals, values, and principles and was substituted by "proper civic training" of what liberal educators and non-elected manipulators thought the Constitution should be reflecting--their ideals rather than what the actual Constitution directed as adopted. Their changes gained traction, and the rapid erosion and (read watering down) politicization of our children's concept of civics has changed until today. It has damaged generations of citizens of the United States.

I find something interesting about *Education Secretary Arne Duncan*, who served from 2009 to 2015, releasing a press release on Civic Education in March 2011 with several points. He stated that the DoE was moving in an "effort to strengthen and reinvigorate civics education." He also spoke before the Civics Educating for Democracy in a Digital Age conference and gave some takeaway points I will condense.

Civics is not a luxury but a necessity civics that cannot just be dismissed by educators and pushed aside in schools. Our students need a sense of citizenship, an understanding of history and government, and a commitment to democratic values.

Young people find civics dusty and dull; it's time to revitalize and update civic education for the 21st century.

Authors note: I ask, was he thinking of liberalizing the Constitution's real meaning, we can only wonder, or can we accept a serious conclusion? I observe the deterioration of our three branches of government riddled with people not really caring about the Constitution and the effect their personal agendas are having on our political process. I have visions of the framers turning over in their graves as so-called Congressmen and Senators misuse the intent that I find thinly veiled of the written law and their use of it to destroy people. I am literally ashamed of my government for this abuse for personal gain. I take solace in the hope that "We the People" are watching and will act as the framers decided, that it is in the people's hands to correct through the election process they instituted.

The article defines Participatory Politics as interactive, peer-based acts through which individuals and groups seek to exert both voice and influence on issues of public concern. Examples include starting new political groups, creating petitions, and mobilizing social networks on behalf of a cause.

Do you think we could suggest that this could mean "down with the standard model of civic education through political activism by those who would seek to circumvent the Constitution and the Bill of Rights?" Can we be in fear of losing our Constitution, Bill of Rights, and Declaration of Independence? It's looking bad, folks.

I am sure by now that you have recognized that this is not as simple a problem as you would believe, with public institutions producing anemic and watered-down civics and most other educational subject matters. One bright spot is that most private schools do recognize civics education as being critical for the knowledge base of what our government is and how it works. This is comforting to know and to realize that we have some people we can draw on.

How Bad is the Effect of a CIVICS Deficit?

Many other CIVICS problems are highlighted in an article written and published by Dr. Sheila Kennedy, The School of Public and Environmental Affairs, Indiana University, Purdue University Indianapolis, titled Civic Literacy: Charting the Dimensions and Consequences of a Civic Deficit, June 6, 2011, she writes, "Available data gives evidence of a widespread lack of constitutional competence and civic literacy in the United States," and she lays it out for us. "The consequence of this ignorance is profound; the current polarization in American political discourse has been significantly enabled by widespread ignorance of the most basic American constitutional principles." She goes on to say, "It is important that citizens know the history and philosophy of their governing institutions." Strong ties and a common devotion to constitutional principles are critical to the formation of national identity. I suggest that those who are not native to the United States need a genuine understanding of the history and the context of our constitutional documents, such as the Constitution, the Bill of Rights, and its amendments.

Let's look at some other observations and studies highlighting the critical need for CIVICS knowledge as associations and organizations recognize CIVICS deficit issues.

This political condition, however, is not just within the massive immigration issue. It exists with our students and the general population. *An Annenberg study in 2007* is depressing. Only 36% of adults could name the three main branches of government: Executive, Legislative, and Judicial; fewer than half of students in the 12th grade knew the meaning of federalism. *NAEP National Assessment of Educational Progress 2006.*

Federalism definition - the distribution of power in an organization, such as a government, between a central authority and the constituent population.

How to use *federalism* in a sentence. The distribution of power in an organization (such as a government) between a central authority and the constituent units

Federalism

Only 35.5% of teens could identify *"We the People"* as the first words of the Constitution (*National Constitution Center 1998*). Our educational system is producing this today, and it is a far cry from what we should require for informed, civic-minded citizens.

Another NEAEP report spanning 1979 through 2010 and addressing grades 8 – 12 shows a declining scaled report of roughly 50% proficiency in civics. This has been going on for some time, and our educational systems in the US are failing us but costing us more educational dollars each fiscal year.

This stunning report from the *National Constitution Center in 1998 (Civic Literacy, Kennedy)* pitted the knowledge of American teenagers with the following: they were able to name the Three Stooges rather than the three branches of government 59% to 41%, and then this, more knew the Prince of Bel-Air than the *Chief Justice of the Supreme Court (William Rehnquist (Wikipedia).*

With 94.7 vs 2.2%. However, 58.3% were able to identify Bill Gates as the "father" of Microsoft, but only 1.8% could identify James Madison as the "Father of the Constitution."

In *2011*, NEWSWEEK MAGAZINE *ran a story, "How Dumb Are We?"* that was said to drove high school teachers to drink; in its survey of 1000 people (a legitimate survey population %), 29% could not name the Vice President of the United States Joseph Biden was the *vice president* of the US in 2011 under Barack Obama. He became the *vice-president* on 2009 January 20.) 73% could not identify the reason for the Cold War, and 44% were unable to define the Bill of Rights. 38% of Americans failed. This test revealed that 61% did not know who held the House majority, and an astounding 77% could not name their state's senators. Astoundingly, one-third could not identify the five rights protected by the First Amendment: freedom of speech, religion, the press, protest, and petition.

Authors Note: Are you convinced yet that we have a civic knowledge deficit?

Might you be concerned that we possibly are doing our nation a high injustice and actually harming our civil and political systems with barely base knowledge of how our government works?

Do you have any questions concerning your local and federal politicians and their knowledge of how our government is supposed to work under our constitution and bill of rights to protect you? I urge you to ask them, really, if they work for you or are supposed to according to their oath. Without constitutional guidance, how can they function as representatives and do the work we voted them into office to do our bidding? I wonder if some of them forget that they are there to take care of home concerns rather than hold their hand out for monies given to buy their votes and to hell with our home-based issues. You know, when I served in the New Hampshire House, it was infected with special interest giveaway lobbyists, people who wanted to buy your vote on a particular bill. Some took the money and, in essence, said, "To hell with my district's interests in the bill," special interests prevailed. I did not cheapen my seat and supported my district's wishes. You would be surprised at how many people approached me to change my stance and work with the consultants, even the Speaker.

This is not really funny, but the lobbyists were restricted from an area leading to the chambers and could not approach members in the bathroom. Ya gotta have some decorum, I guess.

With what has happened in the last years, 2015 through 2024, I wonder how some of them even got elected. I am amazed at the blatant disregard and chicanery concerning our Constitution and Rule of Law and it seems to never end due to political games. I am totally amazed at the hundreds of Congress members and Senators signing onto a bill, HR-109, the New Green Deal, that would, in effect, totally disable our Constitution, Bill of Rights, and our total infrastructure, military structure, all trade, the destruction of our energy industries, vehicles, and drive us into the, as I have labeled it, the dark ages.

You do know, of course, that a number of socialists want to throw out all we have as government foundation documents; yes, that means our Constitution and Bill of Rights and all amendments. With all that is happening today, 6-7/2020, with anarchy, riots, and killings happening everywhere, I wonder if the rabble has any idea of a stabilization government or a continuous free-for-all until we are beaten into a third-world mix of whatever is under a ruthless dictator where a few do well? I immediately think of Venezuela, a rich nation four years ago but a starving nation today with a government in question.

I question anyone on why, with reasoned logic, anybody would want to radically change or perhaps remove protections we have had in place since the Constitution's inception on March 4th, 1789, and the Bill of Rights on December 15, 1791. These bedrock documents were placed in force for our protection and, until recently, it seems, were working instruments until political factions started tearing them apart, making their own rules. I will admit that our country has issues, but as I have said and will say again, there is no sound reason that I can remotely see to throw out a functioning government. I will define later how our rights are being assailed.

Suppose we really care about ETHICALLY preserving our democracy for future generations. In that case, we will stop treating CIVICS education as secondary to math and science instruction and put it back at the core of our school curricula to reestablish historical and future MORAL respect for our country.

Chapter 20

Is our system of government under attack? Is our Democratic Process out of Control, and the Rule of Law Disregarded?

To me, it seems that our 2020-2024/5 administration, from day one, has literally thrown out all of our Rule of Law conditions that are literally the glue that holds our Democratic Republic together. All logical reasoning seems to have disappeared. Our stability in literally all sectors of our government was affected, and radical actions seemed to be the norm. My personal belief is that a pandemic caused unnatural actions, throwing the complete society into upheaval for years. Our family units were abnormally affected, our children were kept from schools, and critical education exposure was not delivered to students in their formative years. We were exposed to abnormal decisions, not normal to run governments smoothly. Spending, which I detailed elsewhere, was out of control, and taxes started to spiral out of control to support out-of-control spending that exceeded our gross national product, and borrowing spun up out of control to levels that will be problematic moving into the future.

In the above case, our government closely resembled the start and functioning of a socialist government, totally disregarding all of our revered Constitutional Democratic Republic and 400-year history. I agree our longevity has been challenged, but this affront seems to totally disregard We the People and the protections our Rule of Law Bill of Rights guaranteed to us that the current administration does not care about the ruling. I admit my belief that it did not care for the populace exampled by extraordinary actions not normal to a constitutional government and the actions of its secretaries and the actions regarding the operation of the House and Senate to block any attempt to normalize the obvious progressive movement that was critically altering the country, I believe will be difficult to repair in short order.

Chapter 21

What Ancient and Current Governmental Systems Did Our Framers Examine?

To frame the U.S. Constitution, our founders examined many civilizations for empirical evidence of content, success, and failure of concepts, both ancient and modern, in Asia, Europe, and Native American governmental systems.

The following were studied.

Credits to Kevin Wandrei.

> **Ancient Greece.** Known as Athenian Democracy, in positive and negative ways. One was negative; it was voting. Only a select group of Greeks were allowed to cast votes. This system in the colonies was also true but not wanted. It only allowed land-owning men to vote. This form of government was rejected, and they selected a representative democracy instead.

> **Ancient Rome.** While Ancient Greece offered workable ideas, the primary ancient civilization studied. It had a Senate and Assembly with separate powers of government, and

this division appealed to the framers. It also had a secret ballot system. The size of the population was also a factor and a better-scaled model.

➢ **British Government.** Even though the founding fathers had led a revolution against Great Britain, they still evaluated the country's major democratic accomplishments. There was the English Bill of Rights and the Magna Charta. In 1215, the Magna Charta established that the Monarchy should be limited and not absolute. In 1628, the English Petition of Rights gave commoners a voice in the English government, guaranteed free elections, and gave rights to people for crimes. These were things the framers wanted to preserve.

➢ **The Iriquois Confederation.** We have given this confederation a lot of ink in the Iroquois chapter, and I refer you to it. However, I wish to mention that Ben Franklin met with the now six nations in 1744 in an attempt to mimic them for a federalist confederacy. The framers also liked the idea that "power comes from We the People." They realized that a disjointed, separated union would be ineffective. A unique democratic experiment Citizens cast votes for legislators digging deeper into the Greek State it ws found that it was the first direct democracy around 508 BCE. It was an experiment where instead of an elected representative, the citizens cast votes for legislation and executive bills.

➢ In search of **Rule of Law** examples for **"We the People"** Rule of Law—**Authors notation;** It is universally accepted that Greece, declared by that upstart Aristotle, is the first to have a Rule of Law that served all peoples fairly in all their "city States." We will examine history deep into the BCE/CE era to see if his claim is valid. I suspect he may be right, but I bet there are societies with progressive rulers that made a herculean attempt to support their political empires with rules that were designed to protect their people as well. We will compare then for the values we seek.

➢ I am acutely aware, and give immense credit, that the framers of our constitution traveled far and wide to gather data to share their findings. I am learning that bits and pieces of this discovered knowledge were thoroughly reviewed and considered for insertion into our documents.

Athens, Greek government examined.

The government in Athens consisted of an assembly, a council of five hundred, and courts. Political distinctions between the ruling class and the working class were eliminated. Citizenship was granted to children of parents who had attained citizenship. A drawback was that only men over 18 who had military service could vote. This form of government only lasted 200 years.

In 507 BCE, an Athenian leader put into force a political reform called demokratia or Rule of Law (rule by the people). Out of a population of 250,000, only 30,000 had full citizenship. Their assembly, open to males only, took place 40 times a year. Women had no role, not something our framers wanted.

The system, due to a protracted war, was replaced with an oligarch during the war, but this experiment failed when Athens lost to Macedonian forces in 322 BCE.

Author notes: As I did a deep dive into Greek governments, I came upon an example, with detail, of the formation of a City State, Tyre, which exampled a form of government that was Democratic and Oligarchic but could have been something the framers may have exampled in their searches of the other city-states. I enclose it for your reading reference as a closely related example of their reported search for a government example.

Queen Elissar, a princess of Tyre, founded Carthage. Her metropolis rose in its high noon to be called a "shining city." It ruled 300 other cities around the western Mediterranean and led the Phoenician Punic World.

Author notes: Reminds me of President Reagan saying: From **Winthrop's "city upon a hill" sermon** would become "the shining city on a hill" of President Reagan: a celebration of individual freedom, material prosperity, and American power—above all, a call for Americans to renew their optimism and believe in themselves again.

Background and Origin

Andrea Sacchi, Didone Abandonnée, Musée des Beaux-Arts, Cae

In the harbor of ancient Tyre in Phoenicia, the fisherman chant, *"Ela--eee--sa, Ela--eee--sa,"* as they haul in their nets. They cannot say why; maybe it's for luck, or maybe it's a lament for their princess who left her homeland never to return.

Elissar or Elissa (Elishat, in Phoenician) was a princess of Tyre. She was Jezebel's grandniece — Princess Jezebel of Tyre was Queen of Israel. Her brother, Pygmalion, king of Tyre, murdered her husband, the high priest. She escaped tyranny in her country and founded Carthage and, thereafter, its Phoenician Punic dominions. Carthage later became a great center of the western Mediterranean in its high noon. One of its most famous sons was Hannibal, who defied Rome.

Details of her life are sketchy and confusing; however, the following is what one can deduct from various sources. According to Justin, Princess Elissar was the daughter of King Matten or Muttoial of Tyre (Belus II of classical literature). After his death, the throne was jointly bequeathed to her and her brother, Pygmalion. She was married to her uncle Acherbas (Sychaeus of classical literature), High Priest of Melqart and a man of authority and riches like that of a king. Tyrannical Pygmalion, a lover of gold and intrigue, was eager to acquire the authority and fortune of Acherbas. He assassinated him in the Temple and kept his evil deed a secret for a long time from his sister. He cheated her with fiction about his death. Meanwhile, the people of Tyre were pressing for a single sovereign, which caused dissensions within the royal family.[14]

Carthaginian Government, City State of Tyre

The emigrants to Carthage were civilized Tyrinians versed in culture, knowledge, and law. They elected magistrates and established the Oligarchic Constitution with a governor who reported to the king of Tyre. They also elected parliament. **_Aristotle wrote ca. 340 B.C. in his "On the Constitution of Carthage" that it is to be held up as a model._**

"The Carthaginians are also considered to have an excellent form of government, which differs from that of any other state in several respects, though it is in some very like the Spartan. Indeed, all three states---the Spartan, the Cretan, and the Carthaginian---nearly resemble one another and are very different from any others. Many of the Carthaginian institutions are excellent. The superiority of their constitution is proved by the fact that the common people remain loyal to the constitution. The Carthaginians have never had any rebellion worth speaking of and have never been under the rule of a

---

[14] https://phoenicia.org/PIRC/index.html

tyrant. Among the points in which the Carthaginian constitution resembles the Spartan are the following: The common tables of the clubs answer to the Spartan phiditia and their magistracy of the Hundred-Four to the Ephors; but, whereas the Ephors are any chance persons, the magistrates of the Carthaginians are elected according to merit---this is an improvement. They also have their kings and their Gerousia, or council of elders, who correspond to the kings and elders of Sparta. Their kings, unlike the Spartans, are not always of the same family, nor that an ordinary one, but if there is some distinguished family, they are selected out of it and not appointed by seniority---this is far better. Such officers have great power and, therefore, if they are persons of little worth, do a great deal of harm, and they have already done harm to Sparta.

"Most of the defects or deviations from the perfect state, for which the Carthaginian constitution would be censured, apply equally to all the forms of government which we have mentioned. But of the deflections from aristocracy and constitutional government, some incline more to democracy and some to oligarchy. The kings and elders, if unanimous, may determine whether they will or will not bring a matter before the people, but when they are not unanimous, the people decide on such matters as well. And whatever the kings and elders bring before the people is not only heard but also determined by them, and anyone who likes may oppose it; now, this is not permitted in Sparta and Crete. That the magistrates of five who have under them many important matters should be co-opted, that they should choose the supreme council of One Hundred, and should hold office longer than other magistrates (for they are virtually rulers both before and after they hold office)---these are oligarchical features; their being without salary and not elected by lot, and any similar points, such as the practice of having all suits tried by the magistrates, and not some by one class of judges or jurors and some by another, as at Sparta, are characteristic of aristocracy.

"The Carthaginian constitution deviates from aristocracy and inclines to oligarchy, chiefly on a point where popular opinion is on their side. For men in general think that magistrates should be chosen not only for their merit, but for their wealth: a man, they say, who is poor cannot rule well---he has not the leisure. If, then, the election of magistrates for their wealth be characteristic of oligarchy, and election for merit of aristocracy, there will be a third form under which the constitution of Carthage is comprehended, for the Carthaginians choose their magistrates and particularly the highest of them---their kings and generals---with an eye both to merit and to wealth. But we must acknowledge that, in thus deviating from aristocracy, the legislator has committed an error. Nothing is more absolutely necessary than to provide that the highest class, not only when in office but when out of office, should have leisure and not disgrace themselves in any way, and to this, his attention should be first directed. Even if you must have regard for wealth in order to secure leisure, it is surely a bad thing that the greatest offices, such as those of kings and generals, should be bought. The law that allows this abuse makes wealth of more account than virtue, and the whole state becomes avaricious.

"For, whenever the chiefs of the state deem anything honorable, the other citizens are sure to follow their example; and, where virtue has not the first place, their aristocracy cannot be firmly established. Those who have been at the expense of purchasing their places will be in the habit of repaying themselves; and it is absurd to suppose that a poor and honest man will be wanting to make gains, and that a lower stamp of man who has incurred a great expense will not. Wherefore they should rule who is able to rule best. And even if the legislator does not care to protect the good from poverty, he should, at any rate, secure leisure for them when in office. It would seem also to be a bad principle that the same person should hold many offices, which is a favorite practice among the Carthaginians, for one business is better done by one man.

What did the founding fathers say about the rule of law?

I found that the framers and signers understood that it was necessary to have a stable justice system – to have rules and laws based on certain lasting fundamental principles, not the arbitrary whims of those holding government power at any moment. Only in this way could we protect ourselves from tyranny.

Attribution by National Geographic, in an article released in 2024, concerning the Greek Rule of Law practiced throughout its city-states. The article's relevant points to this writing were excerpted to support this writing.

Ancient Greek philosopher Aristotle outlines the Rule of Law in this work, 'Politics.' He discovered that there were two questions: Was it wise to be led or to have rules that were common to all, from the bottom to the top, where everyone was accountable to the rules without exception?

I personally find that ridged laws are largely ineffective. No situation is the same, and a ridged law does not apply to all. However, the basic tenet of a written law that represents the main law thread can be adjudicated to fit most situations, and our system of law actually supports this.

The Rule of Law is a principle that all people and organizations within a country, state, or community are held accountable to the same set of laws. The Rule of Law has its origins in ancient Greece and, more specifically, in the philosophy of Aristotle. In his work titled **Politics**, Aristotle raised the question of whether it is better to be ruled by the best leader or the best laws. In exploring this question, he found advantages and disadvantages to both governing methods. His conclusion, however, suggested that laws were appropriate for most societies since they were carefully thought out and could be applied to most situations. Therefore, people should be ruled by the best laws.

In modern times, many countries throughout the world have agreed that the Rule of Law should be followed. In the United States, this means that no one, not even the president, is above the law. The United States federal courts also consider the Rule of Law to apply to corporations and institutions. The courts further state that all people should be held accountable to laws that are publicly accessible and judged independently. Laws should be enforced equally and consistently, adhering also to international human rights principles. The Rule of Law provides modern societies with stability and a clear system for resolving conflicts between citizens within a community of any size.

Rule of Law defined in ancient Persian Empire

Evidence that is recorded. I

RAN commemorates the 2,500-year history of the Persian Empire. Iran promoted the cylinder as the "first charter of human rights." This represents 4,520 years of recorded human rights! Now, don't get misled here; the practice was not globally accepted by all societies.

The **Cyrus Cylinder** is an ancient clay artifact inscribed with a declaration from Cyrus the Great after his conquest of Babylon. It is considered **the world's first charter of human rights**, promoting religious tolerance and freedom. It is now in the British Museum, exemplifying Cyrus's innovative governance and respect for diverse cultures.

In modern times, the Cylinder was adopted as a national symbol of Iran by the ruling Pahlavi dynasty, which put it on display in Tehran in 1971 to commemorate the 2,500-year celebration of the Persian Empire. Princess Ashraf Pahlavi presented United Nations Secretary General U Thant with a replica of the Cylinder. The princess asserted that "the heritage of Cyrus was the heritage of human understanding, tolerance, courage, compassion and, above all, human liberty." Her brother, Shah Mohammad Reza Pahlavi, promoted the Cylinder as the "first charter of human rights," though this interpretation has been described by various historians as "rather anachronistic" and controversial.[15]

Cyrus the Great King of Persia

Persia/Current Iran

Cyrus the Great

From Wikipedia, the free encyclopedia

Cyrus the Great

𒆳 𒆳 𒆳 𒆳 𒆳

- *King of Anshan*

- *King of Persia*

- *King of Media*

- *King of Lydia*

- *King of the World*

- *King of Kings*

- *Great King*

---

[15] https://en.wikipedia.org/wiki/Cyrus_Cylinder

- *King of Babylon*

- *King of Sumer and Akkad*

- *King of the Four Corners of the World*

- *King of the Universe*

"Winged Genius" statue at Pasargadae, with braided hair and a Hemhem crown, traditionally identified as Cyrus[1][a]

King of Kings of the Achaemenid Empire

Reign	550–530 BC

Predecessor	Empire established
Successor	Cambyses II
King of Persia	
Reign	559–530 BC
Predecessor	Cambyses I
Successor	Cambyses II
King of Media	
Reign	549–530 BC
Predecessor	Astyages

Standard of Cyrus the Great (*Derafsh Shahbaz*), founder of the Achaemenid Empire, featuring the Shahbaz (see List of Iranian flags)

Cyrus II of Persia

(Old Persian: 𒐎𒐏 𒐍𒐎𒐏 𒐏 Kūruš; c. 600–530 BC), commonly known as **Cyrus the Great**, was the founder of the Achaemenid Persian Empire. Hailing from Persis, he brought the Achaemenid dynasty to power by defeating the Median Empire and embracing all of the previous civilized states of the ancient Near East,[7] expanding vastly and eventually conquering most of West Asia and much of Central Asia to create what would soon become the largest polity in human history at the time. The Achaemenid Empire's largest territorial extent was achieved under Darius the Great, whose rule stretched from the Balkans (Eastern Bulgaria–Paeonia and Thrace–Macedonia) and the rest of Southeast Europe in the west to the Indus Valley in the east.

After conquering the Median empire, Cyrus led the Achaemenids to conquer the Lydian Empire and eventually the Neo-Babylonian Empire. He also led an expedition into Central Asia, which resulted in major military campaigns that were described as having brought "into subjection every nation without exception"; Cyrus allegedly died in battle with the Massagetae, a nomadic Eastern Iranian tribal confederation, along the Syr Darya in December 530 BC. However, Xenophon of Athens claimed that Cyrus did not die fighting and had instead returned to the city of Pasargadae, which served as the Achaemenid ceremonial capital.[10] He was succeeded by his son Cambyses II, whose campaigns into North Africa led to the conquests of Egypt, Nubia, and Cyrenaica during his short rule.

To the Greeks, he was known as **Cyrus the Elder** (Greek: Κῦρος ὁ Πρεσβύτερος Kŷros ho Presbýteros). Cyrus was particularly renowned among contemporary scholars because of his habitual policy of respecting peoples' customs and religions in the lands that he conquered. He was influential in developing the system of a central administration at Pasargadae to govern the Achaemenid Empire's border satraps, which worked for the profit of both rulers and subjects. Following the Achaemenid conquest of Babylon, Cyrus issued the Edict of Restoration, in which he authorized and encouraged the return of the Jewish people to what had been the Kingdom of Judah, officially ending the Babylonian captivity. He is mentioned in the Hebrew Bible and left a lasting legacy on Judaism due to his role in facilitating the return to Zion, a migratory event in which the Jews returned to the Land of Israel following Cyrus' establishment of Yehud Medinata and subsequently rebuilt the Temple in Jerusalem, which had been destroyed by the Babylonian siege of Jerusalem. According to Chapter 45:1 of the Book of Isaiah, Cyrus was anointed by the Jewish God for this task as a biblical messiah; he is the only non-Jewish figure to be revered in this capacity.[14]

In addition to his influence on the traditions of both the Eastern world and the Western world, Cyrus is also recognized for his achievements in human rights, politics, and military strategy. The Achaemenid Empire's prestige in the ancient world would eventually extend as far west as Athens, where upper-class Greeks adopted aspects of the culture of the ruling Persian class as their own.[15] As the founder of the first Persian empire, Cyrus played a crucial role in defining the national identity of the Iranian nation; the Achaemenid Empire was instrumental in spreading the ideals of Zoroastrianism as far east as China. He remains a cult figure in Iran, with the Tomb of Cyrus at Pasargadae serving as a spot of reverence for millions of the country's citizens. [16]

Etymology

Further information: Cyrus

The name *Cyrus* is a Latinized form derived from the Greek-language name Κῦρος (*Kŷros*), which itself was derived from the Old

---

[16] https://en.wikipedia.org/wiki/Kourosh

Persian name *Kūruš*. The name and its meaning have been recorded within ancient inscriptions in different languages. The ancient Greek historians Ctesias and Plutarch stated that Cyrus was named from the Sun (*Kuros*), a concept which has been interpreted as meaning "like the Sun" (*Khurvash*) by noting its relation to the Persian noun for Sun, *khor*, while using *-vash* as a suffix of likeness. Karl Hoffmann has suggested a translation based on the meaning of an Indo-European root "to humiliate", and accordingly, the name "Cyrus" means "humiliator of the enemy in verbal contest". Another possible Iranian derivation would mean "the young one, child," similar to Kurdish *kur* ("son, little boy") or Ossetian *i-gur-un* ("to be born") and *kur* (young bull). In the Persian language, and especially in Iran, Cyrus' name is spelled as کوروش (*Kūroš*, [kuːˈroʃ]). In the Bible, he is referred to in the Hebrew language as *Koresh* (כורש). Some pieces of evidence suggest that Cyrus is Kay Khosrow, a legendary Persian king of the Kayanian dynasty and a character in *Shahnameh*, a Persian epic.

Some scholars, however, believe that neither Cyrus nor Cambyses were Iranian names, proposing that Cyrus was Elamite in origin and that the name meant "he who bestows care" in the extinct Elamite language. One reason is that, while Elamite names may end in *-uš*, no Elamite texts spell the name this way — only *Kuraš*. Meanwhile, Old Persian did not allow names to end in *-aš*, so it would make sense for Persian speakers to change an original *Kuraš* into the more grammatically correct form *Kuruš*. Elamite scribes, on the other hand, would not have had a reason to change an original *Kuraš* into *Kuruš*, since both forms were acceptable. Therefore, *Kuraš* probably represents the original form. Another scholarly opinion is that *Kuruš* was a name of Indo-Aryan origin, in honor of the Indo-Aryan Kuru and Kamboja mercenaries from eastern Afghanistan and Northwest India that helped in the conquest of the Middle East.

Dynastic history

According to Aristotle (who can argue with him), The Rule of Law is a principle formally established in ancient Greece. The Greeks and Aristotle, borrowing tenants found in ancient history, found that a successful ruling entity that holds all accountable to the same set of laws could control its populations in a fair way so all will have a good system of control.

The Roman Republic

In contrast to the Greek democracy, the framers found that the Roman Republic had a more complex institutional structure.

The eras of ancient Roman history in chronological order are: Roman Kingdom (753 BCE to 509 BCE), Roman Republic (509 BCE to 27 BCE), and Roman Empire (27 BCE to 476 CE in the West, and in the East till 1453 CE as the Byzantine Empire).

Roman Law: Designed to bring order to the republic.

Rome brought conquered lands into the Roman Empire and tried to rule with laws based on reason and justice.

Four Principles of Roman Law

➢ All citizens had the right to equal treatment under the law.

➢ A person was considered innocent until proven guilty.

➢ The burden of proof rests with the accuser, not the accused

➢ Any law that seems unreasonable may be set aside.

The Justinian Code, Or the "Body of Civil Law," is the same basis of law used even today. Developed democracy following the Justinian Code brought forth the "Twelve Tables."

The Twelve Tables of Law, also known as the first code of Roman law, were the foundation of Roman law for a thousand years. They were formally promulgated in 449 BC and consolidated earlier traditions into an enduring set of laws. A committee of ten men wrote down the Twelve Tables called the decemvirs in 451 BCE and were likely posted in the Roman Forum on bronze tablets in 450 BCE.

> ➢ They created executive and legislative branches of government.

> ➢ Public officials were elected to office to serve the public.

> ➢ Citizens were required to pay taxes and serve in the military in exchange for social order.

These laws codes had evolved over a period of 1,000 years

- Laws had evolved by the Senate and interpreted by the Judiciary to meet changing times.

- The emperor became solely responsible for the law.

- Became applicable to conquered territories.

- In the 6 Century CE, the medieval churches based many of their laws on the Roman canon.

Roman Law has had the longest lasting in the field of Law. Even after the Roman collapse, Roman Law still existed and was used by many kingdoms. It became known as Civil Law all over the earth.

Augustus Caesar laid a foundation for a stable government by creating the following.

- Cicil service to enforce laws.

- High-level jobs were opened to men of talent, not just the social class.

- Common coinage

- Secure travel and trade throughout the empire

- Allegiance of cities and provinces by allowing a large measure of self-governance.

- Civil law

- Law of the people; applied to everyone supplemented by civil law.

- Natural Law:

    o Natural order of nature

    o Embodied justice and rights

    o All men are entitled to it.

    o Conceptional but not applied.

Important directly deals with the U.S. Bill of Rights!

The 12 tables were the impetus.

This system of law constantly was rewritten and refined. It is actually regarded as the Basis of Western Law today.

TABLE I	Procedure: for courts and trials
TABLE II	Trials continued.
TABLE III	Debt
TABLE IV	Rights of fathers (*paterfamilias*) over the family
TABLE V	Legal guardianship and inheritance laws
TABLE VI	Acquisition and possession

TABLE VII	Land rights
TABLE VIII	Torts and delicts (Laws of in-jury)
TABLE IX	Public law
TABLE X	Sacred law
TABLE XI	Supplement I

- XII. 5 "Whatever the People have last ordained shall be held as binding by law."

- "There are eight kinds of punishment: fine, fetters, flogging, retaliation in kind, civil disgrace, banishment, slavery, death."

- I. "If he (plaintiff) summons him (defendant) into court, he shall go. If he does not go, (plaintiff) shall call witnesses. Then only he shall take him by force. If he refuses or flees, he (the plaintiff) shall lay hands on him. If disease or age is an impediment, he shall grant him a team (of oxen). He shall not spread with cushions the covered carriage if he does not wish to.

- II. Whoever needs evidence shall go on every third day to call out loud before the witness's doorway."

- III. "When a debt has been acknowledged, or a judgment has been pronounced in court, 30 days must be the legitimate grace period. Thereafter, the arrest of the debtor may be made by the laying on of hands. Bring him into court. If he does not satisfy the judgment (or no one in court offers himself as surety on his behalf), the creditor may take the debtor with him. He may bind him either in stocks or fetters, with a weight of no less than 15 lbs. (or more if he desires)." [After 60 days in custody, the case is returned to the court, and if the debt is not then paid, the debtor can be sold abroad as a slave or put to death.]

- IV. 1 "A dreadfully deformed child shall be killed."

- IV. 2 "If a father surrenders his son for sale three times, the son shall be free."

- V. 1 "Our ancestors saw fit that "females, by reason of levity of disposition, shall remain in guardianship, even when they have attained their majority."

- V. 7 A spendthrift is forbidden to exercise administration over his own goods.

- V. 8 The inheritance of a Roman citizen-freedman is made over to his patron if the freedman has died intestate and has no natural successor.

- VI. 1 When a party shall make a bond or conveyance, what he has named by word-of-mouth shall hold good.

- VI. 2 Marriage by `usage' (*usus*): If a man and woman live together continuously for a year, they are considered to be married; the woman legally is treated as the man's daughter.

- VIII. 1 "If any person has sung or composed against another person a SONG (*carmen*) such as was causing slander or insult.... he shall be clubbed to death."

- VIII. 2 "If a person has maimed another's limb, let there be retaliation in kind unless he agrees to make compensation with him." (*Lex talionis*)

- VIII. 21 "If a patron shall defraud his client, he must be solemnly forfeited ('killed')."

- VIII. 23 "Whoever is convicted of speaking false witness shall be flung from the Tarpeian Rock."

- VIII. 26 "No person shall hold meetings in the City at night."

- IX. 3 "The penalty shall be capital punishment for a judge or arbiter legally appointed who has been found guilty of receiving a bribe for giving a decision."

- IX. 6 "Putting to death... of any man who has not been convicted, whosoever he might be, is forbidden."

- X. 4 "Women must not tear cheeks or hold chorus of 'Alas!' on account of a funeral."

- X. 6a "Anointing by slaves is abolished, and every kind of drinking bout... there shall be no costly sprinkling, no long garlands, no incense boxes."

- XI. 1 "Marriage shall not take place between a patrician and a plebeian."

- XII. 5 "Whatever the People have last ordained shall be held as binding by law."

- ? "There are eight kinds of punishment: fine, fetters, flogging, retaliation in kind, civil disgrace, banishment, slavery, death."

Chapter 22

Other Major Contributions to the Formation of our Constitution Exist.

Magna Charta

In Yorkshire and in England itself, John the King was known as an arbitrary and capricious ruler, and those were the kind words. In 1209, a simpler charter of a Magna Charta was presented by Peter de Brus that Hugh Thomas thought was a statement of good governing than a statement for Langberg Wapentake (a clear definition of this in research was vague, but it is believed to be a district in England} which would not be global England and not what was intended for reigning in the King.

Author note: I am very closely involved with this event because there were ten witnesses, and it is written that Walter Boynton was one of them. Walter Boynton was a senior statesman of Yorkshire. Also in attendance was Ingraham Boynton, also spelled Ingraham de Bouinton, a knight who was a signer of the Magna Charta. It might be interesting to know that our family can accurately trace our heredity from Burgandy, France, to what is now Boynton in Yorkshire, from slightly before 1030, when our Count ancestor built our first home. The "de" in Ingraham's name is related to royalty.

I wish this book could further detail both Walter and Ingraham's fantastic story. Let's just leave it with "a small-town boy makes good." He went off to make war with the King and returned a historic hero with a 1215 copy of the Magna Carta in his pocket, which, by the way, an original copy is at the ancestral home of Burton Agnes. Oh yeah, he married the richest girl on the block.

As for my position in the family's historic story, I am the person who is eligible, according to a British Earl on the royalty board, to be the 16th Baronet of the Boynton Family.

Since the Magna Charta was a British document, the framers chose to example. I would like to include it in this book's pages, but its 88 warranties would be too much to display. The whole document is fantastic reading, and I encourage all of you to see what the framers considered for our Constitution and Bill of Rights.

The Magna Charta

In 1215, the despotic King John of England was confronted by an assembly of barons demanding that traditional rights be recognized, written down, confirmed with the royal seal, and sent to each of the counties to be read to all freemen. The king agreed, binding himself and his heirs to grant "to all freemen of our kingdom" the rights and liberties described in the great charter, or Magna Carta. From 1215 through 1297, the king's successors reissued Magna Carta. In 1297, to meet his debts from foreign wars, King Edward I imposed new and harsher taxes, provoking another confrontation with the barons. This resulted not only in the reissue of Magna Carta, but, for the first time, its entry into the official Statute Rolls of England.

The 1297 document represents the transition of Magna Carta from a brokered agreement to the foundation of English law, establishing the idea that people possess certain unalienable rights that cannot be overruled, even by a king. Magna Carta also guaranteed due process of law, freedom from arbitrary imprisonment, trial by a jury of peers, and other fundamental rights that inspired and informed the Founding Fathers of our nation when they wrote the Declaration of Independence, the United States Constitution, and the Bill of Rights.

A full-scale civil war then broke out between John and his barons. It only ended after John's death from illness in 1216.

Henry III issued a second version of the Magna Carta in 1225, which was granted explicitly in return for a tax payment from the whole kingdom.

Why is it significant today?

The Magna Carta is considered one of the first steps taken in England towards establishing parliamentary democracy.

In the century after Henry III's version of the Magna Carta, parliament interpreted the document's message as a right to a fair trial for all subjects.

During the Stuart period, and particularly in the English Civil War, the Magna Carta was used to restrain the power of monarchs at a time when monarchs on the continent were supremely powerful.

There are strong influences from the Magna Carta in the American Bill of Rights, written in 1791. To this day, there is a 1297 copy in the National Archives in Washington, DC.

Even more recently, the basic principles of the Magna Carta are clearly seen in the Universal Declaration of Human Rights, penned in 1948, just after the Second World War.

Author note: An aerial picture of Burton Agnes, the ancestral home of the Boynton's since 1030. Off to the left is a small building that actually is the first structure built in 1030. The large building to the right was built in 1598.

This estate, **Burton Agnes Hall**, is a magnificent example of Elizabethan architecture, built in 1598 by Sir Henry Griffith and over 600 acres. The beautiful proportions of the Hall and its adherence to the principles of Tudor Renaissance architecture (Commodity, Firmness, and Delight) confirm that a professional hand drew up the designs. The architect was, in fact, Robert Smythson - Master Mason to Queen Elizabeth I and builder of such other famous houses as Longleat, Wollaton, and Hardwick. It is the only Smythson house where the plan still exists in the RIBA collection. In his definitive book on Smythson, Mark Girouard called Burton Agnes a 'splendid and glittering composition.' In the historic buildings, it ranks #3 as the most beautiful ancient buildings in England.

Original copy of the Magna Charta

Important Magna Charta or "Great Charter" takeaways included in our constitutional documents from the 1215 and 1297 versions.

CATO'S LETTER VOL. 13 NO. 3 Excerpted for brevity due to space constriction but duly acknowledged

The complete text of the Magna Carta

I am including the full text because this document's tenets were largely used in our constitutional documents as they related to "We the People" in context.

Tapestry depicting King John

Text of the Magna Carta

The king and the rebel barons negotiated a peace settlement in June 1215. The king agreed to accept the terms of Magna Carta, which is dated 15 June 1215.

Transcript

Clauses marked (+) were repeated in the charter of 1225, but with minor changes. Clauses marked (*) were omitted in all later reissues of the charter. In the charter itself the clauses are not numbered, and the text reads continuously.

JOHN, by the grace of God, King of England, Lord of Ireland, Duke of Normandy and Aquitaine, and Count of Anjou, to his archbishops, bishops, abbots, earls, barons, justices, foresters, sheriffs, stewards, servants, and to all his officials and loyal subjects, Greeting.

KNOW THAT BEFORE GOD, for the health of our soul and those of our ancestors and heirs, to the honour of God, the exaltation of the holy Church, and the better ordering of our kingdom, at the advice of our reverend fathers Stephen, archbishop of Canterbury, primate of all England, and cardinal of the holy Roman Church, Henry archbishop of Dublin, William bishop of London, Peter bishop of Winchester, Jocelin bishop of Bath and Glastonbury, Hugh bishop of Lincoln, Walter bishop of Worcester, William bishop of Coventry, Benedict bishop of Rochester, Master Pandulf subdeacon and member of the papal household, Brother Aymeric master of the knighthood of the Temple in England, William Marshal earl of Pembroke, William earl of Salisbury, William earl of Warren, William earl of Arundel, Alan of Galloway constable of Scotland, Warin fitz Gerald, Peter fitz Herbert, Hubert de Burgh seneschal of Poitou, Hugh de Neville, Matthew fitz Herbert, Thomas Basset, Alan Basset, Philip Daubeny, Robert de Roppeley, John Marshal, John fitz Hugh, and other loyal subjects:

+ (1) FIRST, THAT WE HAVE GRANTED TO GOD, and by this present charter have confirmed for us and our heirs in perpetuity, that the English Church shall be free, and shall have its rights undiminished, and its liberties unimpaired. That we wish this so to be observed appears from the fact that of our own free will, before the outbreak of the present dispute between us and our barons, we granted and confirmed by charter the freedom of the Church's elections – a right reckoned to be of the greatest necessity and importance to it – and caused this to be confirmed by Pope Innocent III. This freedom we shall observe ourselves, and desire to be observed in good faith by our heirs in perpetuity. TO ALL FREE MEN OF OUR KINGDOM, we have also granted, for us and our heirs forever, all the liberties written out below, to have and to keep for them and their heirs, of us and our heirs:

(2) If any earl, baron, or other person that holds lands directly of the Crown for military service shall die, and at his death, his heir shall be of full age and owe a 'relief,' the heir shall have his inheritance on payment of the ancient scale of 'relief.' That is to say, the heir or heirs of an earl shall pay £100 for the entire earl's barony, the heir or heirs of a knight 100s. At most for the entire knight's 'fee,' and any man that owes less shall pay less, in accordance with the ancient usage of 'fees.'

(3) But if the heir of such a person is under age and a ward when he comes of age, he shall have his inheritance without 'relief' or fine.

(4) The guardian of the land of an heir who is under age shall take from it only reasonable revenues, customary dues, and feudal services. He shall do this without destruction or damage to men or property. If we have given the guardianship of the land to a sheriff or to any person answerable to us for the revenues, and he commits destruction or damage, we will exact compensation from him, and the land shall be entrusted to two worthy and prudent men of the same 'fee,' who shall be answerable to us for the revenues, or to the person to whom we have assigned them. If we have given or sold to anyone the guardianship of such land, and he causes destruction or damage, he shall lose the guardianship of it, and it shall be handed over to two worthy and prudent men of the same 'fee,' who shall be similarly answerable to us.

(5) For so long as a guardian has guardianship of such land, he shall maintain the houses, parks, fish preserves, ponds, mills, and everything else pertaining to it from the revenues of the land itself. When the heir comes of age, he shall restore the whole land to him, stocked with plough teams and such implements of husbandry as the season demands and the revenues from the land can reasonably bear.

(6) Heirs may be given in marriage but not to someone of lower social standing. Before a marriage takes place, it shall be made known to the heir's next of kin.

(7) At her husband's death, a widow may have her marriage portion and inheritance at once and without trouble. She shall pay nothing for her dower, marriage portion, or any inheritance that she and her husband held jointly on the day of his death. She may remain in her husband's house for forty days after his death, and within this period, her dower shall be assigned to her.

(8) No widow shall be compelled to marry so long as she wishes to remain without a husband. But she must give security that she will not marry without royal consent if she holds her lands of the Crown or without the consent of whatever other lord she may hold them of.

(9) Neither we nor our officials will seize any land or rent in payment of a debt so long as the debtor has movable goods sufficient to discharge the debt. A debtor's sureties shall not be distrained upon so long as the debtor himself can discharge his debt. If, for lack of means, the debtor is unable to discharge his debt, his sureties shall be answerable for it. If they so desire, they may have the debtor's lands and rents until they have received satisfaction for the debt that they paid for him, unless the debtor can show that he has settled his obligations to them.

* (10) If anyone who has borrowed a sum of money from Jews dies before the debt has been repaid, his heir shall pay no interest on the debt for so long as he remains under age, irrespective of whom he holds his lands. If such a debt falls into the hands of the Crown, it will take nothing except the principal sum specified in the bond.

* (11) If a man dies owing money to Jews, his wife may have her dower and pay nothing towards the debt from it. If he leaves children who are underage, their needs may also be provided for on a scale

appropriate to the size of his holding of lands. The debt is to be paid out of the residue, reserving the service due to his feudal lords. Debts owed to persons other than Jews are to be dealt with similarly.

* (12) No 'scutage' or 'aid' may be levied in our kingdom without its general consent, unless it is for the ransom of our person, to make our eldest son a knight, and (once) to marry our eldest daughter. For these purposes, only a reasonable 'aid' may be levied. 'Aids' from the city of London are to be treated similarly.

+ (13) The city of London shall enjoy all its ancient liberties and free customs, both by land and by water. We also will grant that all other cities, boroughs, towns, and ports shall enjoy all their liberties and free customs.

* (14) To obtain the general consent of the realm for the assessment of an 'aid' – except in the three cases specified above – or a 'scutage,' we will cause the archbishops, bishops, abbots, earls, and greater barons to be summoned individually by letter. To those who hold lands directly of us, we will cause a general summons to be issued, through the sheriffs and other officials, to come together on a fixed day (of which at least forty days' notice shall be given) and at a fixed place. In all letters of summons, the cause of the summons will be stated. When a summons has been issued, the business appointed for the day shall go forward in accordance with the resolution of those present, even if not all those who were summoned have appeared.

* (15) In future we will allow no one to levy an 'aid' from his free men, except to ransom his person, to make his eldest son a knight, and (once) to marry his eldest daughter. For these purposes, only a reasonable 'aid' may be levied.

(16) No man shall be forced to perform more service for a knight's 'fee' or another free holding of land than is due from it.

(17) Ordinary lawsuits shall not follow the royal court around but shall be held in a fixed place.

(18) Inquests of novel disseisin, mort d'ancestor, and darrein presentment shall be taken only in their proper county court. We ourselves, or in our absence abroad, our chief justice, will send two justices to each county four times a year, and these justices, with four knights of the county elected by the county itself, shall hold the assizes in the county court, on the day and in the place where the court meets.

(19) If any assizes cannot be taken on the day of the county court, as many knights and freeholders shall afterward remain behind, of those who have attended the court, as will suffice for the administration of justice, having regard to the volume of business to be done.

(20) For a trivial offence, a free man shall be fined only in proportion to the degree of his offence, and for a serious offence correspondingly, but not so heavily as to deprive him of his livelihood. In the same way, a merchant shall be spared his merchandise and a villein the implements of his husbandry if they fall upon the mercy of a royal court. None of these fines shall be imposed except by the assessment on oath of reputable men of the neighborhood.

(21) Earls and barons shall be fined only by their equals and in proportion to the gravity of their offence.

(22) A fine imposed upon the lay property of a clerk in holy orders shall be assessed upon the same principles without reference to the value of his ecclesiastical benefice.

(23) No town or person shall be forced to build bridges over rivers except those with an ancient obligation to do so.

(24) No sheriff, constable, coroners, or other royal officials are to hold lawsuits that should be held by the royal justices.

* (25) Every county, hundred, wapentake, and tithing shall remain at its ancient rent, without increase, except the royal demesne manors.

(26) If at the death of a man who holds a lay 'fee' of the Crown, a sheriff or royal official produces royal letters patent of summons for a debt due to the Crown, it shall be lawful for them to seize and list movable goods found in the lay 'fee' of the dead man to the value of the debt, as assessed by worthy men. Nothing shall be removed until the whole debt is paid when the residue shall be given over to the executors to carry out the dead man's will. If no debt is due to the Crown, all the movable goods shall be regarded as the property of the dead man, except the reasonable shares of his wife and children.

* (27) If a free man dies intestate, his movable goods are to be distributed by his next-of-kin and friends under the supervision of the Church. The rights of his debtors are to be preserved.

(28) No constable or other royal official shall take corn or other movable goods from any man without immediate payment unless the seller voluntarily offers postponement of this.

(29) No constable may compel a knight to pay money for castleguard if the knight is willing to undertake the guard in person, or with reasonable excuse to supply some other fit man to do it. A knight taken or sent on military service shall be excused from castle guard for the period of this service.

(30) No sheriff, royal official, or other person shall take horses or carts for transport from any free man without his consent.

(31) Neither we nor any royal official will take wood for our castle or for any other purpose without the consent of the owner.

(32) We will not keep the lands of people convicted of a felony in our hand for longer than a year and a day, after which they shall be returned to the lords of the 'fees' concerned.

(33) All fish weirs shall be removed from the Thames, the Medway, and throughout the whole of England, except on the sea coast.

(34) The writ called precipe shall not in future be issued to anyone in respect of any holding of land if a free man could thereby be deprived of the right of trial in his own lord's court.

(35) There shall be standard measures of wine, ale, and corn (the London quarter) throughout the kingdom. There shall also be a standard width of dyed cloth, russet, and haberject, namely two ells within the selvedges. Weights are to be standardized similarly.

(36) In future, nothing shall be paid or accepted for the issue of a writ of inquisition of life or limbs. It shall be given gratis, and not refused.

(37) If a man holds land of the Crown by 'fee-farm,' 'socage,' or 'burgage,' and also holds land of someone else for knight's service, we will not have guardianship of his heir, nor of the land that belongs to the other person's 'fee,' by virtue of the 'fee-farm,' 'socage,' or 'burgage,' unless the 'fee-farm' owes knight's service. We will not have the guardianship of a man's heir or of land that he holds of someone else by reason of any small property that he may hold of the Crown for a service of knives, arrows, or the like.

(38) In future, no official shall place a man on trial upon his own unsupported statement without producing credible witnesses to the truth of it.

+ (39) No free man shall be seized or imprisoned, or stripped of his rights or possessions, or outlawed or exiled, or deprived of his standing in any way, nor will we proceed with force against him, or send others to do so, except by the lawful judgment of his equals or by the law of the land.

+ (40) To no one will we sell, to no one deny or delay right or justice.

(41) All merchants may enter or leave England unharmed and without fear, and may stay or travel within it, by land or water, for purposes of trade, free from all illegal exactions, in accordance with ancient and lawful customs. This, however, does not apply in times of war to merchants from a country that is at war with us. Any such merchants found in our country at the outbreak of war shall be detained without injury to their persons or property until we or our chief justice have discovered how our own merchants are being treated in the country at war with us. If our own merchants are safe, they shall be safe too.

* (42) In future, it shall be lawful for any man to leave and return to our kingdom unharmed and without fear, by land or water, preserving his allegiance to us, except in time of war, for some short period, for the common benefit of the realm. People that have been imprisoned or outlawed in accordance with the law of the land, people from a country that is at war with us, and merchants – who shall be dealt with as stated above – are excepted from this provision.

(43) If a man holds lands of any 'escheat' such as the 'honor' of Wallingford, Nottingham, Boulogne, Lancaster, or of other 'escheats' in our hand that are baronies, at his death, his heir shall give us only the 'relief' and service that he would have made to the baron, had the barony been in the baron's hand. We will hold the 'escheat' in the same manner as the baron held it.

(44) People who live outside the forest need not in future appear before the royal justices of the forest in answer to general summonses unless they are actually involved in proceedings or are sureties for someone who has been seized for a forest offense.

* (45) We will appoint as justices, constables, sheriffs, or other officials, only men that know the law of the realm and are minded to keep it well.

(46) All barons who have founded abbeys and have charters of English kings or ancient tenure as evidence of this may have guardianship of them when there is no abbot, as is their due.

(47) All forests that have been created in our reign shall at once be disafforested. River banks that have been enclosed in our reign shall be treated similarly.

*(48) All evil customs relating to forests and warrens, foresters, warreners, sheriffs and their servants, or river-banks and their wardens, are at once to be investigated in every county by twelve sworn knights of the county, and within forty days of their enquiry, the evil customs are to be abolished completely and irrevocably. But we, or our chief justice if we are not in England, are first to be informed.

* (49) We will at once return all hostages and charters delivered up to us by Englishmen as security for peace or for loyal service.

* (50) We will remove completely from their offices the kinsmen of Gerard de Athée, and in future they shall hold no offices in England. The people in question are Engelard de Cigogné, Peter, Guy, and Andrew de Chanceaux, Guy de Cigogné, Geoffrey de Martigny and his brothers, Philip Marc and his brothers, with Geoffrey his nephew, and all their followers.

* (51) As soon as peace is restored, we will remove from the kingdom all the foreign knights, bowmen, their attendants, and the mercenaries that have come to it, to its harm, with horses and arms.

* (52) To any man whom we have deprived or dispossessed of lands, castles, liberties, or rights, without the lawful judgment of his equals, we will at once restore these. In cases of dispute, the matter shall be

resolved by the judgment of the twenty-five barons referred to below in the clause for securing the peace (§61). In cases, however, where a man was deprived or dispossessed of something without the lawful judgment of his equals by our father King Henry or our brother King Richard, and it remains in our hands or is held by others under our warranty, we shall have respite for the period commonly allowed to Crusaders, unless a lawsuit had been begun, or an enquiry had been made at our order before we took the Cross as a Crusader. On our return from the Crusade, or if we abandon it, we will at once render justice in full.

* (53) We shall have similar respite in rendering justice in connexion with forests that are to be disafforested, or to remain forests when these were first afforested by our father Henry or our brother Richard; with the guardianship of lands in another person's 'fee,' when we have hitherto had this by virtue of a 'fee' held of us for knight's service by a third party; and with abbeys founded in another person's 'fee,' in which the lord of the 'fee' claims to own a right. On our return from the Crusade, or if we abandon it, we will at once do full justice to complaints about these matters.

(54) No one shall be arrested or imprisoned on the appeal of a woman for the death of any person except her husband.

* (55) All fines that have been given to us unjustly and against the law of the land, and all fines that we have exacted unjustly, shall be entirely remitted or the matter decided by a majority judgment of the twenty-five barons referred to below in the clause for securing the peace (§61) together with Stephen, archbishop of Canterbury, if he can be present, and such others as he wishes to bring with him. If the archbishop cannot be present, proceedings shall continue without him, provided that if any of the twenty-five barons has been involved in a similar suit himself, his judgment shall be set aside, and someone

else chosen and sworn in his place, as a substitute for the single occasion, by the rest of the twenty-five.

(56) If we have deprived or dispossessed any Welshmen of land, liberties, or anything else in England or in Wales without the lawful judgment of their equals, these are at once to be returned to them. A dispute on this point shall be determined in the Marches by the judgment of equals. English law shall apply to holdings of land in England, Welsh law to those in Wales, and the law of the Marches to those in the Marches. The Welsh shall treat us and ours in the same way.

* (57) In cases where a Welshman was deprived or dispossessed of anything, without the lawful judgment of his equals, by our father King Henry or our brother King Richard, and it remains in our hands or is held by others under our warranty, we shall have respite for the period commonly allowed to Crusaders, unless a lawsuit had been begun, or an enquiry had been made at our order before we took the Cross as a Crusader. But on our return from the Crusade, or if we abandon it, we will at once do full justice according to the laws of Wales and the said regions.

* (58) We will at once return the son of Llywelyn, all Welsh hostages, and the charters delivered to us as security for the peace.

* (59) With regard to the return of the sisters and hostages of Alexander, king of Scotland, his liberties, and his rights, we will treat him in the same way as our other barons of England, unless it appears from the charters that we hold from his father William, formerly king of Scotland, that he should be treated otherwise. This matter shall be resolved by the judgment of his equals in our court.

(60) All these customs and liberties that we have granted shall be observed in our kingdom in so far as concerns our own relations with

our subjects. Let all men of our kingdom, whether clergy or laymen, observe them similarly in their relations with their own men.

* (61) SINCE WE HAVE GRANTED ALL THESE THINGS for God, for the better ordering of our kingdom, and to allay the discord that has arisen between us and our barons, and since we desire that they shall be enjoyed in their entirety, with lasting strength, forever, we give and grant to the barons the following security:

The barons shall elect twenty-five of their number to keep and cause to be observed with all their might, the peace and liberties granted and confirmed to them by this charter.

If we, our chief justice, our officials, or any of our servants offend in any respect against any man or transgress any of the articles of the peace or of this security, and the offense is made known to four of the said twenty-five barons, they shall come to us – or in our absence from the kingdom to the chief justice – to declare it and claim immediate redress. If we, or in our absence abroad, the chief justice, make no redress within forty days, reckoning from the day on which the offense was declared to us or to him, the four barons shall refer the matter to the rest of the twenty-five barons, who may distrain upon and assail us in every way possible, with the support of the whole community of the land, by seizing our castles, lands, possessions, or anything else saving only our own person and those of the queen and our children, until they have secured such redress as they have determined upon. Having secured the redress, they may then resume their normal obedience to us.

Any man who so desires may take an oath to obey the commands of the twenty-five barons for the achievement of these ends and to join with them in assailing us to the utmost of his power. We give public and free permission to take this oath to any man who so desires, and at no time will we prohibit any man from taking it. Indeed, we will compel any of our subjects who are unwilling to take it to swear it at our command.

If one of the twenty-five barons dies or leaves the country or is prevented in any other way from discharging his duties, the rest of them shall choose another baron in his place, at their discretion, who shall be duly sworn in as they were.

In the event of disagreement among the twenty-five barons on any matter referred to them for decision, the verdict of the majority present shall have the same validity as a unanimous verdict of the whole twenty-five, whether these were all present or some of those summoned were unwilling or unable to appear.

The twenty-five barons shall swear to obey all the above articles faithfully and shall cause them to be obeyed by others to the best of their power.

We will not seek to procure from anyone, either by our own efforts or those of a third party, anything by which any part of these concessions or liberties might be revoked or diminished. Should such a thing be procured, it shall be null and void and we will at no time make use of it, either ourselves or through a third party.

* (62) We have remitted and pardoned fully to all men any ill-will, hurt, or grudges that have arisen between us and our subjects, whether clergy or laymen, since the beginning of the dispute. We have, in addition, remitted fully, and for our own part, have also pardoned, to all clergy and laymen, any offenses committed as a result of the said dispute between Easter in the sixteenth year of our reign (i.e., 1215) and the restoration of peace.

In addition, we have caused letters patent to be made for the barons, bearing witness to this security and to the concessions set out above, over the seals of Stephen, archbishop of Canterbury, Henry, archbishop of Dublin, the other bishops named above, and Master Pandulf.

* (63) IT IS ACCORDINGLY OUR WISH AND COMMAND that the English Church shall be free, and that men in our kingdom shall have and keep all these liberties, rights, and concessions, well and peaceably in their fullness and entirety for them and their heirs, of us and our heirs, in all things and all places forever.

Both we and the barons have sworn that all this shall be observed in good faith and without deceit. Witness the abovementioned people and many others.

Given by our hand in the meadow that is called Runnymede, between Windsor and Staines, on the fifteenth day of June in the seventeenth year of our reign (i.e., 1215: the new regnal year began on 28 May).

Translation by the British Library

Americans need to acknowledge the immense debt we owe to the nobles and clergy who met at Runnymede to wrest from King John several of the rights we enjoy today, to say nothing of the rule of law that followed, however unevenly.

Yes, we're also fond of believing that in 1776, America sprang fully formed, and that was not true; much work was needed to assemble our country's foundational documents. As we celebrate the 4th, we should also recognize that for all their work, America's Founders drew much from the English nation we left years ago.

The Magna Carta gave our framers the language that people can assert their rights against an oppressive ruler and that the power of government can be limited to protect those rights. This concept is foundational and central to both the Declaration of Independence and the United States Constitution.

This brought on the following three other forms of rights: petitions, bills, and an act defining people's rights.

The English Petition of Right

Represented by parliament. It also supports the Magna Carta, the Petition of Right, and the Habeas Corpus Act of 1679. A similar Act, the Claim of Right Act of 1689, applies. The Bill of Rights of 1689 was created on May 8th, 1628, by Sir Edward Coke, representing the protection of civil liberties. It was passed on June 7th, 1628. A major document in constitutional law in 1628 in England set out specific liberties that the King was prohibited from exercising. He rejected the motion but relented under pressure. Both houses joined together and the King fully passed the Petition. This was regarded as the most famous constitutional document equal in value to the Magna Carta and the Bill of Rights of 1689. It remains in force in the UK, Australia, and New Zealand. It influenced the Massachusetts Body of Liberties and was a predecessor to the Third, fifth, sixth, and seventh amendments to the Constitution of the United States.

English Bill of Rights A follow-up of the English Petition of Rights is the Bill of Rights, which Parliament passed and affirmed by Royal assent in 1689, limits the power of the monarch, sets the rights of parliament, regular parliamentary meetings, free elections, freedom of speech, prohibition of cruel and unusual punishment and allowed rights of Protestants to have arms for their defense within the rule of law. It also has no right of taxation without parliament's agreement. It condemned the misdeeds of James II. Most importantly, it restated the requirements of the crown to seek the consent of the people Act applies in Scotland, the model for the US Bill of Rights of 1789. The Act of Settlement in 1701 is still in effect.

The Act of Abjuration or Plakkaat. In English, the Act of Aburation. In short, when the ruler does not defend the subjects from oppression and violence and ignores their ancient customs and privileges, and extracts Slavic compliance, he is no longer a prince but a tyrant. If this is done deliberately they may disallow his authority and legally choose another prince for their defense.

This is similar to the Declaration of Independence. When a President designs to reduce them under despotism, it is their right, it is their duty, to throw off that government for their future security. Speculation is that the framers used this as a model, and they are similar.

Chapter 23

The Mayflower Compact

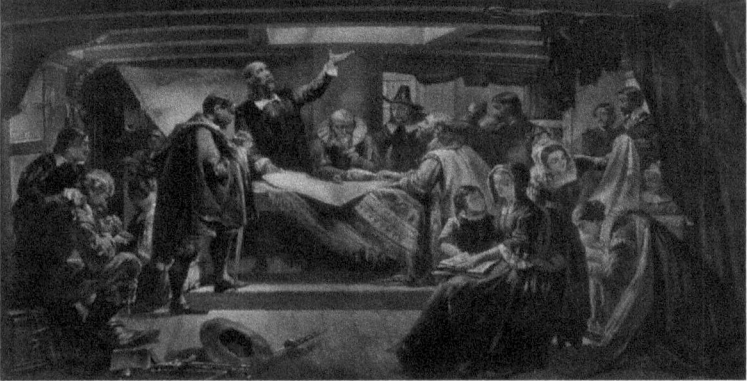

The Mayflower Compact signed aboard ship on November 11, 1620

Author special note: I am proud to say I am an invading alien from the shores of Cape Cod at Plymouth Colony on the first voyage as a relative of John Alden. Call me a plank owner. I was one of 41 of the ship's 101 passengers.

They were originally bound for the Virginia Colony, but a storm forced them to anchor off Cape Cod in Massachusetts. Provisions were running short, so they decided to exercise their own liberty. No one had power over them, so they were determined to form their own government, even keeping their allegiance with England.

The compact was based on a majoritarian model and allegiance to the King. It was a social contract deciding to follow the community's rules for the sake of order and survival.

The Mayflower Compact

IN THE NAME OF GOD, AMEN. We, whose names are underwritten, the Loyal Subjects of our dread Sovereign Lord King James, by the Grace of God, of Great Britain, France, and Ireland, King, Defender of the Faith, &c. Having undertaken for the Glory of God, and Advancement of the Christian Faith, and the Honor of our King and Country, a Voyage to plant the first Colony in the northern Parts of Virginia, Do by these Presents, solemnly and mutually, in the Presence of God and one another, covenant and combine ourselves together into a civil Body Politick, for our better Ordering and Preservation, and Furtherance of the Ends aforesaid: And by Virtue hereof do enact, constitute, and frame, such just and equal Laws, Ordinances, Acts, Constitutions, and Officers, from time to time, as shall be thought most meet and convenient for the general Good of the Colony; unto which we promise all due Submission and Obedience.

IN WITNESS whereof we have hereunto subscribed our names at Cape-Cod the eleventh of November, in the Reign of our Sovereign Lord King James, of England, France, and Ireland, the eighteenth, and of Scotland the fifty-fourth, Anno Domini; 1620.

John Carver

William Bradford

Edward Winslow

William Brewster

Isaac Allerton

Myles Standish

John Alden

John Turner

Francis Eaton

James Chilton

John Craxton

John Billington

Moses Fletcher

John Goodman

Samuel Fuller

Christopher Martin

William Mullins

William White

Richard Warren

John Howland

Stephen Hopkins

Digery Priest

Thomas Williams

Gilbert Winslow

Edmund Margesson

Peter Brown

Richard Britteridge

George Soule

Edward Tilly

John Tilly

Francis Cooke

Thomas Rogers

Thomas Tinker

John Ridgdale

Edward Fuller

Richard Clark

Richard Gardiner

Mr. John Allerton

Thomas English

Edward Doten

Edward Liester

The document was not titled initially but, over time, became known as the "Mayflower Compact." The original document has been lost, but a copy was published in 1622 in *Mourt's Relation* by Edward Winslow and in William Bradford's *Of Plymoth Plantation*. In 1669, Nathaniel Morton published it and included the names of the signers. The document was brought out to be read publicly at government meetings in Plymouth Colony several times a year.

Chapter 24

Virginia Declaration of Rights June 12, 1776

Authors Geoge Mason, Robert Carter Nicholas, and James Madison, Thomas Ludwell Lee

The Virginia Declaration of Rights

Thomas Jefferson drew upon Virginia's Declaration of Rights for the opening paragraphs of the Declaration of Independence. It was widely copied by the other colonies and became the basis of the Bill of Rights. Written by George Mason, it was adopted by the Virginia Constitutional Convention on June 12, 1776.

A Declaration of Rights

It is made by the representatives of the good people of Virginia, assembled in full and free convention whose rights do pertain to them and their posterity as the basis and foundation of government.[17]

Section 1

Section 1. That all men are by nature equally free and independent and have certain inherent rights, of which, when they enter into a state of society, they cannot, by any compact, deprive or divest their posterity; namely, the enjoyment of life and liberty, with the means of acquiring and possessing property and pursuing and obtaining happiness and safety.

Section 2

---

[17] The Virginia Declaration of Rights | National Archives

That all power is vested in, and consequently derived from, the people; that magistrates are their trustees and servants and at all times amenable to them.

Section 3

That government is, or ought to be, instituted for the common benefit, protection, and security of the people, nation, or community; of all the various modes and forms of government, that is best which is capable of producing the greatest degree of happiness and safety and is most effectually secured against the danger of maladministration. And that, when any government shall be found inadequate or contrary to these purposes, a majority of the community has an indubitable, inalienable, and indefeasible right to reform, alter, or abolish it in such manner as shall be judged most conducive to the public weal.

Section 4

That no man, or set of men, is entitled to exclusive or separate emoluments or privileges from the community, but in consideration of public services; which, nor being descendible, neither ought the offices of magistrate, legislator, or judge to be hereditary.

Section 5

That the legislative and executive powers of the state should be separate and distinct from the judiciary, and that the members of the two first may be restrained from oppression by feeling and participating in the burdens of the people, they should, at fixed periods, be reduced to a private station, return into that body from which they were originally taken, and the vacancies be supplied by frequent, certain, and regular elections, in which all, or any part, of the former members, to be again eligible, or ineligible, as the laws shall direct.

Section 6

That elections of members to serve as representatives of the people in assembly ought to be free; and that all men, having sufficient evidence of permanent common interest with, and attachment to, the community, have the right of suffrage and cannot be taxed or deprived of their property for public uses without their own consent or that of their representatives so elected, nor bound by any law to which they have not, in like manner, assented, for the public good.

Section 7

That all power of suspending laws, or the execution of laws, by any authority, without consent of the representatives of the people, is injurious to their rights and ought not to be exercised.

Section 8

That in all capital or criminal prosecutions, a man has a right to demand the cause and nature of his accusation, to be confronted with the accusers and witnesses, to call for evidence in his favor, and to a speedy trial by an impartial jury of twelve men of his vicinage, without whose unanimous consent he cannot be found guilty; nor can he be compelled to give evidence against himself; that no man be deprived of his liberty except by the law of the land or the judgment of his peers.

Section 9

That excessive bail ought not to be required, nor excessive fines imposed, nor cruel and unusual punishments inflicted.

Section 10

That general warrants, whereby an officer or messenger may be commanded to search suspected places without evidence of a fact committed or to seize any person or persons not named, or whose offense is not particularly described and supported by evidence, are grievous and oppressive and ought not to be granted.

Section 11

That in controversies respecting property and in suits between man and man, the ancient trial by jury is preferable to any other and ought to be held sacred.

Section 12

That the freedom of the press is one of the great bulwarks of liberty, and can never be restrained but by despotic governments.

Section 13

That a well-regulated militia, composed of the body of the people, trained to arms, is the proper, natural, and safe defense of a free state; that standing armies, in time of peace, should be avoided as dangerous to liberty; and that in all cases the military should be under strict subordination to, and governed by, the civil power.

Section 14

That the people have a right to uniform government; and, therefore, that no government separate from or independent of the government of Virginia ought to be erected or established within the limits thereof.

Section 15

That no free government, or the blessings of liberty, can be preserved to any people but by a firm adherence to justice, moderation, temperance, frugality, and virtue and by frequent recurrence to fundamental principles.

Section 16

That religion, or the duty which we owe to our Creator, and the manner of discharging it, can be directed only by reason and conviction, not by force or violence; and therefore, all men are equally entitled to the free exercise of religion, according to the dictates of conscience; and that it is the mutual duty of all to practice Christian forbearance, love, and charity toward each other.

This declaration proclaimed the rights of men, the right to reform and abolish "inadequate" government. It influenced a number of later documents, including the Declaration of Independence (1776) and the United States.

Author Notes:

Systems, I agree, can be very complex, and I marvel at the wisdom of the framers. They buy-in-large they were young men, average under 26. That they had the ability to well, "pull a rabbit out of a hat" and give us guiding directions to formulate a working government is mind boggling even today. I myself would, at my mid to advanced age, if tasked, do the same and sample working models and select the best that, in theory, they thought would be sustainable, defensible, works for the people with protections, and has teeth to take care of the downside with a "borrowed" legal system. They didn't do so badly with roads, building construction, and world opinion, but then, of course, they had ancient organizations to lean on as well.

I can see in the writings I have included in this text from the sources that seemed to "float to the top" for consideration, taken from three prime examples, that there were sufficient materials to put into the "kettle of creation" for a workable government. Much discussion to be divulged in this writing will define this along with the body politic's actions and public opinion. Of course, we have conventions and more discussion, and well, let's see what else I can tell you about what I have gleaned from history.

I do not brush aside the controversy of key members of the framers. Some comments were pros and cons. Here are a few examples. **James Madison** did not want a chaotic, anarchic system, whereas Thomas

Paine wanted to embrace ancient democracy and defend it, thinking it could be improved upon. This comment prompted the colonists to think a democratic republic might be in order.

The basic tenet of government is an implicit contract between the government and the populace. The contract between the two is the populace agrees to give up some freedoms in exchange for protection from the government. This was a theory of **Thomas Hobbs** and exposed a full explanation of the basic tenets of a workable government. If it did not hold up its end of the bargain, **Locke** stated that the people had a right to revolt and overthrow the government and return the whole state back to **Nature,** an interesting proposal. The populace would then be obliged to create a new social contract.

Chapter 25

RIGHTS WERE AT THE HEART OF THE DEC-LARATION OF INDEPENDENCE.

Thomas Jefferson was inspired by **Thomas Locke's** explanation of the social contract when he wrote:

> *"We hold these truths to be self-evident, that all men are created equal, that they are endowed by their Creator with unalienable Rights, that among these are Life, Liberty and the pursuit of Happiness."*

It is said that Locke preferred property instead of unalienable rights, but Ben Franklin preferred the use of "pursuit of Happiness." Thomas Jefferson, in writing the Declaration of Independence, was acutely aware of the actions of Great Britain's King George that violated the social contract with the people in the American Colonies. Locke's ideas became the justification for the Revolutionary War.

Jefferson, at the Constitutional Convention, experimented with Locke's theories of "We the People," and James Madison used Locke's ideas when drafting the Constitution. From its first words, the American government is created by the American people to serve the public good and protect their freedom. Madison also drew on French philosopher **Baron de Montesquieu with the idea** of checks and balances for each branch of government and that none would be supreme. In effect, no small group could take over the government, keeping private interests in check for the good of the public. Locke was most influential with the founders of American democracy.

The above was contributed to excerpt fashion by Jennifer Mueller and we thank her.

There were a number of documents that our founders drew upon to support ideas of self-government.

The Petition of Right

As a precondition to granting any future taxes, in 1628, Parliament forced the King to assent to the Petition of Right. This asked for a settlement of Parliament's complaints against the King's non-parliamentary taxation and imprisonments without trial, plus the unlawfulness of martial law and forced billets. However, the King ensured that the Petition was enrolled in such a way that there would be doubts about its force as law: it was granted by his grace rather than 'of right.'

> ➤ That set limits on non-parliamentary taxation and made it illegal to imprison citizens without cause. Other documents gave self-government. The Magna Charta and the English Bill of Rights of 1688 and the Mayflower Compact, Constitution Society: Bill of Rights 1689

> ➤ From these and other forms of researched governments, our Declaration of Independence was produced on July 4, 1776.

The Petition of Right

Authors comment

I draw on Locke's comment to present this example.

In effect, no small group could take over the government, keeping private interests in check for the good of the public. A violation of the social contract with "We the People? It does not follow "rights" in our constitution."

As an example of prohibiting full public involvement in the legislative process, I contend that the following events may have violated the separation of powers in an unlawful attempt at accumulating power in an attempt at an overthrow of a legally elected president and the manipulation of an upcoming national election and the destruction of a legal government.

Authors note: I also note that this right can be applied across the whole spectrum of our government and is equally applicable throughout any administration, be it government or parties wishing to alter the normalcy of a voted-upon process or procedure in any social contract anywhere.

Author Note: Current events of January – February 2020, an inappropriate Power Grab, I might add, totally unconstitutional "not in the light of day," as they say.

This is a prime example of the assumption of too much power recently arising when the partisan Democrats in the House of Representatives held what many called an unconstitutional trial of a sitting president in what I would label a rogue impeachment process. These were obvious one-sided partisan kangaroo courts where the accused were not freely allowed to call witnesses in the Intelligence Committee and then further in the Judicial Committee, both ruled by heavy-handed chairmen. The defense legal counsel was not even allowed to be present. Chairmen of the Intelligence and Judicial committees were, I will say, not in proper decorum and made remarks alleging, some say, improper and not-factual remarks where rebuttal was not allowed and freely overridden by chairmen. Closed-door sessions were held in ultra-secure rooms where the accused party representatives were not invited to attend and were not made aware of the outcomes.

The impeachment votes that were taken were split in favor of the majority party in the Congressional House, were clearly partisan, and were not in accordance with the strict guidelines of the Constitution. In my opinion, using the high bar guidelines and very clear definitions of the allegations to be used clearly stated in the Constitution were not met. The charges were specious, clearly weak with no obvious crime definitely specified. Clearly, they were outside the bounds of Constitutional guidance. The powers of the House were abused in setting up an awkward process, setting up precedence to impeach any President in the future, regardless of party affiliation, on any charge at the will of any political party without adhering to the Constitutional conditions. This created a situation not in accordance with the Constitutional direction and in an "I'll do it myself fashion" and incorrectly bastardized the complete process. Not only did they not meet the high bar on the charges, but they sat on the completely partisan passed charges for a month before moving them to the Senate for the next phase of the impeachment process. This clearly, in my mind, is not a proper role of the House of Representatives. They figured they knew better, but we will see.

Please look at the requirements to impeach a president; they are found in.

Article II, Section IV of the Constitution. It states that the President, Vice President and all civil Officers of the United States shall be removed from office on impeachment for, and conviction of, treason, bribery, or other high crimes and misdemeanors.

After the long-awaited and unexplained thirty-day hold on the delivery of the two articles, the House Managers finally delivered the charges to the Senate with unprecedented pomp and circumstance.

The protocol of the Senate, defined by the Constitution, required that all charges be fully vetted by the House when given to the Senate for a trial. It immediately became unclear if more witnesses were required raising major contention between both houses' members. It's ridiculous for Kabuki theatre to deliver, out of established protocol rules, to deliver incomplete charges concerning an impeachment to Senate members who expected that this was done following strict constitutional guidelines, but this was not the case. This became a serious point of contention for the House managers who wanted witnesses when the Senate objected.

The Senate procedural requirements were already pre-established with protocol following Constitutional guidelines submitted and approved by the Supreme Court Judge. Each Senate leadership member gave opening statements defining the parties' position. The House managers were then entitled to twenty-four hours of presentation, with many asking for more witnesses. Remember, this actually was supposed to be completed during the House Intelligence and Judiciary committees, but the House managers had not done their jobs, wanted more, and expected the Senate to comply and do their job for them.

NOTE: along with witnesses, they wanted to expand the charges outside of the voted and passed articles of impeachment wholly against the rules established by the Constitution, one that would severely limit the President's powers and actually make it a simple task to impeach anyone on simple charges. This would change the intent of the Constitution. It was debated away as dangerous to our future government's ability to govern.

The President's staff then presented their side of what they considered corrections to the House testimony and gave legal and constitutional interpretations of the article's validity.

The next element of the trial involved each party in the Senate asking questions of the President's staff and House managers. The next segment involved voting on each article, with each Senate member giving a voice vote. Both articles were voted down by a partisan split between parties. The Supreme Court judge then declared vindication for the President, and the trial ended with his full acquittal.

As a former Independent minded politician, this activity is of interest to me; my wife calls me a political junkie. Of course, I have an opinion about the whole matter. I found it to be an unmitigated fiasco, one that never should have seen the light of day, foreign to the guidelines laid out in the Constitution, and clearly an affront to its very existence. It was clearly one-sided partisanship with little relief to the defense party. The Chairs of the Intelligence and Judicial committees became very forward dictatorial at times. I wondered if they were trying to aggrandize themselves with their powers; it did not impress me or many others. I believe it had a definite negative outcome for the articles they presented to the Senate floor for trial for the balance of the process.

Citizens of the United States saw a failure of Constitutional CIVICS and ETHICS in our society. I personally saw a blatant disregard for the Rule of Law we have fought to preserve.

I am sickened by the thought that some would throw these revered documents to the wind while falsely professing they "lived and died" by its tenets, which was obvious to me as blatant lies. We can only hope the voting public, "We the People," will remedy this in the next election cycle and give us Representatives and Senators who are not blind sheep partisans but true constitutional representatives working for us.

AUTHOR A final thought and an important one.

WHERE WAS THE SUPREME COURT WHEN THIS ALL CAME DOWN? CAN ANYONE TELL ME? A LAW NEEDED TO BE PASSED DOWN OSTRCISING THE VIOLATING PARTIES SO, THIS COULD HAVE HARDENED OUR LAWS AGAINST THIS TYPE OF ACTION.

Chapter 26

Peoples of Ancient Governments gave us exampled laws

Can we presuppose how basic ancient governments, or let's loosely call them mutual assistance associations, basically represent the formation of organizations to serve the people they designed to represent?

I will review a number of forms of government from the BCE era, which stands for "Before Common Era (BC)," "Before Christian Era (CE)," and represents the time before the last 2024 years. In this book, I researched functional governments back to 4,520 years ago.

This book will strive to give you knowledge of the many ancient and very interesting governments you probably never studied in school or college unless you are a history major or an in-depth history buff. I can assure you that my research is not exhaustive, as many governmental forms have evolved over the ages, but what I will present will be more than enough to give you a solid review of what formed our government's "Rule of Law" documents and who and what was involved.

Let's start with very early populations.

Do you recall LUCY, a skeleton found in an African cave that was said to be 3 million years old? Now, I can speculate, but they say she was placed there as a burial. So, can we theorize that there was a collective society with rules as we know them?

This may be a bit of a stretch for some, but if we look at very early civilizations, let's say millions of years ago, when the cradle of civilization had pockets of individuals, not really sure what to call them, were wandering around and running into other individuals and, hypothetically let's say, they said "let's get together for mutual protection. I'll bet my prehistoric battle axe they said yes "but let's have some basic rules – AH-HA, we'll share hunting yields, and the ladies can grow veggies, and just think those bullies across the veldt better not harm us because we are a serious threat to them and we have our act together.

Well, with that simple civic action, they just formed a cohesive gathering of consenting parties in what is a basic functioning government with maybe a rock tablet etched with the rules of conduct. WOW!

Ironically, something just surfaced to my attention that lends credence to the above supposition. On page 61 of the January/February 2020 edition of Discover magazine, it was noted that skulls were found in two locations in Greece in the Apidima cave named fossil 1. The skulls were of H. Sapiens origin, suggested to be 210,000 years old and coming from Africa.

In Israel, at a site in Misliya, another H. Sapiens, 177,000 to 194,000 years old, along with fossils from China dating 120,000 years old, were discovered.

Now, in the Grecian cave Apidima 2, just a foot apart from Apidima 1, at the age of just 40,000 years younger, this strongly suggests there was a definite association with Neanderthal hominids.

Could we now change our hypothesis about intermingling populations migrating out of Africa and forming associations with others? I believe we could make a strong case.

Chapter 27

Formations of Societal Governments

I believe we have positively ascertained that there is empirical evidence (up to maybe 30 million years ago (archaeological evidence)) of ancient migration and that populations grew in size in Asia, Australia, Europe, the Middle East, France, and England, and beyond and that these populations, through the ages, formed well-documented evidence of societal governments in many diverse forms. I would like to present these to you and what we know of them, their recorded forms of government, how these populations came to life, and their contributions to the rules of law, similar perhaps to what we have now.

OK, but first, let's build a presupposed government using what we know about people in general. It's a start, and it's where all governments emanate from. I know I am old, but not that old, but I needed an example. Give me a break.

We have this band of folks wandering around having no real structure, you know, men, women, and children with no obvious roots, security, no steady food supply, no leadership to speak of, and no place to call home. Definitely not a good picture. Well, in my mind, there is hope. There is this person who they follow who helps others, can find water sources, and hunts and shares his catch. To us, that person has qualities we can define, such as caring for others (moral behavior), treating people as they would treat him (ethics), and helping others solve issues within the group (civic tendency); well, folks, we have identified a leader, one that others can follow. The people respect that person and make them someone who can give the wandering tribe cohesiveness and elevate them to a high position, says Chief; well, that person in leading needs to develop common rules for them to follow so everyone knows what is expected of them, and they know what they can expect from that leader. This person needs to consider security for the group, Establish This is the **foundation of the Rule of Law** as basic as it can be.

Your Mother and Father had the responsibility to teach you about rules. If you were Catholic and went to Catholic school, the Nun's had this ruler, I know, and made you follow rules. When you first go to any school as a child, you follow the rules. As a member of an organization there are leaders and rules. Go to work, and you need to follow the rules. Join the service, and you will certainly find structure and rules. We are a rules-based world with very diverse varying degrees of rules.

The following are definitions of representative governmental and bureaucratic forms of ruling. They all point to complex, evolving, and often conflicting ideas about how we should live with one another and within a larger society with largely varying rules.

Strone Club is an unsubstantiated form of rule by brute force found in very, very ancient times.

Anarchy defined, a state of disorder due to absence or <u>nonrecognition</u> of authority or other controlling systems or an the organization of society on the basis of voluntary cooperation, without political institutions or <u>hierarchical</u> government; <u>anarchism</u>. Envision a hoard of people ravaging without central leadership.

Aristocracy defined, an aristocracy is a form of government where a small group of elites rule. Example a king of a country.

Bureaucracy defined, A bureaucracy is a form of work organization. The historical meaning of the term refers to a body of non-elected government officials. Think of your workplace or a social project.

Capitalism defined, an economic and political system in which a country's trade and industry are controlled by private owners for profit.

Colonialism defined, the policy or practice of acquiring full or partial political control over another country, <u>occupying</u> it with <u>settlers</u>, and <u>exploiting</u> it economically. This was the rule the American colonies were under

Communism defined, a political theory derived from Karl Marx, <u>advocating</u> class war and leading to a society in which all property is publicly owned and each person works and is paid according to their abilities and needs.

Democracy defined, Democracy (from Ancient Greek: δημοκρατία, romanized: dēmokratía, dēmos 'people' and kratos 'rule') is a system of government in which state power is vested in the people or the general population of a state.

Republic defined, representatives of the citizen body. Modern republics are founded on the idea that sovereignty rests with the people, though who is included and excluded from the category Republic defined, form of government in which a state is ruled by of the people has varied across history.

Democratic republic defined, A democratic republic is *a form of government operating on principles adopted from a republic and a democracy*. As a cross between two similar systems. This is the form of government the United States has under our constitution.

Federalism defined, he Constitution of the United States divides the federal government into three branches: legislative, executive, and judicial. This ensures that no individual or group will have too much power.

Feudalism defined, Feudalism was a system in which people were given land and protection by people of higher rank, and worked and fought for them in return.

Kleptocracy defined, a society or system ruled by people who use their power to steal their country's resources. Example: "there are too many entrenched dictatorships and kleptocracies in the region". Example: A corrupt self-serving government who use their power to steal their country's resources. The ruling party is highly sensitive to allegations of corruption and kleptocracy by the public."

Meritocracy defined, A meritocracy is a political, social, or economic system where people are given positions of power, influence, or reward based on their abilities and achievements, rather than their social, cultural, or economic background. In a meritocracy, people are assessed based on their performance, which can be measured through examinations or demonstrated achievements.

Military Dictatorship defined, a form of government in which the military exerts total control of a country, usually after seizing power by overthrowing the previous rulers in a coup. Military dictatorships are typically marked by brutal human rights abuses, such as killings, torture, and disappearances.[18]

Monarchy defined, Monarchy is a political system in which supreme authority is vested in the monarch, an individual ruler who functions as head of state. It typically acts as a political-administrative organization and as a social group of nobility known as "court society." political system based upon the undivided sovereignty or rule of a single person. The term applies to states in which supreme authority is vested in the monarch, an individual ruler who functions as the head of state and who achieves his or her position through heredity. Most monarchies allow only male succession, usually from father to son. England and most monarchies in Europe and countries like Japan have this system.

Oligarchy defined, Many Greek city-states were governed by oligarchies. Rather than investing all the power in the hands of a king or in the hands of an assembly of all citizens, oligarchies instead chose to allow only a handful of individuals to govern. I chose this definition because of our founding fathers looked at this form of rule but discarded it for our democratic republic form of government.

Author Note: The last form of rule actually was control of a different sort found in the world, but I gave examples found.

Plutocracy defined, simply government by the wealthy. a country or society governed by the wealthy. "no one can accept public

---

[18] https://www.britannica.com/topic/military-dictatorship

policies which turn a democracy into a plutocracy" an elite or ruling class of people whose power derives from their wealth. "Officials were drawn from the new plutocracy."

In our own country, there were wealthy financial barons like Ford, Edison, and the following.

According to Thought Co, **John D. Rockefeller** is one of the most notorious "**robber barons**" in US history, controlling much of the American oil industry in the late 19th century. Other "robber barons" include:

- Andrew Carnegie

A captain of industry in 19th century America, Carnegie helped build the American steel industry.

- Cornelius Vanderbilt

Known for his business tactics and strategies, which allowed him to create a transportation empire.

- Jay Gould

An infamous gold and railroad speculator who bought and reorganized the Erie Railroad.

J. P. Morgan

The de facto leader of the Morgan dynasty, Morgan revolutionized numerous industries, including electricity, railroad, and steel.

Charles Crocker

One of the four major barons of the Central Pacific Railroad, Crocker was one of the wealthiest men in America.

Leland Stanford

A "robber baron" and great philanthropist, Stanford got his start in business as a merchant during the California Gold Rush.

James Fisk

A major force on Wall Street, Fisk was dubbed a robber baron due to his unscrupulous financiers.

Jay Cooke

An influential Wall Street banker who played a vital role in brokering federal bonds during the Civil War.

Republicanism defined, By **Robert Longley** history and Government Expert

- B.S., Texas A&M University Updated on May 02, 2024

In both a republic and a democracy, citizens are empowered to participate in a representational political system. They elect people to represent and protect their interests in how the government functions.

Key Takeaways

- Republics and democracies both provide a political system in which citizens are represented by elected officials who are sworn to protect their interests.
- In a pure democracy, laws are made directly by the voting majority, leaving the rights of the minority largely unprotected.

- In a republic, laws are made by representatives chosen by the people and must comply with a constitution that protects the rights of the minority from the will of the majority.
- The United States, while basically a republic, is best described as a "representative democracy."
- In a republic, laws are made by representatives chosen by the people and must comply with a constitution that protects the rights of the minority from the will of the majority.
- The United States, while basically a republic, is best described as a "representative democracy."

Socialism defined, What is socialism theory simplified?

Socialism is an economic and political philosophy encompassing diverse economic and social systems characterised by social ownership of the means of production, as opposed to private ownership. It describes the economic, political, and social theories and movements associated with the implementation of such systems.

Theocracy defined, Theocracy is a form of government where it is believed that a god, deity, or group of deities, or a deity is in charge. The supreme being is usually thought to rule through human figures, like politicians and clergy, who are believed to be in direct contact with and/or of direct descent from the supreme being. Examples of this is the Dali Lama and formerly the Emperor of Japan.

Totalitarianism and Tribalism defined.

Michael Burke

What is tribalism? These days it's used as an insult; it's generally used to describe insular small mindedness and fear of outsiders but I'm from a small town in the west of Ireland and I really don't see it that way. My town feels very tribal in that we all look out for each other and come to each other's aid in a crisis. We also accept new members into our tribe regularly to replace the ones that leave.

Tribes are a natural state for human groups to be in, a collection of families and individuals working for the common good of the tribe. Self-interest becomes somewhat universal for the group. The modern consumerist society separates us out into individuals, when humans are isolated and alone they are vulnerable to everything from predators to con men. The modern world has sort of erased that tribal nature calling it backwards but it's made us all more vulnerable, instead of acting locally with a tribe by our side we are thrust onto a larger stage where we're alone in a sea of voices.

Acting as a tribe people are harder to ignore. As microcosms they are better able to get a fair deal and get things done.

Ireland and the United States would have been an island of tribes for a long time before the concept of nations or even empires were a thing. While those tribes fought each other they also lived in peace a lot of the time too, they traded and socialized with each other. They were not just savage groups that only wanted to fight all the time. I would like to see Ireland as a nation of tribes, where we are all more involved at a local level and less dependent on a national government that just wants to stay in power and where our words as tribes carry more weight. I know socialism would be the obvious modern comparison, but it feels too much like a one size fits all approach. With tribalism everyone can do what they like and only have to come together and agree on major issues.

I relate this to the colonies and the Iroquois and the commonality they shared.

Totalitarianism defined, Totalitarianism is a form of rule in which the government attempts to maintain 'total' control over society, including all aspects of the public and private lives of its citizens. It became a popular subject following World War II and during the peak years of the Cold War. Although totalitarian regimes have existed in other nations including China, North Korea, and Iraq, they began in Europe and were characterized by leaders with strong personalities, such as Hitler in Nazi Germany and Stalin in the Soviet Union. Common qualities existed among all the regimes which defined them as totalitarian, but the implementation of control appeared differently in each country. In Western cultures, where freedom and individuality are valued as guiding principles of governments, totalitarianism is generally seen as a negative and oppressive form of control.

This concludes the examination of the types and styles of governments and social bureaucratic forms of rule. As defined above you can clearly see that our move to a governmental system, one of a Rule of Law, had many pathways that our founders could have accepted for our growing population. I for one can clearly see that this form, introduced by the examination of world societies from the BCE era and the Iroquois Constitution, in my opinion, was the best choice. It gives We the People the rights we deserve in a participative form of government.

Not that I am expert on governments, but while serving in the military from 1959 to 1978, I actually had the experience of being in countries with forms of governments not like our own but my having to function within their lawful structures which was strange to me in some cases. The commands I served with visited and sometimes were tasked to serve as station ships in in various countries where I literally was immersed in their cultures. Countries such as Hong Kong (2) times (two months), where I had to interact with a mixed British and Chinese system and while there I had to do work on the Chinese mainland in Kowloon(British/Communist), the Philippines, (US Territory) , Taiwan 1 Month (Feudalism), Japan 7 months, 1959/60(change from a oligarchic and militaristic system) to US Occupation in 1946, Korea 2 Months in 1960 a Democratic regime, South Africa at Cape Town a **Aristocracy**, Congo, under the UN flag, 1 Month on Congo River in 1960 (at war). It had a democratically elected government (UN Controls), Malaysia 1961,1 Month, British and Malayan Federal Governments, Borneo, 1960 1 Month, British Colony. Other forms of governments in Central and South America were other forms under Presidents or Dictators but were confidential involvements but observed and understood.

What Civilization's Governments Were Studied by the Constitutional Framers?

Excerpts contributed by Kevin Wandrei, Classroom

Considering that there are many types of government, both ancient and modern, listed above, in framing the U.S. Constitution, the Founding Fathers had what I would call an overwhelming and daunting task to identify and define what issues they wanted to address, not wanting to experience again the injustice's levied upon them by Britain. in the forming of a new nation. In fact, they were all learned men and had knowledge of the many types of governments they needed to review. They wanted tried and true practices and laws practiced and exampled over, in some cases, many thousands of years.

Obviously, they could not clearly reference, with any certainty, the Aboriginal migration through Africa, Europe and over the Beringia Bridge, but they closely studied many civilizations that settled and formed durable governments. Many populations, through melding of minor societies into major assemblies, established its rules and laws through trial and error. Some efforts being tumultuous, but eventually successful in developing Rule of Law for the people of interest to our founding fathers and the 13 colonies declarations of purpose for their citizens.. Some others, found to be worthy of inclusion in foundational discussion, will be exampled in this manuscript.

In framing the U.S. Constitution, the Founding Fathers closely studied the governments of countries, both ancient and modern, with a special emphasis on those in Europe, but others were studied. The ones they primarily focused on are listed below and comprehensive details will follow further on as we examine them for their contributions to the framers.

Ancient Greece 508 BC Ancient Rome 509 BC Ancient Macedonia 332 BC

Ancient England 1215 AD Magna Carta Mayflower   Compact 1620 AD

English Bill of Rights 1689 AD the Iroquois Nation 1744 AD

Dutch Republic 1581 AD Virginia Declaration of Rights 1776 AD
the Bible

Ben Franklin Albany Plan of Union Articles of Confederation between states 1777-1781

There are others that contributed unique rules of governance that will be discussed within each focused government example.

Personal Contributors to the Founding Documents and Papers

When anyone mentions the Constitution, Bill of Rights, Rule of Law or the Declaration of Independence they always mention key individuals or the framers but as they sing in the song "Is that all there is" well, in research, I found that there are many individuals, some I myself did not know, or identify, as key contributors to the foundation of our country. I will list them as befitting their very important contribution and will detail what they did for contributions towards the formation of our government, with an accompanying picture. There are several others who contributed to various key contributing roles such as Paul Revere, the leaders, and delegates of the colonies but these individuals listed below were the major contributors.

While the men who were active are posted there were a couple that seemed to be most active contributing much to the formation of our democratic government and deserve biographical exposure to herald their accomplishment.

Oh yes, I cannot forget the ladies at my peril.

I acknowledge that many women during the period of our nations actions to develop into a Democratic Republic supported their husbands. Not all had an active role in their actions and held the home hearths together. I will focus on the ladies who had a noted active role to support their spouces in carrying out their roles.

One very special lady pictured below was finally discovered in 1929.

Anna Smith Strong (1740–1812) was a Patriot during the American Revolution. She used her laundry to relay signals for General George Washington's missions. A black petticoat on her clothesline indicated a whaler's location, while handkerchiefs specified which of six coves he was hidden in.

Meet the Hero: *Anna Smith Strong/Spy*

Anna Smith Strong was born on April 14, 1740, and married Selah Strong III in 1760. Selah was a delegate to the first three provincial congresses in colonial New York and was a captain in the New York militia in 1776. In 1778, at the height of the Revolutionary War, Selah was imprisoned in the sugar house of New York City and, later, on the HMS *Jersey* for "surreptitious correspondence with the enemy." The British thought he was a spy.

Little did the British know that it was Anna who would become the spy of the family. But first, Anna used her wealthy Tory (British loyalists) family members to bribe British officials to parole her husband to Connecticut, where he stayed for the remainder of the war with their children. Anna remained alone on Strong's Neck (a hamlet on Long Island) for the rest of the war. She stayed to take care of the family home, as empty homes were subject to greater destruction and abuse by British forces—she had another reason too, though.

Major Benjamin Tallmadge from Setauket, Long Island (due south of Strong's Neck), was asked by General George Washington to recruit spies who could be trusted to collect information from New York City. This group of spies was referred to as the "Culper Spy Ring," which operated primarily in New York City, Long Island, and Connecticut. Tallmadge asked for Anna's enlistment—the two were already friends, having both grown up in Setauket—and thus, she became the only female spy in the Culper Spy Ring.

Anna's job was dangerous—she was to relay information to Abraham Woodhull, another Culper spy who lived in Setauket, about the whereabouts of yet another spy, Caleb Brewster. Brewster, a known spy to British forces, rowed his whaleboat across the Long Island Sound to and from Connecticut and needed to deliver information from Woodhull to Tallmadge. Tallmadge then would decide which pieces of information would make their way to General Washington's headquarters in Westchester County, New York.

Given her location, Anna's job was to give the signal to Woodhull that Brewster had arrived. For this, she pinned a black petticoat up on her clothesline, which was easily visible to both Brewster and Woodhull. However, the coastline was riddled with small coves in which Brewster could hide himself and his boat, and Woodhull needed to know which cove Brewster was in to expedite the information-sharing process—with Brewster being a known spy, Woodhull needed to be quick.

Anna's system was simple. There were six coves used by Brewster for cover. She would hang white handkerchiefs up, with the number of handkerchiefs corresponding to which cove Brewster hid. One handkerchief meant that he was in the first cove, two meant that he was in the second, and so on. By counting the number of white handkerchiefs on the line, Woodhull knew which cove Brewster was in.

In part due to Anna's simple and discreet system, the Culper Spy Ring was responsible for the discovery of Benedict Arnold's infamous act of treason, wherein he devised a plot to surrender West Point to the British for 20,000 pounds and a place in the British command. This information was relayed to General Washington, though by that time, Arnold had fled.

Although members of the ring were subjected to intense British scrutiny, and though several were arrested during the war, not a single member was ever outed. The ring was kept in such great secrecy that General Washington did not know the identities of all of his spies, and the ring's existence was virtually unknown to the public until the discovery of correspondence in 1929.

After the war, Anna was reunited with Selah, and they had their tenth child, George Washington Strong.

From left: Elizabeth Hamilton, Deborah Read, Dolley Madison, Martha Washington, but there were more. As researched, I will post them as it fits their roles.

Elizabeth Hamilton (1757-1854)

Long-suffering yet intensely loyal, Elizabeth Hamilton buried her sister, her eldest son, her husband, and her father in three turbulent years. She would spend much of her long widowhood working to secure Hamilton's place as President.

American history. Courtesy: Library of Congress

"I Meet You in Every Dream"

Elizabeth Schuyler was born on August 7, 1757, in Albany, New York, the second daughter of a wealthy landowner and Revolutionary War general Philip Schuyler. Almost none of Elizabeth's own correspondence has survived, so her personality is gleaned largely from the impressions of others. Good-natured though somewhat serious, she was at ease in the outdoors and devout in her Christian faith. A dutiful daughter, she eschewed the elopements chosen by three of her sisters and instead conducted a traditional, if whirlwind, courtship with the dashing young aide she found at George Washington's headquarters in February 1780. They had met briefly a few years before, but now Alexander Hamilton was smitten, "a gone man," in the words of another aide. "I meet you in every dream," Hamilton wrote in one of his swooning letters, "and when I wake, I cannot close my eyes for ruminating on your sweetness." In a joking letter to a fellow aide, he sounded more dispassionate: "Though not a genius, she has good sense enough to be agreeable, and though not a beauty, she has fine black eyes, is rather handsome, and has every other requisite of the exterior to make a lover happy."

A Happy Union

Alexander and Elizabeth (he called her Eliza or Betsey) were married at the Schuyler home on December 14 of that same year, and Hamilton was warmly received into the family. He had particularly fond dealings with Philip Schuyler and Elizabeth's eldest sister Angelica, a beautiful and charming woman. In one letter, Angelica told Elizabeth that she loved Hamilton "very much and, if you were as generous as the old Romans, you would lend him to me for a little while." Whether Elizabeth received this as sisterly banter or something more serious is not known; one of her few surviving letters does say that marriage made her "the happiest of women. My dear Hamilton is fonder of me every day."

Mother, Supporter, Humiliated Wife

Elizabeth gave birth to their first child, Philip, in 1782, and seven more would follow over the next two decades; the Hamiltons also raised the orphaned daughter of a friend for 10 years. A firm but affectionate mother, Elizabeth made sure her children had a religious upbringing and ran the household so efficiently that an associate told Hamilton she "has as much merit as your treasurer as you have as treasurer of the wealth of the United States." She was present at such historic moments as when Hamilton began to write The Federalist and composed his defense of a national bank. Elizabeth also spent many months separated from her husband. During one such interlude, in the summer of 1791, Hamilton began an affair with Maria Reynolds that, when publicly revealed six years later, exposed Elizabeth to a humiliation augmented both by Hamilton's insistence on airing the adultery's most lurid details and a hostile press that asked, "Art thou a wife? See him, whom thou has chosen for the partner of this life, lolling in the lap of a harlot!!" Ashamed of his conduct,

Hamilton began to pay closer attention to his family. But a series of events would soon rip that family apart.

Losses

The first blow was struck in March 1801, when Elizabeth lost her sister Peggy after a long illness. Her eldest son Philip died that November in a reckless duel, and Hamilton himself followed fewer than three years later. Thrust into harsh financial straits, Elizabeth then witnessed her father's death in November 1804 and had to use both strength and ingenuity to keep her remaining family afloat. A slight inheritance from Philip Schuyler helped with that, as did the private raising of money from Hamilton's friends that enabled Elizabeth to stay in the house she and Hamilton had shared.

Active Widowhood

Elizabeth did not spend her days in sorrow or self-pity. Instead, she immersed herself in charitable work, helping found New York's first private orphanage in 1806 and embarking on a decades-long campaign to ensure "her Hamilton" received the historical laurels she was sure he deserved. She recruited biographers to do proper work on her husband (the task eventually fell to a son), hired assistants to organize his papers and even wore a little bag around her neck with pieces of a sonnet he had composed for her in 1780. She moved to Washington, D.C., in 1848 to live with a daughter, became a celebrated guest at the White House, and died just a few months after her 97th birthday.

Deborah Read

From Wikipedia, the free encyclopedia

Deborah Read Franklin (c. 1708 – December 19, 1774) was the common-law wife of Benjamin Franklin, a polymath and one of the Founding Fathers of the United States.

Early years

Little is known about Read's early life. She was born around 1708, most likely in Birmingham, England (some sources state she was born in Philadelphia)[1] to John and Sarah Read, a well-respected Quaker couple. John Read was a moderately prosperous building contractor and carpenter who died in 1724. Read had three siblings: two brothers, John and James, and a sister, Frances.[2] The Read family immigrated to British America in 1711, settling in Philadelphia.[3]

Marriages

In October 1723, Read met then-17-year-old Benjamin Franklin when he walked past the Read home on Market Street one morning.[2] Franklin had just moved to Philadelphia from Boston to find employment as a printer. In his autobiography, Franklin recalled that at the time of their meeting, he was walking while carrying "three great puffy rolls". As he had no pockets, Franklin carried one roll under each arm and was eating the third. Read (whom Franklin called "Debby") was standing in the doorway of her home and was amused by the sight of Franklin's "most awkward ridiculous appearance."

A romance between Read and Franklin soon developed. When Franklin was unable to find appropriate living accommodations near his job, Read's father allowed him to rent a room in the family home. Read and Franklin's courtship continued, and in 1724, Franklin proposed marriage. However, Read's mother, Sarah, would not consent to the marriage, citing Franklin's pending trip to London and financial instability.

Read and Franklin postponed their marriage plans, and Franklin traveled to England. Upon arriving in London, Franklin decided to end the relationship. In a terse letter, he informed Read that he had no intention of returning to Philadelphia. Franklin subsequently became stranded in London after Sir William Keith failed to follow through on promises of financial support.

In Franklin's absence, Read was persuaded by her mother to marry John Rogers, a British man who has been identified variously as a carpenter or a potter. Read eventually agreed and married Rogers on August 5, 1725, at Christ Church, Philadelphia. The marriage quickly fell apart as the "sweet-talking" Rogers could not hold a job and had incurred a large amount of debt before their marriage. Four months after they were married, Read left Rogers after a friend of Rogers' visiting from England informed her that Rogers had a wife in his native England. Read refused to live with or recognize Rogers as her husband. While the couple were separated, Rogers spent Read's dowry, incurred more debt, and used the marriage to further his own schemes. In December 1727, Rogers stole a slave and disappeared.[9] Soon afterward, unconfirmed reports circulated that Rogers had made his way to the British West Indies, where he was killed in a fight. In his autobiography, Franklin also claimed that Rogers died in the British West Indies. John Rogers' true fate has never been proven.

Despite his previous intention to remain in London, Franklin returned to Philadelphia in October 1727. He and Read eventually resumed their relationship and decided to marry. While Read considered her marriage to her first husband to be over, she was not able to legally remarry. At that time, the law in the Province of Pennsylvania would not grant a divorce on the grounds of desertion, nor could Read claim to be a widow, as there was no proof that Rogers was dead. If Rogers returned after Read legally married Franklin, she faced a charge of bigamy, which carried the penalty of thirty-nine lashings on the bare back and life imprisonment with hard labor.

To avoid any legal issues, Read and Franklin decided upon a common-law marriage. On September 1, 1730, the couple held a ceremony for friends and family in which they announced they would live as husband and wife. They had two children together: Francis Folger "Franky" (born 1732), who died of smallpox in 1736 at the age of four, and Sarah "Sally" (born 1743). Read also helped to raise

Franklin's illegitimate son <u>William</u>, whose mother's identity is still unknown.

Later years and death

By the late 1750s, Benjamin Franklin had established himself as a successful printer, publisher, and writer. He was appointed the first postmaster of Philadelphia and was heavily involved in social and political affairs that would eventually lead to the establishment of the United States. In 1757, Franklin embarked on the first of numerous trips to Europe. Read refused to accompany him due to a fear of ocean travel. While Franklin stayed overseas for the next five years, Read remained in Philadelphia where, despite her limited education, she successfully ran her husband's businesses, maintained their home, cared for the couple's children, and regularly attended Quaker Meetings.

Franklin returned to Philadelphia in November 1762. He tried to persuade Read to accompany him to Europe, but she again refused. Franklin returned to Europe in November 1764 where he would remain for the next ten years.[17] Read would never see Franklin again.

In 1768, Read suffered the first of a series of strokes that severely impaired her speech and memory. For the remainder of her life, she suffered from poor health and depression. Despite his wife's condition, Franklin did not return to Philadelphia even though he had completed his diplomatic duties.[18] In November 1769, Read wrote Franklin saying that her stroke, declining health, and depressed mental state were a result of her "dissatisfied distress" due to his prolonged absence.[19] Franklin still did not return but continued to write to Read. Read's final surviving letter to Franklin is dated October 29, 1773. Thereafter, she stopped corresponding with her husband. Franklin continued to write to Read, inquiring as to why her letters had ceased, but still did not return home.[18]

On December 14, 1774, Read suffered a final stroke and died on December 19. She was buried at <u>Christ Church Burial Ground</u> in

Philadelphia. Franklin was buried next to her upon his death in 1790.

Dolley Madison (born May 20, 1768, Guilford County, North Carolina [U.S.]—died July 12, 1849, Washington, D.C., U.S.) was an American first lady (1809–17), the wife of James Madison, fourth president of the United States. Raised in the plain style of her Quaker family, she was renowned for her charm, warmth, and ingenuity. Her popularity as manager of the White House made that task a responsibility of every first lady who followed.

Dolley was one of eight children of John Payne, a merchant, and Mary Coles Payne. Soon after her birth, her father's business fell on hard times, and the family moved to eastern Virginia, where they were active members of the Society of Friends. When she was 15 her family moved to Philadelphia, where Dolley married a young lawyer, John Todd, in 1790. The couple had two children, but in 1793, her youngest son and husband died during an epidemic of yellow fever, widowing Dolley at 25.[19]

---

[19] Deborah Read - Wikipedia

Dolley Madison

Dolley Madison, engraving from a painting by Gilbert Stuart.

A few months later, Aaron Burr, then a United States senator from New Jersey, introduced Dolley to James Madison, who was 17 years her senior; though a small man physically, he was a towering political figure. There was a mutual, immediate, and strong attraction between James and Dolley, and they wed on September 15, 1794, at her sister's home in Virginia. Because her husband was Episcopalian, however, the Quakers disowned her. Soon after their marriage, accompanied by her son, the Madisons moved to Philadelphia, then the nation's capital, where James served as a member of the House of Representatives. During the presidency of <u>John</u>

Adams (1797–1801), the Madisons lived on James's estate, Mont-pellier (now Montpelier), in Virginia. Soon after the election of Thomas Jefferson in 1800, they relocated to Washington, D.C., where James served as secretary of state, and Dolley assisted the wid-owed Jefferson as a hostess at official events, giving her ample prep-aration for her future role as first lady.

The first president's wife to preside over the White House for any significant amount of time, Dolley Madison set many precedents. She established the tradition that the mansion would reflect the First Lady's tastes and ideas about entertainment. With the help of Ben-jamin Latrobe, architect, and surveyor of public buildings, she deco-rated and furnished the house so that it was both elegant and com-fortable. Unfortunately, not many Americans had the chance to see it before the British burned the mansion in August 1814 during the War of 1812. Dolley underscored the First Lady's responsibility for caring for the mansion and its contents when she directed the removal and safe storage of precious holdings, including the fa-mous Gilbert Stuart portrait of George Washington that still hangs in the East Room.

Dolley Madison

Dolley Madison, painting by Rembrandt Peale.

As hostess, Dolley Madison carefully balanced two competing traditions in the new nation: the democratic emphasis on equal treatment and the elitist notion that the president's house was the province of the privileged few. At weekly receptions she opened the doors to virtually anyone who wanted to come and then moved among the guests, greeting all with charming ease. In her stylish turbans and imported clothes, she became enormously popular and much imitated. Although most Americans approved, she did have her critics, including Elijah Mills, a senator from Massachusetts, who complained that she mixed "all classes of people…greasy boots and silk stockings."

Although she eschewed taking public stands on controversial issues, Dolley had a shrewd political sense and cultivated her husband's enemies as carefully as his friends. When President Madison dismissed his secretary of state, Robert Smith, she invited him to dinner; when he failed to accept she went to call on him personally. In the election of 1812, when many Americans complained that Madison had led them into an unnecessary war, she used her invitation lists to win him favor and a second term, according to some historians.

She insisted on visiting the household of every new representative or senator, a task that proved very time-consuming as the nation grew and the number of congressmen increased. Since many representatives chose to bring their families to Washington, dozens of households expected a call from the president's wife. Her successors found the practice too burdensome and stopped it.

Dolley Madison

Dolley Madison enjoyed a happy marriage; different as she and her husband were in personality, they doted on each other. However, her relationship with her son, John Payne Todd, was a different matter. He spent money recklessly and expected his mother to cover his debts and losses.

When James's second term ended in 1817, he and Dolley moved back to Montpellier, where they lived until his death in 1836. James's last decades were not prosperous, and the debts of young Payne Todd depleted the family's resources. To supplement Dolley's income after James's death, a sympathetic and grateful Congress appropriated $30,000 to purchase the Madison papers.

In 1837, Dolley moved back to Washington. Living in a home opposite the White House, she was the nation's most prestigious hostess. Presidents and social leaders called on her, and she was a frequent White House guest. But her profligate son continued to try her patience and deplete her purse. In 1842, she traveled to New York City to arrange a loan from the wealthy fur magnate John Jacob Astor, and Congress came to her aid once more by agreeing to buy the remaining Madison papers for $25,000, but only on the condition that the money be placed in trust so that her son could not get it.

When Dolley Madison died in 1849 she was one of the most popular figures in Washington and the nation's favourite first lady. At her funeral Pres. Zachary Taylor, his cabinet, the diplomatic corps, and members of Congress lined up to pay their respects. She was buried beside James Madison at a family plot near Montpelier.

Martha Washington

Martha Dandridge Custis Washington (June 2, 1731 O.S. – May 22, 1802) was the wife of George Washington, the first president of the United States. Although the title was not coined until after her death, she served as the inaugural first lady of the United States, defining the role of the president's wife and setting many precedents that future first ladies would observe. During her tenure, she was referred to as "Lady Washington". Washington is consistently ranked in the upper half of first ladies by historians.

Martha Dandridge married <u>Daniel Parke Custis</u> on May 15, 1750, and the couple had four children, only one of whom survived to adulthood.[1] She was widowed in 1757 at the age of 26, inheriting a large estate. She was remarried to George Washington in 1759, moving to his plantation, <u>Mount Vernon</u>. Her youngest daughter died of epilepsy in 1773, and the Washingtons were unable to conceive any children of their own. Washington became a symbol of the <u>American Revolution</u> after her husband was appointed <u>commander-in-chief</u> of the <u>Continental Army</u>, and she took on a matronly role while visiting encampments when fighting stalled each winter. Her only surviving child, John, died from a camp illness during the war. After the war ended in 1783, Washington sought retirement at Mount Vernon, but she was returned to public life when her husband became president of the United States in 1789.

Washington took on the social role of the president's wife reluctantly, becoming a national celebrity in the process. She found this life unpleasant, feeling that she was restricted and wishing for retirement. In addition to hosting weekly social events, Washington understood that how she composed herself would reflect on the nation, both domestically and abroad. As such, she struck a careful balance between the dignity associated with a <u>head of state</u>'s wife and the humility associated with <u>republican</u> government. The Washingtons returned to Mount Vernon in 1797, and she spent her retirement years greeting admirers and advising her successors. She was widowed for a second time in 1799, and she died two and a half years later in 1802.

Early life (1731–1748)

Dandridge at age eight

Martha Dandridge Custis in 1757: mezzotint by John Folwell
(1863) after a portrait by John Wollaston

Martha Dandridge was born on June 2, 1731, on her parents' tobacco plantation in <u>Chestnut Grove</u> Plantation in <u>New Kent</u>
<u>County</u> the <u>Colony of Virginia</u>. She was the oldest daughter of <u>John</u>
<u>Dandridge</u>, a Virginia planter and county clerk who <u>immigrated</u>

from England, and Frances Jones, the granddaughter of an Anglican rector. Martha had three brothers and four sisters: John (1733–1749), William (1734–1776), Bartholomew (1737–1785), Anna Maria "Fanny" Bassett (1739–1777), Frances Dandridge (1744–1757), Elizabeth Aylett Henley (1749–1800), and Mary Dandridge (1756–1763). As the oldest of eight, including one sister that was 25 years her junior, Dandridge played a maternal and domestic role beginning early in life. Dandridge may have also had an illegitimate half-sister born into slavery, Ann Dandridge Costin, and an illegitimate white half-brother, Ralph Dandridge.

Dandridge's father was well-connected with the Virginia aristocracy despite his relative lack of wealth, and she was taught to behave as a woman of the upper class. She received a relatively high quality education for the daughter of a planter, though it was still inferior to that of her brothers. She took to equestrianism, at one point riding her horse up and down the stairs of her uncle's home and escaping chastisement because her father was so impressed by her skill.

Marriage to Daniel Parke Custis (1749–1757)[edit]

In 1749, Dandridge met Daniel Parke Custis, the son of a wealthy planter in Virginia. They wished to marry, but the father of Dandridge's prospective groom, John Custis, was highly selective of what woman would marry into the family's fortune. She eventually won his approval, and Dandridge married Custis, who was two decades her senior, on May 15, 1750. After they were married, Custis moved with her husband to his residence at White House Plantation on the Pamunkey River. Here they had four children: Daniel, born 1751; Frances, born 1753; John, born 1754; and Martha, born 1756. Daniel died in 1754 and Frances died in 1757. Daniel Parke Custis was one of the wealthiest men in the Virginia colony as well as one of the largest slaveowners, owning nearly 300 slaves.[11]

Custis became a widow at the age of 26 when her husband died (possibly from a severe infection of the throat).[12] Upon his death, she inherited the large estate that he had previously inherited from his father.[7] After his death in 1757, she received one-third of his estate outright, and the remaining two-thirds was granted to their two young children. The total inheritance amounted to approximately $33,000 (equivalent to $1,104,439 in 2023), 17,000 acres of land, and hundreds of slaves. The legal and financial matters of the inheritance presented a considerable burden on Custis while she was raising her two surviving children and grieving the loss of her husband and her children as well as that of her father.[10]:4 She was also left with the responsibility of managing the farmland and overseeing the well-being of the slaves.[3]:2 According to her biographer, "she capably ran the five plantations left to her when her first husband died, bargaining with London merchants for the best tobacco prices."

Marriage to George Washington (1758–1774)

Courtship and wedding

The Marriage of Washington to Martha Custis by Junius Brutus Stears (1849)

By one account Custis met George Washington during the Williamsburg social season, and they courted over the following months during his leaves from the military. By another, they were introduced by Colonel Chamberlayne, a mutual acquaintance, when they both stayed the night at his home in May 1758. They married on January 6, 1759, at the White House plantation.

The couple honeymooned at the Custis family's White House plantation, followed by a stay in Williamsburg where her husband was a representative in the House of Burgesses before setting up house at his Mount Vernon estate. At the time of their wedding, she was one of the wealthiest widows in the Thirteen Colonies. Their marriage remained happy over the following 40 years, in part because of their similar worldviews.[10]:4 It was a marriage based on mutual respect and shared habits, with both maintaining similar schedules in day-to-day life and both prioritizing family and image over-excitement and vice.

Mount Vernon

From 1759 to 1775, the Washingtons lived at Mount Vernon, where they tended to their plantation.[7] Washington ran the household and regularly entertained visitors. She knitted and oversaw the making of clothes, and she became talented in curing meat in their smokehouse. Washington entertained almost daily, having visitors for dinner or for longer stays as the family became more prominent in the political and social life of Virginia. Washington's husband used her wealth to expand their home at Mount Vernon and turn it into a profitable estate.

The Washingtons had no children together, but they raised Martha's two surviving children. She was highly protective of them, especially after her two previous children had died and Patsy was found to have epilepsy. In 1773, Patsy died when she was 17 during an epileptic seizure. Washington's last surviving child, John, left King's College that fall and married Eleanor Calvert in February 1774. The Washingtons hoped for more children throughout their marriage, but they were unable to conceive.

American Revolution (1775–1789)[

Early revolution

Martha Washington by <u>Rembrandt Peale</u>, circa 1856, based on a portrait by his father, <u>Charles Willson Peale</u>

Life for the Washingtons was interrupted as the <u>American Revolution</u> escalated in the 1770s.[3]:4 Though rumors were spread that she was a <u>Loyalist</u>, Washington consistently shared her husband's political beliefs.[9]:3–4 She strongly supported his role in the <u>Patriot</u> movement and his work to advance his beliefs in the cause. She stayed at Mount Vernon when he was appointed <u>commander-in-chief</u> of the <u>Continental Army</u> in 1775, overseeing the construction of new wings to their home. She then moved to the home of her brother-in-law so as not to be so conspicuous a target during the <u>American Revolutionary War</u>.

The revolution was the first time in their marriage that they were apart for an extended period. In the fall of 1775, Washington traveled to Massachusetts to meet with her husband. On the journey north, she experienced her newfound celebrity status for the first time as the wife of a famed general. She joined him in <u>Cambridge</u>, from where he and the other Continental Army officers were operating. While staying in Cambridge, she served as a hostess for guests of the officers. She would also sew clothes for the soldiers while at camp, encouraging other officers' wives to do the same, leading to the creation of a <u>sewing circle</u> that contributed to the war effort. Though she hid it from those around her, Washington was frightened by the gunfire that could be heard from the nearby <u>Siege of Boston</u>. She accompanied her husband when operations were relocated to New York, but she was sent to Philadelphia as British forces came closer. Each spring, when conflict resumed, she returned to Mount Vernon.

Independent United States

The American Revolution became increasingly stressful for Martha after the signing of the <u>Declaration of Independence</u>, as George faced increased risks on the battlefield. Each winter, Washington would join her husband at his encampment while fighting was stalled. The quality of her housing varied during these visits, both in comfort and in safety. <u>General Lafayette</u> observed that she loved "her husband madly". Washington was kept informed of the war's developments by her husband, sometimes performing clerical work for him, and she was even permitted to know military secrets. She became a symbol of the war effort, alongside George Washington, as a grandmotherly figure that cared for the soldiers.

The Continental Army settled in Valley Forge, the third of the eight winter encampments of the Revolution, on December 19, 1777. Washington traveled 10 days and hundreds of miles to join her husband in Pennsylvania. On April 6, Elizabeth Drinker and three friends arrived at Valley Forge to plead with the General to release their husbands from jail; the men, all Quakers, had refused to swear a loyalty oath to the American revolutionaries. Because the commander was not available at first, the women visited with Martha. Drinker described her later in her diary as "a sociable pretty kind of Woman".

The Washingtons' son John was serving as a civilian aide to his father during the <u>siege of Yorktown</u> in 1781 when he died of "camp fever", a contemporary diagnosis for <u>epidemic typhus</u>. After his death, the Washingtons took in the youngest two of his four children, <u>Eleanor (Nelly) Parke Custis</u> and <u>George Washington Parke (Washy) Custis</u>. The Washingtons also provided personal and financial support to the children of many of their relatives and friends.

Postwar retirement

The Washingtons returned to Mount Vernon in 1783. They stayed at Mount Vernon for much of the Confederation period, living in retirement with their nephew, nieces, and grandchildren. Washington, now in poorer health, believed that her husband was finished with public service.[3]:6 She spent her time raising their grandchildren, constantly worried for their health after having all four of her children and many other relatives die of illness. She also resumed hosting company at Mount Vernon, recruiting several of her nieces and other young women to assist her, as the house was overwhelmed with visitors. Their life at Mount Vernon was interrupted again when he was asked to participate at the Constitutional Convention in 1787 and again when he was chosen as the first president of the United States in 1789.

First lady of the United States (1789–1797)

Republican Court, or, Lady Washington's Reception Day by Daniel Huntington (c. 1861)

After the war, Washington was not fully supportive of her husband's agreeing to be president of the newly formed United States. She did not immediately join him at the capital in New York City, only arriving in May 1789. The journey was followed by the press, which was unprecedented in the attention that it paid to a woman's actions, and the entourage was met with admirers and fanfare in each town that it passed through. It was during this journey that she gave her only public speech as first lady, thanking those that came to see her. She arrived on the presidential barge, escorted by her husband, immediately establishing the president's wife as a public figure. After arriving at the capital, Washington became the inaugural first lady of the United States, though the term would not be used until later. Instead, she was referred to as "Lady Washington".

As the inaugural first lady, many of Washington's practices in the White House became traditions for future first ladies, including the opening of the White House to the public on New Year's Day, a practice that would continue until the Hoover administration. She hosted many affairs of state at New York City and Philadelphia during their years as temporary capitals. Taking her responsibility as the lady of the house seriously, Washington returned the official calls of every lady that left her card at the heavily-trafficked presidential home to ensure that everyone could reach the president, always doing so within three days.

Washington was also tasked by her husband with the responsibility of hosting drawing room events on Fridays in which ladies were permitted to attend. She would remain seated during such events while the president greeted their guests. The guests were at first uncertain as to whether they should follow the royal custom of waiting for the hostess to leave before they do, and she resolved the issue by announcing her husband always retired at nine. She was careful during these events to avoid political talk, encouraging a change of subject when it came up. The social circles that developed among those in American politics at this time became known as the Republican Court.

Personal life

The Washington Family by <u>Edward Savage</u>

The first presidential residence was a house on <u>Cherry Street</u>, followed by a house on <u>Broadway</u>. The capital was moved to <u>Philadelphia</u> in 1790, and the presidential residence again moved, this time to a house on High Street (now <u>Market Street</u>). Washington much preferred the Philadelphia residence, as it had a greater social life and was closer to Mount Vernon. Early in her husband's presidency, she had little opportunity to go out, as any action she took would have political implications. After their move to Philadelphia, the Washingtons loosened their self-imposed limits on personal activity.

While serving as first lady, Washington became close to Polly Lear, the wife of her husband's secretary <u>Tobias Lear</u>. She also associated with <u>Lucy Flucker Knox</u>, wife of war secretary <u>Henry Knox</u>, and <u>Abigail Adams</u>, the <u>second lady</u>. The time she spent with her grandchildren was another high point for Washington, who would sometimes take them to shows and museums. She also made a point of frequently attending church, owing to her firm <u>Episcopalian</u> beliefs.

Washington was forced to take control of the presidential residence at one point shortly after her husband's presidency began, forbidding guests from entering, as he was undergoing the removal of a tumor. In July 1790, artist <u>John Trumbull</u> gave Washington a full-length portrait painting of her husband as a gift. It was displayed in their home at Mount Vernon in the New Room. When Washington learned that her husband might take on a second term as president, she uncharacteristically protested against the decision. Despite her opposition, he was reelected in 1793, and she reluctantly accepted four more years as the wife of the president. The young Georges Washington de La Fayette joined the Washington family in 1795 while his father, Marquis de Lafayette, was held as a political prisoner in France. He would live with the Washingtons until fall of 1797.

In 1796, Washington's slave and personal maid Oney Judge escaped and fled to New Hampshire. Despite Washington's insistence to her husband that Judge should be returned and again should be Washington's slave, the president did not attempt to pursue Judge.[8] Washington's tenure as first lady ended in 1797

Lady Washington by Charles Willson Peale (date unknown)

As the wife of both the head of government and the head of state, Washington was immediately faced with the pressure of representing the United States. She had to present the United States as a dignified nation to establish credibility among the countries of Europe, but she also had to respect the spirit of democracy by refusing to present herself as a queen. She was also aware that the precedent she set would be inherited by future presidential wives. Washington balanced these responsibilities by playing the role of a social hostess at presidential events, a role that would become the primary function of the first lady. In turn, this made the position of first lady an important point of contact between the president and the people.

Washington presented an image of herself as an amiable wife, but privately she complained about the restrictions placed on her life. She found the pageantry of the presidency to be boring and artificial. Washington was not exempt from the political attacks often levied at her husband's administration by opposition-owned newspapers. While her social role was celebrated by her husband's supporters, the anti-Federalists criticized her as emulating royalty and encouraging aristocracy. At the same time, other critics accused her social activities of being too informal. To her displeasure, she found that she was constantly the subject of public attention, and she was forced to pay increased attention to her hair and clothes each day. Despite this, she still opted to dress simply in homespun clothes, feeling that it was more appropriate in a republic.

Later life and death (1797–1802)

Washington's chambers after her husband's death

The Washingtons left the capital immediately after the inauguration of John Adams, making the return journey to Mount Vernon, which by then had begun to decay. Again they went into retirement, and they saw to several renovations for their home. In the years after the presidency, the Washingtons received more visitors than ever, from friends and strangers alike. They eventually took in one of the former president's nephews, Lawrence Lewis, to serve as secretary, and he would eventually marry Washington's granddaughter Nelly.

Washington feared that her husband would again be called away to lead a provisional army against France, but no such conflict took place. Her husband died of a severe throat infection on December

14, 1799 at the age of 67. As a widow, Washington spent her final years living in a garret where she knitted, sewed, and responded to letters. Though she was the legal owner of her husband's property, she gave control of its business affairs to her relatives. She also inherited her husband's slaves on the condition that they be freed upon her death. Fearing that these slaves might hurt her, she freed them. She did not have the authority to free her dower slaves, and she chose not to free the one slave, Elish, whom she personally owned.

Washington retained an interest in the presidency after her tenure as first lady, beginning the tradition of advising her successors. The Washington family long disliked Thomas Jefferson and Jeffersonian politics, in part because of the central role he played in criticizing the Washington administration. Washington took offense when Jefferson became president, as she felt that he did not give adequate respect to the office.

Tomb of George Washington (Right) and Martha Washington (Left)

Washington's health, always somewhat precarious, declined after her husband's death. She had anticipated her death since that of her husband. When she developed a fever in 1802, she burned all of her husband's letters to her, summoned a clergyman to administer last communion, and chose her funeral dress. Two and a half years after the death of her husband, Washington died on May 22, 1802, at the age of 70. Following her death, Washington's body was interred in the original Washington family tomb vault at Mount Vernon. In 1831, the surviving executors of George's estate removed the bodies of the Washingtons from the old vault to a similar structure within the present enclosure at Mount Vernon.

Legacy

Just as her husband had set the precedent for the presidency, Washington established what would eventually become the role of first lady. She was prominent in the ceremonial aspects of the presidency, assisting her husband in his role as head of state, but she had very little public involvement in his administrative role as head of government. This would be the standard of presidential wives for the next century. Washington was recognized for her humility and her mild-mannered nature, to the point that her contemporaries were often taken by surprise when meeting her. No personal records of Washington exist from before the death of her first husband, and she destroyed many letters that she had written since then. Many recipients of her letters kept them, however, and those letters have been preserved in archives such as at Mount Vernon and the Virginia Historical Society. Several collections of these letters have been published.

Honors

Martha Washington 1902 issue stamp

During the Revolutionary War, one of the regiments at Valley Forge named themselves "Lady Washington's Dragoon" in her honor. The Martha Washington College for Women was founded in Abingdon, Virginia in 1860. It was merged with Emory & Henry College in 1918, and the main original building of Martha Washington College was converted to the Martha Washington Inn. Martha Washington Seminary, a finishing school for young women in Washington, DC, was opened in 1905, and it ceased operations in 1949.

A postage stamp featuring Martha Washington, the first stamp to honor an American woman, was issued as part of the 1902 stamp series. An 8-cent stamp, it was printed in violet-black ink. The second stamp issued in her honor, a 4-cent definitive stamp printed in yellow-brown ink, was released in 1923. A $1+\frac{1}{2}$-cent stamp was issued in 1938 to honor Washington as part of the Presidential Issue series. Washington's image was featured on the one-dollar silver certificate banknote beginning in 1886, making her the second woman to appear on an American banknote after Pocahontas. To prevent confusion with existing coinage, pattern coins testing new metals have been produced by the U.S. mint, or a company contracted to it, with Martha Washington on the obverse.[20]

OUR FIRST PRESIDENTS

GEORGE WASHINGTON

George Washington President - General of the Armies Continental Army February 22, 1732 – December 14, 1799

---

[20] Deborah Read - Wikipedia

George Washington by Charles Willson Peale, 1776. White House Historical Foundation.

Few figures loom as large in American military history as George Washington. In many ways, he is viewed almost as a mythical figure and is typically remembered for his momentous achievements. He led the Continental Army to victory in the Revolutionary War, helped create the U.S. Constitution, and served as the first president of the United States. In particular, his superb leadership qualities allowed him to succeed throughout his life. Though not without faults, he established a precedent of selfless service and moral integrity in the American armed forces, a legacy that lives on in the nation he helped create.

Born on February 22, 1732, to Augustine and Mary Ball Washington, the future president grew up in Virginia. His father, a justice of the peace, died in 1743, and Washington inherited part of his estate at Ferry Farm near Fredericksburg. Born into moderate wealth, Washington did not attend school but received a robust education in mathematics and land surveying. He began working as a surveyor in 1748 and completed several expeditions to the Shenandoah Valley. By the age of 20, Washington was a socially connected, well-educated, wealthy landowner. Yet, Washington desired military service and received a commission in the Virginia Militia in 1752.

Washington, then a major, inadvertently started the French and Indian War in 1754 when his forces attacked and killed a French officer in a scouting party in the Ohio River Valley. French and Native

American forces retaliated, defeating Washington's militia force. The following year, Washington fought at the disastrous Battle of Monongahela on July 9, 1755, where the French and their Indian allies routed a large British and militia force. He continued to serve in the war, leading provincial units until he resigned in 1758. Though the British won the war, Washington's reputation was far from certain. British leadership regarded him as a poor commander, while colonists viewed him as a hero for his bravery and steady leadership in battle.

After the war, he returned to Mount Vernon, which he would inherit from his brother Lawrence in 1761. He wished to make the farm profitable and spent considerable money to expand the property. Using the labor of over one hundred enslaved individuals, Washington successfully developed Mount Vernon into a prosperous plantation. In 1758, he was elected to a seat in the Virginia legislature. The following year, he married Martha Dandridge Custis, a wealthy widow. She and her two young children joined Washington at Mount Vernon. As the years went on, Washington grew increasingly interested in politics. By 1771, Washington openly criticized the British for what he viewed as oppressive tax policies towards the colonies. He was elected by the Virginia legislature to represent the colony at the First Continental Congress in 1774. After the eruption of open conflict in Massachusetts in April 1775, Washington attended the Second Continental Congress. On June 14th, Congress resolved to create a Continental Army. The following day, Washington was selected as the new army's commander-in-chief. His personal integrity, military experience, and hero status all contributed to his selection. In many ways, he was viewed as the only man who could do the job.

On July 2, 1775, Washington arrived outside Boston to take command of the forces gathering there and create a regular army out of a ragtag band of poorly equipped militiamen and volunteers. Washington rapidly organized the Continental Army and selected several officers from the ranks, such as Maj. Gen. Henry Knox. Under Washington's direction, Knox daringly moved 59 cannons over 300 miles from Fort Ticonderoga, New York, to Dorchester Heights outside of Boston. The plan worked, and the British left Boston in March 1776. Though he had won his first major confrontation of the war, Washington and the Continental Army's success was short-lived. Attempting to capture New York, British general Sir William Howe decimated the Continental Army in a series of battles. By the end of 1776, Washington's Army was demoralized and shaken. Ninety percent of the troops he had commanded in Boston were either killed, wounded, captured, or had left the Army. With morale low, Washington launched a surprise attack on December 26, 1776 against the British allied Hessian forces camped in New Jersey at Trenton and Princeton. Caught by surprise, the Americans routed the Hessian forces and Washington achieved an important victory for his Army.

Over the course of the next few years, Washington enjoyed few battlefield successes as he was regularly defeated by superior British forces. Yet, Washington's stalwart leadership, integrity, and dignity held the Army together, presenting a credible threat to the British. After Maj. Gen. Horatio Gates' army defeated the British at the battles of Saratoga in September and October 1777, France entered the war and allied with the Americans in 1778. This provided Washington with the weapons, supplies, and reinforcements he needed to achieve a decisive victory.

After a large French force commanded by the Comte de Rochambeau joined Washington's forces in 1781, the two generals planned a pivotal strike. Though Washington favored attacking New York, Rochambeau and the French believed the Chesapeake Bay in Virginia to be the best target to isolate and capture an entire British army. After a French fleet commanded by the Comte de Grasse successfully blockaded the Chesapeake Bay, the Franco-American forces besieged a large British army at Yorktown, Virginia. The British surrendered on October 19, 1781, effectively ensuring victory in war and independence.

Near the end of war, Washington successfully stopped a coup attempt by Continental Army officers at Newburgh, New York, in

March 1783. Yet again, Washington's personal qualities and leadership proved invaluable. On September 3, 1783, the Revolutionary War officially ended with the signing of the Treaty of Paris. Some believed Washington might not resign his commission and attempt to seize power, as he was extremely popular with the troops and the public. However, Washington resigned his commission and returned to Mount Vernon, bowing to Congress in a short ceremony on December 23, 1783, at Annapolis, Maryland. For this act alone, King George III called Washington, "the greatest man in the world."

Initially, Washington intended to enjoy his retirement from public service, content to spend his life as a farmer at Mount Vernon. However, his retirement was interrupted when he was once again called on to serve his country. Washington was a unanimous choice to head the Constitutional Convention in 1787. His stalwart leadership, hero status, and dignified manner made him perhaps the only person capable of leading the assembly. He worked with the delegates for over a year to create and ratify the Constitution. Washington continued to lead and was unanimously elected the first President of the United States.

Washington reluctantly accepted a position of power once again, serving two full terms as president. His qualities as a natural and dignified leader made him an ideal choice for the job. Working closely with Secretary of the Treasury Alexander Hamilton, who had served under Washington in the Revolutionary War, Washington created an energetic and centralized federal government, setting a precedent for the new American experiment. He helped establish a national bank, suppressed the Whiskey Rebellion, and established a trade relationship with Great Britain. After eight years in office, Washington again willingly stepped away from power, establishing the precedent of American presidents only serving two terms. He penned an emotional farewell address in 1796, where he warned against the dangers of political parties, foreign influence, and valuing a single state over the entire nation. He retired to Mount Vernon in 1797.

Washington devoted himself to improving Mount Vernon in his retirement. On December 12, 1799, he became ill after riding his horse through rain and sleet. His condition rapidly worsened and he died on December 14, 1799. At his funeral, Maj. Gen. Henry "Light Horse Harry" Lee stated that Washington was, "First in war, first in peace, and first in the hearts of his countrymen." These words accurately summarize Washington's legacy. He was first in war as the commander-in-chief of the Continental Army, leading the charge for American independence. He was first in peace as a farmer, a husband, and the first President of the United States. And he was first in the hearts of his countrymen as a beloved hero for all Americans. His superb leadership abilities and humble example of giving up power set a precedent for Army leadership that continues to this day.

A.J. Orlikoff

Lead Education Special

John Adams – President of the United States

From Wikipedia, the free encyclopedia

John Adams (October 30, 1735 – July 4, 1826) was an American statesman, attorney, diplomat, writer, and <u>Founding Father</u> who served as the second <u>president of the United States</u> from 1797 to 1801. Before <u>his presidency</u>, he was a leader of the <u>American Revolution</u> that achieved independence from <u>Great Britain</u>. During the latter part of the <u>Revolutionary War</u> and in the early years of the new nation, he served the <u>U.S. government</u> as a senior diplomat in Europe. Adams was the first person to hold the office of <u>vice president of the United States</u>, serving from 1789 to 1797. He was a dedicated diarist and regularly corresponded with important contemporaries, including his wife and adviser <u>Abigail Adams</u> and his friend and political rival <u>Thomas Jefferson</u>.

A lawyer and political activist prior to the Revolution, Adams was devoted to the <u>right to counsel</u> and <u>presumption of innocence</u>. He defied anti-British sentiment and successfully defended British soldiers against murder charges arising from the Boston Massacre. Adams was a Massachusetts delegate to the Continental Congress and became a leader of the revolution. He assisted Jefferson in drafting the Declaration of Independence in 1776 and was its primary advocate in Congress. As a diplomat he helped negotiate a peace treaty with Great Britain and secured vital governmental loans.[21] Adams was the primary author of the Massachusetts Constitution in 1780, which influenced the United States Constitution, as did his essay *Thoughts on Government*.

Adams was elected to two terms as vice president under President George Washington and was elected as the United States' second president in 1796. He was the only president elected under the banner of the Federalist Party. Adams's term was dominated by the issue of the French Revolutionary Wars, and his insistence on American neutrality led to fierce criticism from both the Jeffersonian Republicans and from some in his own party, led by his rival Alexander Hamilton. Adams signed the controversial Alien and Sedition Acts, and built up the Army and Navy in the undeclared naval war with France. He was the first president to reside in the White House.

In his bid in 1800 for reelection to the presidency, opposition from Federalists and accusations of despotism from Jeffersonians led to Adams losing to his vice president and former friend Jefferson, and he retired to Massachusetts. He eventually resumed his friendship with Jefferson by initiating a continuing correspondence. He and Abigail generated the Adams political family, including their son John Quincy Adams, the sixth president. John Adams died on July 4, 1826 – the fiftieth anniversary of the adoption of the Declaration of Independence. Adams and his son are the only presidents of the first twelve who never owned slaves. Historians and scholars have favorably ranked his administration.

Early life and education

---

[21] https://artsandculture.google.com/entity/john-adams/m03_js?hl=en

Further information: Adams political family

Adams's birthplace in present-day Quincy, Massachusetts

John Adams was born on October 30, 1735, to <u>John Adams Sr.</u> and <u>Susanna Boylston</u>. He had two younger brothers, Peter and <u>Elihu</u>. Adams was <u>born on the family farm</u> in <u>Braintree</u>, Massachusetts. His mother was from a leading medical family of present-day <u>Brookline, Massachusetts</u>. His father was a <u>deacon</u> in the <u>Congregational Church</u>, a farmer, a <u>cordwainer</u>, and a lieutenant in the <u>militia</u>. Adams often praised his father and recalled their close relationship. Adams's great-great-grandfather <u>Henry Adams</u> immigrated to Massachusetts from <u>Braintree, Essex</u>, England, around 1638.

Adams's formal education began at age six at a <u>dame school</u>, conducted at a teacher's home and centered on *The New England Primer*. He then attended Braintree Latin School under Joseph Cleverly, where studies included Latin, rhetoric, logic, and arithmetic. Adams's early education included incidents of truancy, a dislike for his master, and a desire to become a farmer, but his father commanded that he remain in school. Deacon Adams hired a new schoolmaster named Joseph Marsh, and his son responded positively. Adams later noted that "As a child I enjoyed perhaps the greatest of blessings that can be bestowed upon men – that of a mother who was anxious and capable to form the characters of her children."

College education and adulthood

At age sixteen, Adams entered <u>Harvard College</u> in 1751, studying under <u>Joseph Mayhew</u>. As an adult, Adams was a keen scholar, studying the works of ancient writers such as <u>Thucydides</u>, <u>Plato</u>, <u>Cicero</u>, and <u>Tacitus</u> in their original languages. Though his father expected him to be a minister, after his 1755 graduation with an <u>A.B. degree</u>, he taught school temporarily in <u>Worcester</u>, while pondering his permanent vocation. In the next four years, he began to seek prestige, craving "Honour or Reputation" and "more defference from [his] fellows", and was determined to be "a great Man". He decided to become a lawyer, writing his father that he found among lawyers "noble and gallant achievements" but, among the clergy, the "pretended sanctity of some absolute dunces". He had reservations about his self-described "trumpery" and failure to share the "happiness of [his] fellow men".

When the <u>French and Indian War</u> began in 1754, Adams, aged nineteen, felt guilty he was the first in his family not to be a militia officer; he said "I longed more ardently to be a Soldier than I ever did to be a Lawyer".

Law practice and marriage

In 1756, Adams began <u>reading law</u> under James Putnam, a leading lawyer in Worcester. In 1758, he earned an <u>A.M.</u> from Harvard, and in 1759 was admitted to the bar. He developed an early habit of diary writing; this included his impressions of <u>James Otis Jr.</u>'s 1761 challenge to the legality of British <u>writs of assistance</u>, which allowed British officials to search a home without notice or reason. Otis's argument against the writs inspired Adams to the cause of the <u>American colonies</u>.[20]

In 1763, Adams explored aspects of political theory in seven essays written for Boston newspapers. Under the <u>pen name</u> "Humphrey Ploughjogger", he ridiculed the selfish thirst for power he perceived among the Massachusetts colonial elite.[21] Adams was initially less well known than his older cousin <u>Samuel Adams</u>, but his influence emerged from his work as a constitutional lawyer, his analysis of history, and his dedication to republicanism. Adams often found his own irascible nature a constraint in his political career.[14]

Portraits of John and Abigail Adams by Benjamin Blyth, c. 1766

In the late 1750s, Adams fell in love with Hannah Quincy; he was poised to propose but was interrupted by friends, and the moment was lost. In 1759, he met 15-year-old Abigail Smith, his third cousin, through his friend Richard Cranch, who was courting Abigail's older sister. Adams initially was not impressed with Abigail and her two sisters, writing that they were not "fond, nor frank, nor candid".

In time, Adams grew close to Abigail. They were married on October 25, 1764, despite the opposition of Abigail's mother. The pair shared a love of books and proved honest in their praise and criticism of each other. After his father's death in 1761, Adams had inherited a 9+½-acre (3.8 ha) farm and a house where they lived until 1783.

John and Abigail had six children: Abigail (known "Nabby") in 1765, John Quincy in 1767, Susanna in 1768, Charles in 1770, Thomas in 1772, and Elizabeth in 1777. Susanna died when she was one year old, while Elizabeth was stillborn. All three of Adams's sons became lawyers. Charles and Thomas were unsuccessful, became alcoholics, and died at a relatively young age. In contrast, John Quincy excelled and launched a political career, eventually becoming president himself.[22]

Thomas Jefferson - President

From Wikipedia, the free encyclopedia

This article is about the third president of the United States

Thomas Jefferson (April 13, 1743 – July 4, 1826) was an American statesman, diplomat, lawyer, architect, philosopher, and Founding Father who served as the third president of the United States from 1801 to 1809. He was the primary author of the Declaration of Independence. Following the American Revolutionary War and prior to becoming president in 1801, Jefferson was the nation's first U.S. secretary of state under George Washington and then the nation's second vice president under John Adams. Jefferson was a leading proponent of democracy, republicanism, and individual rights, and produced formative documents and decisions at the state, national, and international levels. His writings and advocacy for human rights, including freedom of thought, speech, and religion, served as substantial inspirations to the American Revolution and subsequent Revolutionary War in which the Thirteen Colonies succeeded

---

[22] https://en.wikipedia.org/wiki/John_Adams#:~:text=Adams%20was%20elected%20to%20two,banner%20of%20the%20Federalist%20Party.

in breaking from <u>British America</u> and establishing the United States as a sovereign nation.

During the American Revolution, Jefferson represented <u>Virginia</u> at the <u>Second Continental Congress</u> and served as the second <u>governor of Virginia</u> from 1779 to 1781. In 1785, <u>Congress</u> appointed Jefferson <u>U.S. minister to France</u>, where he served from 1785 to 1789. President Washington then appointed Jefferson the nation's first secretary of state, where he served from 1790 to 1793. During this time, in the early 1790s, Jefferson and <u>James Madison</u> organized the <u>Democratic-Republican Party</u> to oppose the <u>Federalist Party</u> during the formation of the nation's <u>First Party System</u>. Jefferson and Federalist John Adams became both friends and political rivals. In the <u>1796 U.S. presidential election</u> between the two, Jefferson came in second, which made him Adams' vice president under the electoral laws of the time. Four years later, in the <u>1800 presidential election</u>, Jefferson again challenged Adams, and won the presidency. In <u>1804</u>, Jefferson was reelected overwhelmingly to a second term.

As president, Jefferson assertively defended the nation's shipping and trade interests against <u>Barbary pirates</u> and aggressive British trade policies, promoted a western expansionist policy with the <u>Louisiana Purchase</u>, which doubled the nation's geographic size, and was able to reduce military forces and expenditures following successful negotiations with France. In his second presidential term, Jefferson was beset by difficulties at home, including the trial of his former vice president <u>Aaron Burr</u>. In 1807, Jefferson implemented the <u>Embargo Act</u> to defend the nation's industries from British threats to U.S. shipping, limiting foreign trade and stimulating the birth of the <u>American manufacturing</u> industry. Presidential scholars and historians praise Jefferson's public achievements, including his advocacy of religious freedom and tolerance, his peaceful acquisition of the <u>Louisiana Territory</u> from France, and his leadership in supporting the <u>Lewis and Clark Expedition</u>; they give radically differing interpretations of his <u>views on and relationship with slavery</u>.

He is ranked by both scholars and in public opinion among the up-per-tier of American presidents.

Early life and career

Main article: Early life and career of Thomas Jefferson

Jefferson was born on April 13, 1743 (April 2, 1743, Old Style, Jul-ian calendar), at the family's Shadwell Plantation in the British Col-ony of Virginia, the third of ten children. He was of English and pos-sibly Welsh descent, and was born a British subject. His father, Peter Jefferson, was a planter and surveyor who died when Jefferson was fourteen; his mother was Jane Randolph. Peter Jefferson moved his family to Tuckahoe Plantation in 1745 on the death of William Randolph III, the plantation's owner and Jefferson's friend, who in his will had named Peter guardian of Randolph's children. The Jef-fersons returned to Shadwell before October 1753.

Peter died in 1757, and his estate was divided between his sons Thomas and Randolph. John Harvie Sr. became 13-year-old Thom-as' guardian. Thomas inherited approximately 5,000 acres (2,000 ha; 7.8 sq mi), which included Monticello, and he assumed full legal authority over the property at age 21.

Education and early family life

Jefferson began his education together with the Randolph children at Tuckahoe under tutors. Thomas' father Peter, who was self-taught and regretted not having a formal education, entered Thomas into an English school at age five. In 1752, at age nine, he attended a local school run by a Scottish Presbyterian minister and also began study-ing the natural world, which he grew to love. At this time he began studying Latin, Greek, and French, while learning to ride horses as well. Thomas also read books from his father's modest library.[17] He was taught from 1758 to 1760 by the Reverend James Maury near Gordonsville, Virginia, where he studied history, sci-ence, and the classics while boarding with Maury's

226

family.[18][17] Jefferson came to know various American Indians, including the Cherokee chief Ostenaco, who often stopped at Shadwell to visit on their way to Williamsburg to trade.[19][20] In Williamsburg, the young Jefferson met and came to admire Patrick Henry, eight years his senior, and shared a common interest in the playing of the violin.

The Wren Building at the College of William & Mary, where Jefferson studied

Jefferson entered the College of William & Mary in Williamsburg, Virginia, in 1761, at the age of eighteen, and studied mathematics, metaphysics, and philosophy with William Small. Under Small's tutelage, Jefferson encountered the ideas of the British Empiricists, including John Locke, Francis Bacon, and Isaac Newton. Small introduced Jefferson to George Wythe and Francis Fauquier. Small, Wythe, and Fauquier recognized Jefferson as a man of exceptional ability and included him in their inner circle, where he became a regular member of their Friday dinner parties. Jefferson later wrote that, while there, he "heard more common good sense, more rational & philosophical conversations than in all the rest of my life".

During his first year at the college, Jefferson spent considerable time attending parties and dancing and was not very frugal with his expenditures; in his second year, regretting that he had squandered away time and money in his first year, he committed to studying fifteen hours a day.[23] While at William & Mary, Jefferson became a member of the Flat Hat Club.

Jefferson concluded his formal studies in April 1762.[25] He read the law under Wythe's tutelage while working as a law clerk in his office. Jefferson was well-read in a broad variety of subjects, which, along with law and philosophy, included history, natural law, natural religion, ethics, and several areas in science, including agriculture. During his years of study under the watchful eye of Wythe, Jefferson authored a *Commonplace Book*, a survey of his extensive readings. Wythe was so impressed with Jefferson that he later bequeathed his entire library to him.

On July 20, 1765, Jefferson's sister Martha married his close friend and college companion Dabney Carr, which was greatly pleasing to Jefferson. In October of that year, however, Jefferson mourned his sister Jane's unexpected death at age 25; he wrote a farewell epitaph for her in Latin.

Jefferson treasured his books and amassed three sizable libraries in his lifetime. He began assembling his first library, which grew to 200 volumes, in his youth. It included books inherited from his father and left to him by Wythe. In 1770, however, Jefferson's first library was destroyed in a fire at his Shadwell home. His second library replenished the first. It grew to 1,250 titles by 1773, and to nearly 6,500 volumes by 1814. Jefferson organized his books into three broad categories corresponding with elements of the human mind: memory, reason, and imagination. After British forces burnt the Library of Congress during the 1814 Burning of Washington, Jefferson sold his second library to the U.S. government for $23,950, hoping to help jumpstart the Library of Congress' rebuilding. Jefferson used a portion of the proceeds to pay off some of his large debt. However, Jefferson soon resumed collecting what amounted to his third personal library, writing to John Adams, "I cannot live without books." By the time of his death a decade later, the library had grown to nearly 2,000 volumes.

Lawyer and House of Burgesses

House of Burgesses in Williamsburg, Virginia, where Jefferson served from 1769 to 1775

Jefferson was admitted to the Virginia bar in 1767, and lived with his mother at Shadwell.[He represented <u>Albemarle County</u> in the Virginia <u>House of Burgesses</u> from 1769 until 1775. He pursued reforms to slavery, including writing and sponsoring legislation in 1769 to strip power from the royal governor and courts, instead providing masters of slaves with the discretion to emancipate them. Jefferson persuaded his cousin <u>Richard Bland</u> to spearhead the legislation's passage, but it faced strong opposition in a state whose economy was largely agrarian.

Jefferson took seven cases of freedom-seeking slaves and waived his fee for one he claimed should be freed before the minimum statutory age for emancipation. Jefferson invoked <u>natural law</u>, arguing "everyone comes into the world with a right to his own person and using it at his own will ... This is what is called personal liberty, and is given him by the author of nature, because it is necessary for his own sustenance." The judge cut him off and ruled against his client. As a consolation, Jefferson gave his client some money, which was conceivably used to aid his escape shortly thereafter. However, Jefferson's underlying intellectual argument that all people were entitled by their creator to what he labeled a "natural right" to liberty is one he would later incorporate as he set about authoring the Declaration of Independence. He also took on 68 cases for the General Court of

Virginia in 1767, in addition to three notable cases: *Howell v. Netherland* (1770), *Bolling v. Bolling* (1771), and *Blair v. Blair* (1772).

Jefferson wrote a resolution calling for a "Day of Fasting and Prayer" and a boycott of all British goods in protest of the <u>British Parliament</u> passing the <u>Intolerable Acts</u> in 1774. Jefferson's resolution was later expanded into *<u>A Summary View of the Rights of British America</u>*, in which he argued that people have the right to <u>govern themselves</u>.

Monticello, marriage, and family

Monticello, Jefferson's home near Charlottesville, Virginia

In 1768, Jefferson began constructing his primary residence, Monticello, whose name in Italian means "Little Mountain", on a hilltop overlooking his 5,000-acre (20 km²; 7.8 sq mi) plantation. He spent most of his adult life designing Monticello as architect and was quoted as saying, "Architecture is my delight, and putting up, and pulling down, one of my favorite amusements." Construction was done mostly by local masons and carpenters, assisted by Jefferson's slaves. He moved into the South Pavilion in 1770. Turning Monticello into a neoclassical masterpiece in the <u>Palladian</u> style was his perennial project.

On January 1, 1772, Jefferson married his third cousin <u>Martha Wayles Skelton</u>, the 23-year-old widow of Bathurst Skelton. She was a frequent hostess for Jefferson and managed the large household. Biographer Dumas Malone described the marriage as the happiest period of Jefferson's life. Martha read widely, did fine needlework, and was a skilled pianist; Jefferson often accompanied her on the violin or cello. During their ten years of marriage, Martha bore six children: Martha "Patsy" (1772–1836); Jane (1774–1775); an unnamed son who lived for only a few weeks in 1777; Mary "Polly" (1778–1804); Lucy Elizabeth (1780–1781); and another Lucy Elizabeth (1782–1784). Only Martha and Mary survived to adulthood. Martha's father John Wayles died in 1773, and the couple inherited 135 slaves, 11,000 acres (45 km²; 17 sq mi), and the estate's debts. The debts took Jefferson years to satisfy, contributing to his financial problems.

Martha later suffered from ill health, including diabetes, and frequent childbirth weakened her. Her mother had died young, and Martha lived with two stepmothers as a girl. A few months after the birth of her last child, she died on September 6, 1782, with Jefferson at her bedside. Shortly before her death, Martha made Jefferson promise never to marry again, telling him that she could not bear to have another mother raise her children. Jefferson was grief-stricken by her death, relentlessly pacing back and forth. He emerged after three weeks, taking long rambling rides on secluded roads with his daughter Martha, by her description "a solitary witness to many a violent burst of grief".

After serving as U.S. Secretary of State from 1790 to 1793 during Washington's presidency, Jefferson returned to Monticello and initiated a remodeling based on architectural concepts he had learned and acquired in Europe. The work continued throughout most of his presidency and was completed in 1809.

Francis J. Bremer, John Winthrop: America's Forgotten Founding Father (New York: Oxford University Press, 2003), pp. 188 and 191; John Winthrop, journal entry for June 6 and 12, 1630, in The Journal of John Winthrop, 1630–1649, ed. Richard S. Dunn and Laetitia Yeandle (Cambridge, MA: Harvard University Press, 1996), pp. 18, note 24; 25, note 42; and 27. 10June 12, 1630 11 THE SECOND CONTINENTAL CONGRESS ADOPTS A RESOLUTION PRESCRIBING A GENERAL AMERICAN FLAG TO SUPERSEDE THE AD HOC COLLECTION OF FLAGS used by the Continental Army and Navy (and displaying various mottoes: "Don't Tread on Me," "An Appeal to Heaven," "Liberty and Union," and "Liberty or Death") during the two years since the beginning of the American Revolution. In January 1776, George Washington introduced the use of a red-and-white striped flag (similar to one employed by the East India Company) with the British Union Jack in the upper-left corner and known as the Grand Union Flag. The Continental Congress's resolution set the standard for "the flag of the United States" as a field (or fly) of "thirteen stripes, alternate red and white," with a blue upper-left corner (or union) displaying "thirteen stars" in white, "representing a new constellation." The flag remained unaltered until 1794, when Congress passed legislation to add two stars and two stripes to the flag in recognition of the admission of Vermont and Kentucky to the Union. A third statute in 1818 permanently fixed the number of stripes at 13. Because no pattern for the stars in the union was specified in the June 14 resolution, Revolutionary flags alternately displayed the stars as a circlet or a pattern of June 14, 1777 five columns (with alternating three and two stars). In fact, no overall flag code was adopted until 1942. In 1780, Francis Hopkinson claimed to have been the original designer of the flag, and in 1870, the descendants of Betsy Ross advanced the claim that she had sewn the first flag at the behest of George Washington in 1776. Both claims are dubious. Although an early version of the flag may have been used at the Battle of the Brandywine on September 11, 1777.

Revolutionary War

Declaration of Independence

Main article: United States Declaration of Independence

The <u>Declaration of Independence</u>, which Jefferson largely wrote in isolation between June 11 and 28, 1776, from a floor he was renting in a home at 700 <u>Market Street</u> in <u>Center City Philadelphia</u>, are "the most potent and consequential words in American history," historian <u>Joseph Ellis</u> later wrote.

Jefferson was the primary author of the Declaration of Independence. At age 33, he was one of the youngest delegates to the Second Continental Congress beginning in 1775 at the outbreak of the American Revolutionary War, where a formal declaration of independence from Britain was overwhelmingly favored. Jefferson was inspired by the Enlightenment ideals of the sanctity of the individual, and the writings of Locke and Montesquieu.

Jefferson sought out John Adams, a Continental Congress delegate from Massachusetts and an emerging leader in the Congress. They became close friends, and Adams supported Jefferson's appointment to the Committee of Five, charged by the Congress with authoring a declaration of independence. The five were Adams, Jefferson, Benjamin Franklin, Robert R. Livingston, and Roger Sherman. The committee initially thought that Adams should write the document, but Adams persuaded the committee to choose Jefferson.

Jefferson consulted with his fellow committee members, but mostly wrote the Declaration of Independence in isolation between June 11 and 28, 1776, in a home he was renting at 700 Market Street in Center City Philadelphia. Jefferson drew considerably on his proposed draft of the Virginia Constitution, George Mason's draft of the Virginia Declaration of Rights, and other sources. Other committee members made some changes, and a final draft was presented to Congress on June 28, 1776.

The declaration was introduced on Friday, June 28, and Congress began debate over its contents on Monday, July 1, resulting in the removal of roughly a fourth of Jefferson's original draft. Jefferson resented the changes, but he did not speak publicly about the revisions. On July 4, 1776, the Congress ratified the Declaration, and delegates signed it on August 2; in so doing, the delegates were knowingly committing an act of high treason against The Crown, which was deemed the most serious criminal offense and was punishable by torture and death.

Jefferson's preamble is regarded as an enduring statement on individual and human rights, and the phrase "all men are created equal" has been called "one of the best-known sentences in the English language". The Declaration of Independence, historian <u>Joseph Ellis</u> wrote in 2008, represents "the most potent and consequential words in American history".[23]

James Madison - President

president of United States

Print Cite Share Feedback

Also known as: James Madison, Jr.

Written by

Irving Brant

Fact-checked by

The Editors of Encyclopaedia Britannica

Last Updated: May 27, 2024 • <u>Article History</u>

Asher B. Durand: portrait of James Madison

<u>See all media</u>

In full:

---

[23]   https://en.wikipedia.org/wiki/Thomas_Jefferson#:~:text=Thomas%20Jefferson%20(April%2013%2C%201743,of%20the%20Declaration%20of%20Independence.

James Madison, Jr.

Born:

March 16 [March 5, Old Style], 1751, Port Conway, Virginia [U.S.]

Died:

June 28, 1836, Montpelier, Virginia, U.S. (aged 85)

Title / Office:

presidency of the United States of America (1809-1817), United States

House of Representatives (1789-1797), United States

Continental Congress (1780-1783), United States

(Show more)

Political Affiliation:

Democratic-Republican Party

Awards And Honors:

Hall of Fame (1905)

See all related content →

Top Questions

What is James Madison best known for?

What did James Madison accomplish?

What was James Madison's education?

Examine contributions of James Madison to the framing and ratification of the U.S. Constitution and Bill of Rights and to the U.S. prosecution of the War of 1812

Learn about the statesmanship of James Madison, including his contributions to the framing and ratification of the U.S. Constitution and Bill of Rights and his leadership of the U.S. during the War of 1812.(more)

See all videos for this article

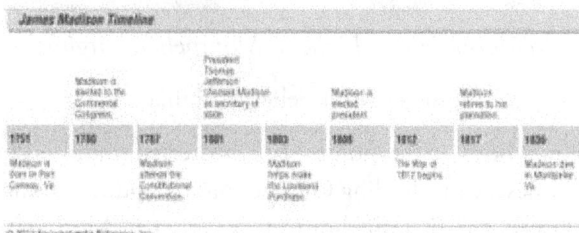

Key events in the life of James Madison

James Madison (born March 16 [March 5, Old Style], 1751, Port Conway, Virginia [U.S.]—died June 28, 1836, Montpelier, Virginia, U.S.) was the fourth president of the United States (1809–17) and one of the Founding Fathers of his country. At the Constitutional Convention (1787), he influenced the planning and ratification of the U.S. Constitution and collaborated with Alexander Hamilton and John Jay in the publication of the Federalist papers. As a member of the new House of Representatives, he sponsored the first 10 amendments to the Constitution, commonly called the Bill of Rights. He was secretary of state under President Thomas Jefferson when the Louisiana Territory was purchased from France. The War of 1812 was fought during his presidency.

Early life and political activities

Madison, James: home in Montpelier, Virginia

James Madison's home in Montpelier, Virginia.

Madison was born at the home of his maternal grandmother. The son and namesake of a leading Orange county landowner and squire, he maintained his lifelong home in Virginia at Montpelier, near the Blue Ridge Mountains. In 1769 he rode horseback to the College of New Jersey (Princeton University), selected for its hostility to episcopacy. He completed the four-year course in two years, finding time also to demonstrate against England and to lampoon members of a rival literary society in ribald verse. Overwork produced several years of epileptoid hysteria and premonitions of early death, which thwarted military training but did not prevent home study of public law, mixed with early advocacy of independence (1774) and furious denunciation of the imprisonment of nearby Dissenters from the established Anglican church. Madison never became a church member, but in maturity he expressed a preference for Unitarianism.

His health improved, and he was elected to Virginia's 1776 Revolutionary convention, where he drafted the state's guarantee of religious freedom. In the convention-turned-legislature he helped Thomas Jefferson disestablish the church but lost reelection by refusing to furnish the electors with free whiskey. After two years on the governor's council, he was sent to the Continental Congress in March 1780.

Charles Willson Peale: portrait of James Madison

James Madison, watercolour on ivory by Charles Willson Peale, 1783.

Five feet four inches tall and weighing about 100 pounds, small boned, boyish in appearance, and weak of voice, he waited six months before taking the floor, but strong actions belied his mild demeanour. He rose quickly to leadership against the devotees of state sovereignty and enemies of Franco-U.S. collaboration in peace negotiations, contending also for the establishment of the Mississippi as a western territorial boundary and the right to navigate that river through its Spanish-held delta. Defending Virginia's charter title to the vast Northwest against states that had no claim to western territories and whose major motive was to validate barrel-of-rum purchases from Indian tribes, Madison defeated the land speculators by persuading Virginia to cede the western lands to Congress as a national heritage.

Following the ratification of the Articles of Confederation in 1781, Madison undertook to strengthen the Union by asserting implied power in Congress to enforce financial requisitions upon the states by military coercion. This move failing, he worked unceasingly for an amendment conferring power to raise revenue and wrote an eloquent address adjuring the states to avert national disintegration by ratifying the submitted article. The chevalier de la Luzerne, French minister to the United States, wrote that Madison was "regarded as the man of the soundest judgment in Congress."

Richard Henry Lee

Richard Henry Lee (1732-1794). Charles Willson Peale (1741-1827). Oil on canvas, c. 1784. Library of Congress, Prints and Photographs Division. Reproduction Number: LC-USZ62-92331.

(1732-1794)

Virginian Richard Henry Lee was a born aristocrat. An active participant in many key events in the Revolutionary War, Lee protested the Stamp Act in Virginia (1765), sat on the committee that named George Washington Commander-in-Chief of the Continental army (1775), and introduced the motion that led to the Declaration of Independence (1776). While in the Continental Congress (1774-1780, 1784-1787) he also worked to stop importation of slaves into the American states.

Yet, despite his experience in the Continental Congress -- America's national legislature -- Lee distrusted a strong national government, fearing that the individual states would lose rights and power. Unconvinced that the Constitution was the answer to the country's problems of government, he worked against its ratification. In Lee's words: "To say that a bad government must be established for fear of anarchy is really saying that we should kill ourselves for fear of dying."

George Mason, the Man

George Mason, 1725-1792

"The fact is unquestionable, that the Bill of Rights, and the Constitution of Virginia, were drawn originally by George Mason, one of our greatest men, and of the first order of greatness."

Thomas Jefferson, friend and contemporary of Mason

The name George Mason is not one that many Americans outside our region would recognize, but the place of George Mason, the man, in our nation's history is of immeasurable importance.

Mason was a plantation owner whose residence was <u>Gunston Hall</u>, a handsome Georgian brick home located in close proximity to Mount Vernon, former home of George Washington, a neighbor and close friend for all but the last years of his life. A prominent figure in his home state and one whose counsel was greatly valued by others of his generation, Mason was the main author of both the Virginia Declaration of Rights and the Constitution of Virginia.

As a delegate to the Constitutional Convention, Mason refused to sign the Constitution and lobbied against its ratification in his home state, believing the document as drafted gave too much power to a central government and was incomplete absent a bill of rights to guarantee individual liberty. His dissent arose in part, too, from what he perceived as the Convention's reluctance to deal more harshly with the institution of slavery (although he himself held slaves).

Mason's refusal to sign the new Constitution cost him greatly, as he lost the friendship of Washington and others over his refusal to endorse the document in its final form. His refusal cost him his rightful place in the annals of history to some extent, as well. Mason is sometimes referred to as the "Forgotten Founder," largely ignored by history books and often uncredited for originating many of the core concepts and much of the language later incorporated in both the Declaration of Independence and the Bill of Rights.

He was the author of the Virginia Declaration of Rights, which was adopted three weeks before the national Declaration of Independence; and in this he charted the rights of human beings much more fully than Jefferson did in the immortal but necessarily compressed paragraph in the more famous document. Of the contemporary impact of Mason's Declaration there can be no possible question. Draftsmen in other states drew upon it when they framed similar documents or inserted similar safeguards of individual liberties in their new constitutions. Universal in its appeal, it directly affected the French Declaration of the Rights of Man and the Citizen of 1789. In our own time it is echoed in the Declaration of Human Rights of the United Nations. Writing in his old age, Lafayette said: "The era of the American Revolution, which one can regard as the beginning of a new social order for the entire world, is, properly speaking, the era of declarations of rights." More than any other single American, except possibly Thomas Jefferson, whom in some sense he anticipated, George Mason may be regarded as the herald of this new era; and in our own age, when the rights of individual human beings are being challenged by totalitarianism around the world, men can still find inspiration in his noble words.

Dr. Joseph Warren

A special post by the author

The following post for Dr. Joseph Warren is fully detailed for a special reason. I myself belong to an organization that I was inducted into back in the 1970's, known as the Order of the Ancient and Honorable Guard of Massachusetts, as a lifetime honorarium as a Sargent. My appointment came from the Battle of Breeds Hill where my ancestor died on the redoubts with Dr. Joseph Warren fighting the British in the third and final attack. My ancestors are memorialized on the monument at that site. I was summoned by the colonel of the Ancient and Honorable and escorted to the Breeds Hill site and shown the monument. He noted my ancestor Thomas Boynton on the monument and gave me the historic details of which I had not been aware of. This honor was extended to me for another organization as a Captain, in The Sons of the American Revolution, of which I am a member of the Greer Chapter of TN.

If I may, some details on Patriot Minuteman Boynton.

Thomas Boynton journal, 19 April- 26 August 1775

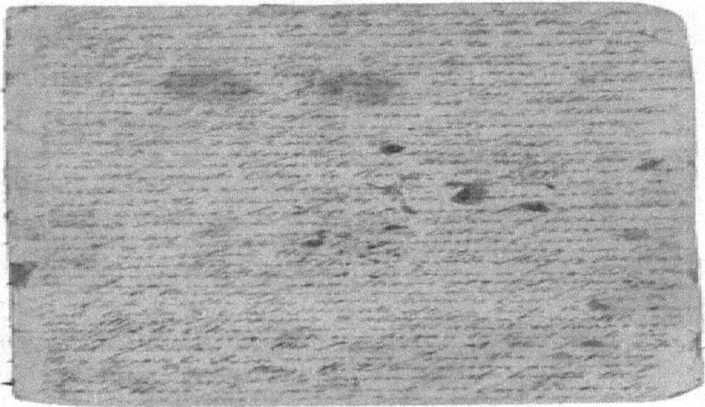

16 cm x 10 cm

From the Thomas Boynton journal.

The Thomas Boyton journal is a fragment of a journal, comprised of two pages.

Author note: The spelling of Boyton is not wrong. Paymasters often recorded names as pronounced. It was common in the Revolutionary War.

This description is from the project: *Coming of the American Revolution*]

A fragment of the journal of Andover minuteman Thomas Boynton, kept in Andover and Charlestown, Mass., 19 April - 26 August 1775. Boynton served under Captain Benjamin Ames in Colonel James Frye's regiment of the Massachusetts Militia. The four brief entries describe the regiment's response to the Lexington alarm and their participation in the Battle of Bunker Hill.

Sounding the Alarm

At 10:00 P.M. on the night of 18 April, approximately 800 (Colonials estimated 1200) British grenadiers and light infantry begin making their way to the Back Bay. Once gathered there, they are ferried across the Charles River basin to Cambridge. Again, they muster, and at two o'clock in the morning they set out in the direction of Concord. As they march, they hear shots in the distance, a signal for minutemen to pick up their arms, for the Regulars are on the move. At 4:30 A.M., when they reach Lexington Green, the Regulars encounter resistance. Eight militiamen are killed and ten wounded, but the Regulars push on and reach Concord by 7 A.M. Along the way they hear more gunshots, church bells, and drum beats sounding the alarm throughout the countryside. In far-flung towns such as Andover, 17 miles northeast of Concord, militiamen like Thomas Boynton rally to assist their brethren.

When retreat to Cambridge was sounded, General Stark's New Hampshire troops cover them in the rear. One of the last to abandon the fort on Breed's Hill, Joseph Warren is killed, recognized by a British officer and unmercifully butchered. As the remaining troops retreat to Cambridge, they morn for Warren and leave behind 140 dead colonial troops and 271 wounded.

Nathan Hale a General George Washington Spy

Search CIA.govSearch

Legom

Library

Nathan Hale: American Patriot. Army Ranger. Spy.

September 1, 2022

In Nathan Hale's time during the early years of the Revolutionary War, spying was not exactly considered honorable. But Hale believed in America and was willing do anything in his power to defend

American freedom. He volunteered to spy on the British Army after reportedly confiding in his classmate that he longed to be useful and that every kind of service for the public good was honorable by being necessary.

Early life of an American Patriot

Nathan Hale was born to a prominent Connecticut family in 1755 and attended Yale University (then known as Yale College) with hopes of becoming a teacher. He graduated with honors in 1773 and began teaching in New London, Connecticut.

When the Revolutionary War began in 1775, Hale recognized the importance serving in the military to fight for America's independence from Britain. He joined the Connecticut militia, becoming a First Lieutenant within five months. For reasons unknown, Hale was unable to join his troops on the battlefront during the Siege of Boston, which deeply troubled him.

Answering the Call to Serve

Hale, intensely eager to go to combat against the Redcoats, leapt at the opportunity to serve in the newly established Knowlton's Rangers. General George Washington, then commander of the Continental Army, established the elite group under the command of Lt. Col. Thomas Knowlton and tasked it with carrying out reconnaissance and raids.

After the Continental Army's defeat at Brooklyn Heights in August 1776, Washington was forced to move his army into Manhattan as the British took control of Long Island. Washington desperately needed intelligence on their next move.

Knowlton gathered his men, updated them on the dire situation, and asked for volunteers willing to go undercover and cross enemy lines. The Rangers voiced their willingness to die in battle but disdain for dying in disguise. Ultimately, only one answered the call. Nathan Hale.

Hale viewed the call to spy against the British as his chance to serve in a meaningful way.

A plaque in Manhattan noting the spot where Nathan Hale was hanged.

The Fateful Mission

On the night of September 15, 1776, Hale left for Long Island outfitted as a schoolmaster and carrying his Yale diploma. He was using the cover story that he was a teacher looking for work.

Details of Hale's espionage activities and capture are scant, though he almost certainly traveled around Long Island taking copious notes of British movements and fortifications just before his discovery.

On the morning of his execution on September 22, 1776, Hale showed great dignity and composure. His final words are purported to be: "I only regret that I have but one life to give to my country."

The Legacy

A statue of Nathan Hale—one of several replicas—was unveiled at CIA Headquarters on 6 June 1973, the bicentennial anniversary of Hale's graduation from Yale.

A CIA statement released on that occasion praised Hale as "the country's first intelligence officer."

Though there is no known portrait of Hale, the sculptor—artist Bela Lyon Pratt who was commissioned by Hale's alma mater, Yale University—used a local man who was the same age as Hale to serve as inspiration. Pratt's original statue of Hale went on display on Yale University campus in 1914.

The statue captures the spirit of the moment before Hale's execution. A 21-year-old man prepared to meet his death for honor and country. His hands and feet bound, face resolute, and gaze fixed on the horizon.

The Agency, steeped in tradition, holds to the legend that placing a quarter—which bears the face of Washington whom Hale served under—around Hale's statue will ensure the safety of officers preparing to leave for an assignment.

Dr. Joseph Warren

From Wikipedia, the free encyclopedia

2nd President of the Massachusetts Provincial Congress

In office

May 2, 1775 – June 17, 1775

Preceded by	John Hancock
Succeeded by	James Warren
Personal details	
Born	June 11, 1741
	Roxbury, Province of Massachusetts Bay, British America
Died	June 17, 1775 (aged 34)
	Breed's Hill, Charlestown, Pro

	vince of Massachusetts Bay, British America
Cause of death	Killed in action
Resting place	Forest Hills Cemetery
Spouse	Elizabeth Hooten
	(m. 1764; died 1773)
Relations	Mercy Scollay (fiancée)
Children	Elizabeth, Joseph, Mary, and Richard
Education	Roxbury Latin School
Alma mater	Harvard College
Occupation	Physician
Signature	*JWarren*

Military service

Allegiance	Massachusetts Bay United Colonies
Branch/service	Massachusetts Patriot militia

Years of service	1775
Rank	Militiaman
	Major general

Dr. Joseph Warren (June 11, 1741 – June 17, 1775), a Founding Father of the United States, was an American physician who was one of the most important figures in the Patriot movement in Boston during the early days of the American Revolution, eventually serving as President of the revolutionary Massachusetts Provincial Congress. Warren enlisted Paul Revere and William Dawes on April 18, 1775, to leave Boston and spread the alarm that the British garrison in Boston was setting out to raid the town of Concord and arrest rebel leaders John Hancock and Samuel Adams. Warren participated in the Battles of Lexington and Concord the following day, the opening engagements of the American Revolutionary War.

Warren had been commissioned a major general in the colony's militia shortly before the June 17, 1775 Battle of Bunker Hill. Rather than exercise his rank, Warren chose to participate in the battle as a private soldier, and was killed in combat when British troops stormed the redoubt atop Breed's Hill. His death, immortalized in John Trumbull's painting, *The Death of General Warren at the Battle of Bunker's Hill, June 17, 1775*, galvanized the rebel forces. Warren has been memorialized in the naming of many towns, counties, streets, and other locations in the United States, by statues, and in numerous other ways.

Biography

GEN. WARREN

Portrait from Boston Monthly Magazine, 1826

Joseph Warren was born in <u>Roxbury</u>, <u>Province of Massachusetts</u> <u>Bay</u>, to Joseph and Mary (née Stevens) Warren. His father was a respected farmer who died in October 1755 when he fell off a ladder while gathering fruit in his orchard. After attending the <u>Roxbury</u> <u>Latin School</u>, Joseph enrolled in <u>Harvard College</u>, graduating in 1759, and then taught for about a year at Roxbury Latin. While teaching at Roxbury, Warren pursued postgraduate studies at Harvard, graduating with a <u>Master of Arts</u> degree in 1763 after defending a thesis against the proposition that all disease was caused by obstruction of bodily vessels. He married 18-year-old heiress Elizabeth Hooten on September 6, 1764. She died in 1773, leaving him with four children: Elizabeth, Joseph, Mary, and Richard.[1] Before his death in 1775, he was engaged to Mercy Scollay.

While practicing medicine and surgery in <u>Boston</u>, he became involved in politics, associating with <u>John Hancock</u>, <u>Samuel Adams</u>, and other leaders of the broad movement labeled <u>Sons of Liberty</u>. He was one of the leaders of Patriot activities during the Liberty

Affair and facilitated an agreement with Hancock and government customs officials prior to the Boston demonstrations.

Warren conducted an autopsy on the body of young Christopher Seider in February 1770, and was a member of the Boston committee that assembled a report on the following month's Boston Massacre. Earlier, in 1768, Royal officials tried to place his publishers Ede's and Gill on trial for an incendiary newspaper essay Warren wrote under the pseudonym *A True Patriot*, but no local jury would indict them.

In 1774, he authored the song "Free America," which was published in colonial newspapers. The poem was set to a traditional British tune, "The British Grenadiers."

Warren owned at least one enslaved person. This unnamed man, formerly held by Joshua Green, helped Warren with his medical practice.

Lexington and Concord

Warren (right) offering to serve General Israel Putnam as a private before the Battle of Bunker Hill

As Boston's conflict with the royal government came to a head in 1773–1775, Warren was appointed to the Boston Committee of Correspondence. He twice delivered orations in commemoration of the Massacre, the second time in March 1775 while the town was occupied by army troops. Warren drafted the Suffolk Resolves, which were endorsed by the Continental Congress, to advocate resistance to Parliament's Coercive Acts, which were otherwise known as the Intolerable Acts. He was appointed President of the Massachusetts Provincial Congress, the highest position in the revolutionary government.

In mid-April 1775, Warren and Benjamin Church were the two top members of the Committee of Correspondence left in Boston. On the afternoon of April 18, the British troops in the town mobilized for a long-planned raid on the nearby town of Concord, and already before nightfall word of mouth had spread knowledge of the mobilization widely within Boston. It had been known to rebel leadership for weeks that General Gage in Boston had plans to destroy munitions stored in Concord by the colonials, and it was also known that they would be taking a route through Lexington. Some unsupported storiesargue that Warren received additional information from a highly placed informant (usually claiming it was from Margaret Kemble Gage, the wife of General Thomas Gage),[1] that the troops had orders to arrest Samuel Adams and John Hancock. However, there is little evidence of this as the troops apparently had no such orders. Regardless, Warren learned there was some British expedition likely to begin that night, and so sent William Dawes and Paul Revere on their famous "midnight rides" to warn Hancock and Adams in Lexington. (There is growing consensus in new scholarship that Mrs. Gage never did conspire against the British and that Warren needed no informant to deduce that the British were mobilizing.)

Warren slipped out of Boston early on April 19, and during that day's Battle of Lexington and Concord, he coordinated and led militia into the fight alongside William Heath as the British Army returned to Boston. When the enemy were returning from Concord, he was among the foremost in hanging upon their rear and assailing their flanks. During this fighting Warren was nearly killed, a musket ball striking part of his wig. When his mother saw him after the battle and heard of his escape, she entreated him with tears again not to risk life so precious. "Wherever danger is, dear mother," he answered, "there will your son be. Now is no time for one of America's children to shrink from the most hazardous duty; I will either set my country free, or shed my last drop of blood to make her so." He then turned to recruiting and organizing soldiers for the Siege of Boston, promulgating the Patriots' version of events, and negotiating with Gen. Gage in his role as head of the Provincial Congress.

Death of General Warren

The Death of General Warren at the Battle of Bunker Hill by John Trumbull (1786)

Warren was commissioned into the Continental Army at the rank of major general by the Second Continental Congress on June 14, 1775. Three days later, he arrived at Charlestown just before the battle of Bunker Hill began and made his way to where Patriot militiamen were forming. Upon meeting General Israel Putnam, Warren asked where he thought the heaviest fighting would be; Putnam responded by pointing to Breed's Hill. Warren subsequently volunteered to join the militia at the rank of private against the wishes of both Putnam and Colonel William Prescott, both of whom unsuccessfully requested that he serve as their commander instead. Warren declined their request due the fact that Putnam and Prescott held more military experience.

During the early stages of the battle, Warren repeatedly stated that "These fellows say we won't fight! By Heaven, I hope I shall die up to my knees in blood!" Defending the Patriot redoubt against two failed attacks by British troops, he kept firing his gun until running out of ammunition and was killed in action during the third and final assault by British gunfire. The man who killed him was possibly Lieutenant Lord Rawdon, who personally recognized him, or by a British officer's servant, an account supported by a forensic analysis conducted in 2011.

After the battle, Warren's body was stripped of his clothing, repeatedly bayoneted and then buried in a shallow ditch by British forces. Captain Walter Laurie, who participated in the battles of Lexington and Concord, later wrote that he "stuffed the scoundrel with another rebel into one hole, and there he and his seditious principles may remain." American soldier Benjamin Hichborn subsequently wrote a letter to John Adams on December 10, 1775, claiming that Lieutenant James Drew, a Royal Navy officer stationed onboard the sloop HMS *Scorpion*, went to Breed's Hill "a day or two" after the battle and exhumed Warren's body, "spit in his face, jumped on his stomach, and at last cut off his head and committed every act of violence upon his body... In justice to the officers in general I must add, that they despised Drew for his Conduct." Warren's body was exhumed again ten months after his death by his brothers and Paul Revere, who identified the remains by an artificial tooth Warren had installed in his jaw. His body was interred in the Granary Burying Ground. In 1825, it was exhumed and reinterred in St. Paul's Church in Boston before being moved one final time in 1855 to his family's vault in Forest Hills Cemetery.[24]

George Wythe

Jefferson described Wythe as "my faithful and beloved mentor in youth and my most affectionate friend through life" and "my ancient master, my earliest and best friend." In 1769, Jefferson added a political career to his practice of law, being elected to the Virginia House of Burgesses.

---

[24] https://en.wikipedia.org/wiki/Joseph_Warren#

George Wythe

1726-1806

Representing Virginia at the Continental Congress

by Ole Erekson, Engraver, c1876, Library of Congress

Born: 1726

Birth- Elizabeth City Co. (Hampton), Va.
place:

Educa- Informal, Law Studies. (Lawyer, Educator)
tion:

Work: Admitted to the Bar in Virginia, 1746; Clerk of the committee on Privileges and Elections of the House of Burgesses, 1747; Attorney General of Virginia, 1753; Member
of the House of Burgesses; 1755-65; Member of the Board
of Visitors, William and Mary, 1761; Professor of Law,
William and Mary, 1769-1789; Elected to Continental

Congress, 1775-76; Speaker of the Virginia House, 1777-78; Judge of the Chancery Court of Virginia, 1789-1806

Died: June 8, 1806

George Wythe was one of the very most distinguished men of his age, yet due to his modesty and quiet dignity, we learn little about him from the history books. He was born in Elizabeth County Virginia, in 1726, of a wealthy agricultural family. His father died when George was three, but his mother, who was extraordinarily well educated for a woman of that day, tutored him in the classics in a manner that would take him far indeed. His mother died when he was still a teenager and his oldest brother, who took no interest in George, inherited the family property. George entered the college of William and Mary but was unable to keep up with the fees. He dropped out and then managed to secure a study of law at the office of a Stephen Dewey. His studies were so successful that he was admitted to the bar in Spottsylvania County in 1746, at the age of 20.

Everyone who came into contact with him was impressed. He was appointed clerk to the Committee which formed the rules of conduct and elections in the House of Burgesses in 1746. In 1753 the Royal Governor of Virginia made him Attorney General, to fill the shoes of Peyton Randolph while he traveled to England. In 1755 Wythe was elected to represent Williamsburg at the House of Burgesses. At that time, his oldest brother died, and he inherited the family farm. Wythe served in the House of Burgesses until it was dissolved, on the eve of the revolution.

His most valuable contribution to the new nation was his involvement in education. This began in 1761 when he was elected to the Board of Visitors at the College of William and Mary. Eight years later the man who could never gain a degree for want of the money to do it with, became America's first Professor of Law. His students included Thomas Jefferson, Henry Clay, James Monroe, John Marshal, and several dozen other distinguished public servants. He taught for twenty years and admitted to no greater love than that of forming young minds.

In 1775 Wythe was elected to attend the Continental Congress. He served for two years, voted in favor of the Resolution, and for the Declaration. In 1776 he was called back to Virginia in order to help form the new government. He was elected Speaker of the Virginia House of Delegates in 1777. The following year he was made one of the three Chancellors of the State of Virginia, a post that he served in for the rest of his life. George Wythe was revered as a man on great honor and integrity. He was a republican in all things, and a quiet abolitionist. He freed his slaves and made provisions for their support until they could earn a living for themselves. This ended in tragedy-and that tragedy would cost Wythe his own life. A young member of his family, on discovering that Wythe had conditionally willed part of the family property to his slaves, decided to enlarge his own share by poisoning them with arsenic. He incidentally murdered George Wythe in the process. Wythe died on June 8, 1806 at the age of 80.

Key Individuals in the Colonies by State, their wives and accomplishments

Connecticut

Roger Sherman

Married Elizabeth Hartwell in 1749. Together they had seven children. She died in 1760.

Sherman married again to **Rebecca Minot Prescott** (1742-1813) on May 12, 1763. Together they had eight more children. Rebecca was friends with **Betsy Ross**, who let her sew three of the stars on the original United States flag. Because of her success in this role, Rebecca was picked to create the first flag of Connecticut. She was also referred to by George Washington as the "most beautiful of the Cabinet ladies." She died in 1813.

Delaware

Gunning Bedford Jr.

Married **Jane "Jenny" Ballareau Parker** in 1772. Jenny* was the daughter of James Parker, a journalist from New Jersey and a friend of Benjamin Franklin's. Franklin famously called Jenny "Jenky." She was classically educated and spoke French fluently, and her natural grace allowed her to catch the eye of Bedford. Together they had five children, two of which died in infancy. Jane Parker died at the age of 85, on July 26, 1831, outliving her husband by 19 years.

John Dickinson

Married **Mary "Polly" Norris**, the daughter of <u>Isaac Norris II</u>, the Speaker of the Pennsylvania General Assembly. She was an accomplished reader, avid correspondent, and an astute gardener. The two were married in secret, as Dickinson did not want to associate with the Society of Friends, a Quaker institution that the Norris family was associated with.* Together they had five children, three of whom died in infancy. Polly died on July 23, 1.

George Read

Married **Gertrude Ross Till** (1733 -September 2, 1802) on January 11, 1763, and together they had five children. Gertrude was the daughter of the Rev. George Ross, the Anglican rector of Immanuel Church in New Castle sister of George Ross a future signer of the Declaration of Independence. Gertrude was a widow, previously married to Thomas Till. She was an avid gardener, and a lover of tulips, and spent many hours tending to them. <u>Gertrude</u> died on September 2, 1802, at her home in New Castle, Delaware.

Dickinson signed the Articles of Confederation, which he had drafted while representing Pennsylvania in the Congress in 1776. Like most Americans, he initially assumed that the political and economic liberties being defended on the battlefield could best be preserved by state governments and military forces created by those state governments. After much debate, Congress adopted the Articles, thereby endorsing his plan for a limited national organization of independent and sovereign states. Dickinson also assisted in drafting both the Articles of Confederation and the U.S. Constitution.

Georgia

William Few

Married **Catherine "Kitty" Nicholson** (August 7, 1764 - 1854) in July of 1788, a fellow New Yorker, the daughter of Commodore James Nicholson of the Royal Navy, and friend of writer **Thomas Paine**.* Together they had three daughters. Kitty died in 1954, out-living her husband by many years.

Maryland

James McHenry

Married **Margaret "Peggy" Allison Caldwell** (October 8, 1762 - November 20, 1833) in 1784 and wrote to her consistently throughout his career. Often his letters contained poetry he had written. They had a very happy marriage, and together had five children, two of whom died young. Peggy was deeply religious, and was not always interested in her husband's affairs, although she always supported him.* She died on November 20, 1833, outliving James by 17 years.

Massachusetts

Rufus King

Married **Mary Alsop** (October 17, 1769 - October 18, 1769) in New York City on March 30, 1786, the only daughter of **John Alsop**, a wealthy merchant, and a delegate for New York to the Continental Congress. Mrs. King was known as being beautiful with gentle manners. She died in Jamaica, New York on October 18, 1769.

New Jersey

William Livingston

Married **Susanna French** in 1747, daughter of a well-to-do New Jersey landowner. Together they had 13 children. According to Livingston's biographer, <u>Susannah</u> had a strong influence on her husband in spite of his unyielding temper. She was a woman of sense and endless tenderness. She died on July 17, 1789.

New York

Alexander Hamilton

Married Elizabeth "Eliza" Schuyler (August 9, 1757 - November 9, 1854) on December 17, 1780, the daughter of American Revolutionary War General <u>Phillip Schuyler</u> and Catherine Van Rensselaer Schuyler of the influential New York Rensselaers. Together, Alexander and Eliza had 8 children. Because of the famous duel between Hamilton and Burr, Eliza outlived her husband for 50 years. She spent most of her life tending to widows and orphans, and co-founded the New York Orphan Asylum Society.

North Carolina

William Blount

Married Mary "Molsey" Grainger on February 12, 1228.* She was the granddaughter of Joshua Grainger, one of the founders of Wilmington, NC. Together, Mary and William had 9 children, three of whom died in infancy. Mary was strongly attached to North Carolina, and when Washington appointed Blount to be governor of Tennessee, she was reluctant to leave. However, Blount built a beautiful home for her and brought her family to the region, and she was able to live out the rest of her days peacefully. She died of Malaria in 1800, only a month or two before her husband died of unhappiness.

The town of Maryville and the county of Grainger are named in honor of her.

Pennsylvania

George Clymer

Married Elizabeth Meredith (1743-1815) on March 18, 1765. Elizabeth was born into a prominent Philadelphia family who were close friends with George Washington. Together they had nine children, five of whom reached adulthood. John Adams, after meeting her at a social dinner, described her in his diary as a "very facetious and social lady.*" She died in 1815, two years after her husband, in their estate in Summerseat, Pennsylvania.

Benjamin Franklin

Entered into a common-law marriage with Deborah Read (February 14, 1708 - December 19, 1774) in 1730. Their marriage would have been legal, except that Deborah was already married to John Rodgers, who had fled to Barbados to avoid paying his debts, never to return. Deborah was pivotal in raising Franklin's first son, and together they had two more children. Their daughter, Sally, died of smallpox as a child. Deborah died of a stroke on December 14, 1774.

Gouverneur Morris

Married Anne "Nancy" Cary Randolph when he was 57. Nancy was the sister of Thomas Mann Randolph, Jr., husband of **Thomas Jefferson**'s daughter, Martha Jefferson Randolph, who was also her cousin. Gouverneur and Nancy had one child together, a son. **Gouverneur Morris** (/ɡʌvərnɪər ˈmɒrɪs/ *guh-vər-NEER MOR-ris*;[1] January 31, 1752 – November 6, 1816) was an American statesman, a Founding Father of the United States, and a signatory to the Articles of Confederation and the United States Constitution. He wrote the Preamble to the United States Constitution and has been called the "Penman of the Constitution".[2] While most Americans still thought of themselves as citizens of their respective states, Morris advanced the idea of being a citizen of a single union of states. He represented Pennsylvania at the 1787 Constitutional Convention in which he advocated a strong central government. He served on the committee that wrote the final draft of the United States Constitution.

Robert Morris

Married Mary White (1749-1827) on March 2, 1769, and together they had seven children. Mary was born to Colonel Thomas and Esther White from a prominent family in Maryland, and her brother was Anglican Bishop William White. Mary was known for her hospitality, and was one of the most well-liked women of her generation. She did in 1827, at the age of 78.

South Carolina

Charles Cotesworth Pinckney

Married Sarah Middleton in 1773, the daughter of a signer of the Declaration of Independence, Henry Middleton.

After Sarah's death, he married **Mary Stead** (November 14th, 1796 to August 29th, 1797) in 1786. She once accompanied Charles to Paris, when he was appointed minister to France.

Virginia

James Madison

Married Dolley Payne Todd (May 20, 1768 - July 12, 1849) on September 15, 1794, a widow who was 16 years his junior. James and Dolley had no children together. Dolley Madison was born into a Quaker family in North Carolina. She married John Todd in 1790, a Quaker from Philadelphia. Together they had two sons. In 1793, yellow fever broke out in the region, causing the death of her husband John Todd and her younger son William.

Dolly was renowned for her social graces. Her hospitable nature contributed to her husband's popularity as president. Famously, when the capitol building burned in 1814, she is credited with saving the Lansdowne Portrait of George Washington.

George Washington

Married Martha Dandridge Custis (June 2, 1731 - May 22, 1802) on January 6, 1759, the widow of Daniel Parke Custis. Martha had four children with her first husband, only two of whom reached adulthood. George and Martha never had children together, but George raised Martha's children as his own.

As the first First Lady, Martha established many of the customs which would be observed by future First Ladies. She died at her home on May 22, 1802. She was 70 years old.

* Retrieved from Janice E. McKenny's book: *Women of the Constitution: Wives of the Signers.* Found at:books.google.com

John Blair

John Blair Jr. (April 17, 1732 – August 31, 1800) was an American Founding Father, who signed the United States Constitution as a delegate from Virginia and was appointed an Associate Justice on the first U.S. Supreme Court by George Washington. In the prelude to the American Revolutionary War, Blair had served as a commissioner of admiralty to enforce regulations promulgated by the Virginia Revolutionary Conventions, then on the committee that prepared the Virginia Declaration of Rights and the Virginia Constitution of 1776. [25]

---

[25] Constitution Day Materials, US Constitution, Pocket Constitution Book, Declaration of Independence, Bill of Rights (constitutionfacts.com)

John Jay

United States statesman and chief justice

Written and fact-checked by

The Editors of Encyclopaedia Britannica

Last Updated: May 13, 2024 • Article History

Jay, John

Born:

 Dec. 12, 1745, New York, N.Y. [U.S.]

Died: May 17, 1829, Bedford, N.Y., U.S. (aged 83)

Title / Office:

governor (1795-1801), New York

Supreme Court of the United States (1789-1795), United States

supreme court (1789-1795), United States

Continental Congress (1774-1774), United States

Role In:

Jay Treaty

John Jay (born Dec. 12, 1745, New York, N.Y. [U.S.]—died May 17, 1829, Bedford, N.Y., U.S.) was a Founding Father of the United

States who served the new nation in both law and diplomacy. He established important judicial precedents as the first chief justice of the United States (1789–95) and negotiated the Jay Treaty of 1794, which settled major grievances with Great Britain and promoted commercial prosperity.

Jay graduated from King's College (now Columbia University) in 1764 and was admitted to the bar in 1768, establishing himself as a successful attorney in New York. Jay deplored the growing estrangement between the colonies and the mother country, fearing that independence might stir up violence and mob rule. Nevertheless, once the revolution was launched, he became one of its staunchest supporters. As a delegate to the First Continental Congress (1774) in Philadelphia, he drafted *The Address to the People of Great Britain,* stating the claims of colonists. He helped assure the approval of the Declaration of Independence (1776) in New York, where he was a member of the provincial Congress. The following year he helped draft New York's first constitution, was elected the state's first chief justice, and in 1778 was chosen president of the Continental Congress.

In 1779 Jay was appointed minister plenipotentiary to Spain, which had joined France in openly supporting the revolutionaries against Britain. His mission—to borrow money and to gain access to the Mississippi River—proved abortive, and he was sent in May 1782 to join Benjamin Franklin in Paris as joint negotiator for peace with Great Britain. In undercover talks with the British, he won surprisingly liberal terms, which were later included essentially intact in the Treaty of Paris (Sept. 3, 1783), which concluded the war.

On his return from abroad, Jay found that Congress had elected him secretary for foreign affairs (1784–90). Frustrated by the limitations on his powers in that office, he became convinced that the nation needed a more strongly centralized government than was provided for by the Articles of Confederation, and he plunged into the fight for ratification of the new federal Constitution, framed in 1787. Using the pseudonym Publius, he collaborated with Alexander

Hamilton and James Madison by writing five essays for *The Federalist*—the classic defense of the new governmental structure. In 1789 Pres. George Washington appointed Jay the country's first chief justice, in which capacity he was instrumental in shaping Supreme Court procedures in its formative years. His most notable case was *Chisholm v. Georgia,* in which Jay and the court affirmed the subordination of the states to the federal government. Unfavourable reaction to the decision led to adoption of the Eleventh Amendment, denying federal courts authority in suits by citizens against a state.

In 1794 Washington sent Jay as a special envoy to Great Britain to help avert war over accumulated grievances. The commercial agreement, called the Jay Treaty (November 19), aroused a storm of protest among the Jeffersonian Republicans, who denounced it as a sellout by pro-British Federalists. Mobs burned Jay in effigy, and opponents denounced him as a traitor. Before the negotiations, Jay at one time had been considered a leading candidate to succeed Washington, but the unpopular treaty ruined whatever chances he had for the presidency. New York Federalists, however, elected him governor (1795–1801), an office from which he retired to spend the remainder of his life on his farm. (In 1800 Jay declined John Adams's offer for reappointment as chief justice.)

John Locke

Author critical critique:

While John Locke was long before the activities of the colonies to be involved in them, in a physical sense, his literary influence as an English philosopher had a powerful and profound influence on the colonial philosophy of government. An interesting theory of his is philosophical empiricism, a concept I personally do not adhere to. His concept of this theory was that the "human mind is in a blank state at birth and that knowledge is based on experience."

My disagreement with this is it is fundamental in approach and does not apply to all levels of education which would or should be coupled with comprehensive education of the masses and be based on historical knowledge. Most would not have been educated in his time period; education was not for the masses, and knowledge was only for the privileged classes to rule the masses.

Those who followed his theism were adhering to his philosophy called liberalism. Coupled with his Social Contract Theory, Liberalism uncoupled is on the pathway to abject socialism.

I see this uncoupling happening in our country today, and it needs to be checked. This opinion is based on what the population has to give up, a natural freedom, and give it to a ruling party.

Hobbes challenges this opinion in "The State of Nature" was, therefore, a state of war, which could be ended only if individuals agreed (in a social contract) to give their liberty into the hands of a sovereign on the sole condition that their lives were safeguarded by sovereign power. This unbalance has many examples in ancient and current examples in the many types of governments posted in this work. Yes, there are successful examples, but many face trials and tribulations.

I also acknowledge we have existed for 400 years with our cherished documents protecting our liberties but there are factions who want to throw all of this out of the window. I refer to the current politics not adhering to our venerable documents and, in my opinion, wanting to shuffle to the left and be ruled without recourse; well, that's not true; we could overthrow the government as is our right. Our borders are open, they want illegals to vote, countries are not certain they can depend on us fully, and I could go on.

What exactly would become of us? At this time, the jury is out on this, and the situation is fearfully fragile, in my humble opinion.

I want to draw your attention to a white paper by Maegan Nation, a Political Science student writing on "Locke's Social Contract: Is It Legitimate?" submitted to Political Science Faculty Advisor Dr. Mary Elizabeth Sullivan, University of Central Arkansas. It has many contrarian opinions of the theory.

John Locke's theories' 10 major points

John Locke (1632—1704)

John Locke was among the most famous philosophers and political theorists of the 17th century. He is often regarded as the founder of a school of thought known as <u>British Empiricism</u>, and he made foundational contributions to modern theories of limited, liberal government. He also was influential in the areas of theology, religious toleration, and educational theory. In his most important work, the *Essay Concerning Human Understanding*, Locke set out to offer an analysis of the human mind and its acquisition of knowledge. He offered an empiricist theory according to which we acquire ideas through our experience of the world. The mind is then able to examine, compare, and combine these ideas in numerous different ways. Knowledge consists of a special kind of relationship between different ideas. Locke's emphasis on the philosophical examination of the human mind as a preliminary to the philosophical investigation of the world and its contents represented a new approach to philosophy, one which quickly gained a number of converts, especially in Great Britain. In addition to this broader project, the *Essay* contains a series of more focused discussions on important and widely divergent philosophical themes. In politics, Locke is best known as a proponent of limited government. He uses a theory of natural rights to argue that governments have obligations to their citizens, have only limited powers over their citizens, and can ultimately be overthrown by citizens under certain circumstances. He also provided powerful arguments in favor of religious toleration. This article attempts to give a broad overview of all key areas of Locke's thought.

Don't think of me as a contrarian; I believe in the Bill of Rights and my country. What we have at this point in time is being attacked, and that is not supposed to happen.

Accomplishments of John Locke

1. Tabula Rasa (Blank Slate) concept

John Locke introduced the concept of tabula rasa, which translates to "blank slate." He argued that the mind is not inherently filled with ideas or knowledge at birth, but rather, it is like a blank slate upon which experiences and perceptions write.

According to Locke, all knowledge and ideas come from sensory experience and observation of the external world. This idea challenged the prevailing belief in innate ideas and emphasized the role of experience and perception in shaping human understanding.

2. Contributed to the development of empiricism

Locke's work played a crucial role in the development of empiricism, a philosophical school of thought that asserts that knowledge is derived from experience. He emphasized the importance of sensory perception and observation in acquiring knowledge.

According to Locke, the mind is initially devoid of any innate knowledge or principles and gradually builds knowledge through sensory experiences.

His emphasis on empirical evidence and observation as the basis for understanding the world had a significant influence on subsequent philosophers and the scientific method.

3. Natural rights and social contract theory

Locke's political philosophy revolved around the concepts of natural rights and social contract theory. He argued that individuals possess natural rights to life, liberty, and property, which are inherent and cannot be legitimately taken away by any authority.

Locke believed that governments are formed through a social contract, a voluntary agreement among individuals to establish a political society. According to this theory, people surrender some of their natural rights to a government in exchange for the protection of their remaining rights.

This concept of a social contract between the governed and the government served as the basis for the legitimacy and limitations of political power, emphasizing the consent of the governed and the duty of the government to protect the rights of its citizens.

Locke's ideas on natural rights and social contract theory influenced the development of democratic principles and the establishment of constitutional governance in many countries, including the United States.

4. Advocated for limited government and separation of powers

Locke advocated for the idea of limited government and the separation of powers as a means to protect individual rights and prevent tyranny. He believed that governments should be based on the consent of the governed and should have their powers limited to specific functions.

Locke argued for the separation of powers into legislative, executive, and judicial branches to ensure a system of checks and balances. This division of power helps prevent any one branch from becoming too dominant and abusing its authority.

Locke's ideas on limited government and separation of powers influenced the political philosophy of many later thinkers and were instrumental in shaping the systems of government in modern democracies.

5. Influence on American Founding Fathers

John Locke's influence on the American Founding Fathers was significant and far-reaching. His ideas provided a philosophical foundation for the principles of liberty and limited government that guided the American Revolution and the drafting of the United States Constitution.

Here are some key ways in which Locke influenced the American Founding Fathers:

1. **Natural Rights**: Locke's concept of natural rights, including the rights to life, liberty, and property, strongly influenced the Founding Fathers' understanding of individual rights. Thomas Jefferson, in drafting the Declaration of Independence, drew heavily from Locke's ideas when he wrote that all individuals are endowed with certain unalienable rights.

2. **Social Contract Theory**: Locke's theory of the social contract, which posited that governments derive their authority from the consent of the governed, informed the Founding Fathers' understanding of the relationship between the people and their government. The idea that government exists to protect the rights and interests of the people resonated with the framers of the Constitution.

3. **Separation of Powers**: Locke's advocacy for the separation of powers and checks and balances heavily influenced the structure of the American government. The Founding Fathers, particularly James Madison, incorporated these principles into the Constitution to ensure that no single branch of government would become too powerful.

4. **Limited Government**: Locke's emphasis on limited government and the protection of individual rights directly influenced the Founding Fathers' vision for the United States. They sought to establish a government that was limited in

its powers and would not infringe upon the natural rights of its citizens.

5. **Revolutionary Justification**: Locke's writings on resistance to tyrannical governments provided intellectual justification for the American Revolution. His arguments that people have the right to overthrow oppressive rulers if their natural rights are violated were echoed in the Declaration of Independence and the American Revolution's spirit of independence.

The Founding Fathers, including Thomas Jefferson, James Madison, and Benjamin Franklin, among others, studied and drew inspiration from Locke's works.

His ideas played a crucial role in shaping the principles and values upon which the United States was founded, making Locke a key intellectual influence on the American Revolution and the establishment of a constitutional republic.

6. Advocated for religious tolerance

Locke's work "A Letter Concerning Toleration" was a significant contribution to the promotion of religious tolerance and freedom of conscience.

He argued that the state should not interfere in matters of religious belief and that individuals have the right to worship according to their own conscience. Locke believed that religious diversity should be accepted and that religious persecution is both morally wrong and politically harmful.

His ideas on religious tolerance had a profound impact on the development of principles related to religious freedom and the separation of church and state.

7. Made contributions to economic thought

Locke made important contributions to economic thought, particularly in relation to property rights and the labor theory of value. He emphasized the importance of private property as a fundamental right, stating that individuals have the right to acquire, possess, and enjoy property.

Locke's labor theory of value posited that individuals acquire property through their own labor and that the value of goods and services is determined by the labor expended in producing them.

These ideas laid the groundwork for classical liberal economic theories and influenced the development of capitalism. Locke's contributions to economic thought helped shape our understanding of property rights, individual liberty, and the role of labor in the economy.

8. Promoted practical and individualized education

Locke's thoughts on education are outlined in his work "Some Thoughts Concerning Education." He emphasized the importance of early childhood education and believed in a practical, individualized approach to learning.

Locke argued that education should focus on developing a child's character, reason, and moral values. He advocated for a balanced curriculum that includes a mix of academic subjects, physical education, and practical skills.

Locke's ideas on education emphasized the importance of nurturing a child's natural abilities and fostering independent thinking, which had a lasting impact on educational philosophy and practices.

9. Contributed to the development of constitutionalism

Locke's ideas played a significant role in the development of constitutionalism, which is the belief in the importance of a constitution as the fundamental law of a nation. His writings provided a theoretical framework for constitutional governance, where power is distributed and controlled through a constitution.

Locke emphasized the idea of limited government, the consent of the governed, and the protection of individual rights through a system of checks and balances.

His ideas on constitutionalism influenced the development of modern democratic systems, including the separation of powers and the protection of individual rights through constitutional provisions.

10. Influenced the Enlightenment movement

Locke's ideas had a profound influence on the Enlightenment, an intellectual and cultural movement of the 17th and 18th centuries. The Enlightenment emphasized reason, individualism, and the importance of the individual's rights and liberties.

Locke's emphasis on individual rights, limited government, and the social contract laid the foundation for many Enlightenment thinkers. His ideas on religious tolerance, natural rights, and the pursuit of knowledge through empirical observation aligned with the core values of the Enlightenment.

Locke's works, particularly "An Essay Concerning Human Understanding" and his political treatises, contributed to the intellectual climate of the Enlightenment and shaped the philosophical, political, and scientific developments of the time.

Thomas Paine (born January 29, 1737, Thetford, Norfolk, England—died June 8, 1809, New York, New York, U.S.) was an English-American writer and political pamphleteer whose *Common Sense* pamphlet and Crisis papers were important influences on the American Revolution. Other works that contributed to his reputation as one of the greatest political propagandists in history were *Rights of Man*, a defense of the French Revolution and republican principles, and *The Age of Reason*, an exposition of the place of religion in society.

Life in England and America

Paine was born to a Quaker father and an Anglican mother. His formal education was meager, just enough to enable him to master reading, writing, and arithmetic. At 13, he began work with his father as a corset maker and then tried various other occupations unsuccessfully, finally becoming an officer of the excise. His duties were to hunt for smugglers and collect the excise taxes on liquor and tobacco. The pay was insufficient to cover living costs, but he used part of his earnings to purchase books and scientific apparatus.

Paine's life in England was marked by repeated failures. He had two brief marriages. He was unsuccessful or unhappy in every job he tried. He was dismissed from the excise office after he published a strong argument in 1772 for a raise in pay as the only way to end corruption in the service. Just when his situation appeared hopeless, he met Benjamin Franklin in London, who advised him to seek his fortune in America and gave him letters of introduction (including one to Franklin's son-in-law, Richard Bache).

Paine arrived in Philadelphia on November 30, 1774. Bache introduced him to Robert Aitkin, whose *Pennsylvania Magazine* Paine helped found and edit for 18 months. In addition, Paine published numerous articles and some poetry anonymously or under pseudonyms. One such article was "African Slavery in America," a scathing denunciation of the African slave trade, which he signed "Justice and Humanity."

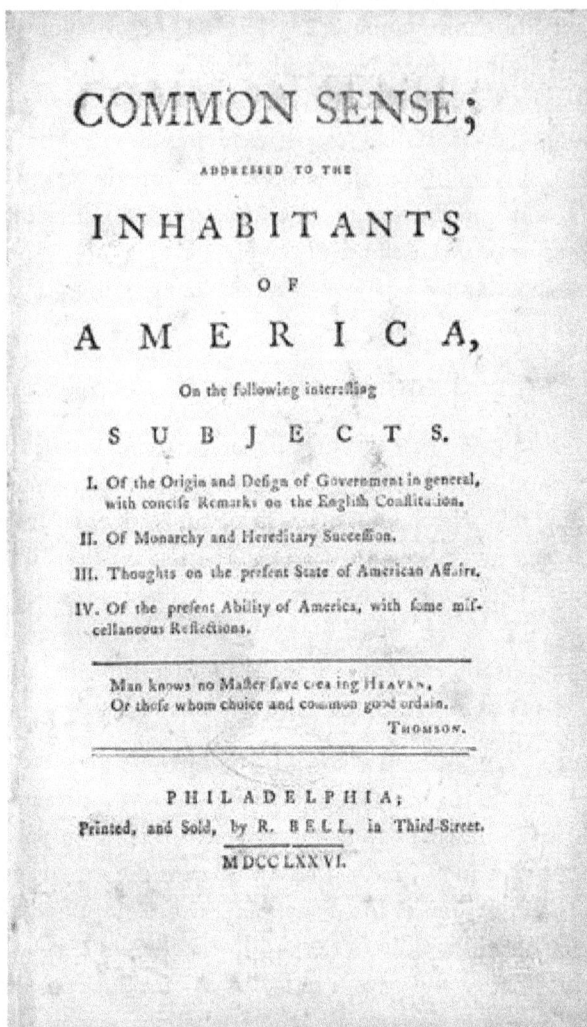

Common Sense Title page from Thomas Paine's pamphlet Common mon Sense, 1776.

Paine had arrived in America when the conflict between the colonists and England was reaching its height. After blood was spilled at the Battles of Lexington and Concord on April 19, 1775, Paine argued that the cause of America should be not just a revolt against taxation but a demand for independence. He put this idea into *Common Sense*, which came off the press on January 10, 1776. The 50-page pamphlet sold more than 500,000 copies within a few months. More than any other single publication, *Common Sense* paved the way for the Declaration of Independence, unanimously ratified on July 4, 1776.

During the war that followed, Paine served as volunteer aide-de-camp to Gen. Nathanael Greene. His great contribution to the patriot cause was the 16 "Crisis" papers issued between 1776 and 1783, each one signed *Common Sense*. "The American Crisis. Number I," published on December 19, 1776, when George Washington's army was on the verge of disintegration, so moved Washington that he ordered it read to all the troops at Valley Forge. Its opening is among the most stirring passages in the literature of the American Revolution:

These are the times that try men's souls. The summer soldier and the sunshine patriot will, in this crisis, shrink from the service of his country, but he that stands it now deserves the love and thanks of man and woman. Tyranny, like hell, is not easily conquered, yet we have this consolation with us—that the harder the conflict, the more glorious the triumph. What we obtain too cheap, we esteem too lightly: It is dearness only that gives everything its value. Heaven knows how to put a proper price upon its goods, and it would be strange indeed if so celestial an article as freedom should not be highly rated. Britain, with an army to enforce her tyranny, has declared that she has a right not only to tax but "to bind us in all cases whatsoever," and if being bound in that manner is not slavery, then is there not such a thing as slavery upon earth? Even the expression is impious, for so unlimited a power can belong only to God.

This paper, combined with the subsequent victory of Washington's army in the Battle of Trenton later in the month, had the probable effect of inspiring many soldiers, whose term of service would expire on January 1, to reenlist.

In 1777 Congress appointed Paine secretary to the Committee for Foreign Affairs. He held the post until early in 1779 when he became involved in a controversy with <u>Silas Deane</u>, a member of the <u>Continental Congress</u>, whom Paine accused of seeking to profit personally from French aid to the United States. But in revealing Deane's machinations, Paine was forced to quote from secret documents to which he had access as secretary of the Committee for Foreign Affairs. As a result, despite the truth of his accusations, he was forced to resign from his post.

Paine's desperate need for employment was relieved when he was appointed clerk of the General Assembly of Pennsylvania on November 2, 1779. In this <u>capacity</u>, he had frequent opportunities to observe that American troops were at the end of their patience because of lack of pay and scarcity of supplies. Paine took $500 from his salary and started a subscription for the relief of the soldiers. In 1781, pursuing the same goal, he accompanied <u>John Laurens</u> to <u>France</u>. The money, clothing, and ammunition they brought back with them were important to the final success of the Revolution. Paine also appealed to the separate states to cooperate for the well-being of the entire nation. In "Public Good" (1780), he included a call for a national convention to remedy the ineffectual <u>Articles of Confederation</u> and establish a strong central government under "a continental constitution."

At the end of the American Revolution, Paine again found himself poverty-stricken. His patriotic writings had sold by the hundreds of thousands, but he had refused to accept any profits in order that cheap editions might be widely circulated. In a petition to Congress <u>endorsed</u> by Washington, he pleaded for financial assistance. Paine's opponents buried it in Congress, but Pennsylvania gave him £500 and New York a farm in <u>New Rochelle</u>. Here, Paine devoted his time to inventions, concentrating on an iron bridge without piers and a smokeless candle.

In Europe: *Rights of Man*

In April 1787, Paine left for Europe to promote his plan to build a single-arch bridge across the wide <u>Schuylkill</u>

River near Philadelphia. But in England, he was soon diverted from his engineering project. In December 1789 he published anonymously a warning against the attempt of Prime Minister William Pitt to involve England in a war with France over the Dutch Republic, reminding the British people that war had "but one thing certain and that is increase of taxes." But it was the French Revolution that now filled Paine's thoughts. He was enraged by Edmund Burke's attack on the uprising of the French people in his *Reflections on the Revolution in France*, and, though Paine admired Burke's stand in favor of the American Revolution, he rushed into print with his celebrated answer, *Rights of Man* (March 13, 1791). The book immediately created a sensation. At least eight editions were published in 1791, and the work was quickly reprinted in the U.S., where the Jeffersonian societies widely distributed it. When Burke replied, Paine came back with *Rights of Man, Part II*, published on February 17, 1792

What began as a defense of the French Revolution evolved into an analysis of the basic reasons for discontent in European society and a remedy for the evils of arbitrary government, poverty, illiteracy, unemployment, and war. Paine spoke out effectively in favor of republicanism as against monarchy and went on to outline a plan for popular education, relief of the poor, pensions for aged people, and public works for the unemployed, all to be financed by the levying of a progressive income tax. To the ruling class Paine's proposals spelled "bloody revolution," and the government ordered the book banned and the publisher jailed. Paine himself was indicted for treason, and an order went out for his arrest. But he was en route to France, having been elected to a seat in the National Convention before the order for his arrest could be delivered. Paine was tried in absentia, found guilty of seditious libel, and declared an outlaw, and the *Rights of Man* was ordered permanently suppressed.

The first years that he spent in France formed a curious episode in his life. He was enthusiastically received, but because he knew little French, translations of his speeches had to be read for him. In France, Paine hailed the abolition of the monarchy but deplored the terror against the royalists and fought unsuccessfully to save the life of King Louis XVI, favoring banishment rather than execution, which he argued would alienate American sympathy. He was to pay for his efforts to save the king's life when the radicals under Maximilien Robespierre took power. Paine was imprisoned from December 28, 1793, to November 4, 1794, when, with the fall of Robespierre, he was released and, though seriously ill, readmitted to the National Convention.

While in prison, the first part of Paine's _Age of Reason_ was published (1794), and Part II followed it after his release (1796). Although Paine made it clear that he believed in a Supreme Being and, as a Deist, opposed only organized religion, the work won him a reputation as an atheist among the orthodox. The publication of his last great pamphlet, _Agrarian Justice_ (1797), with its attack on inequalities in property ownership, added to his many enemies in establishment circles.

Paine remained in France until September 1, 1802, when he sailed for the United States. He quickly discovered that his services to the country had been all but forgotten and that he was widely regarded only as the world's greatest infidel. Despite his poverty and his physical condition, worsened by occasional drunkenness, Paine continued his attacks on privilege and religious superstitions. He died in New York City in 1809 and was buried in New Rochelle on the farm given to him by the state of New York as a reward for his Revolutionary writings. Ten years later, William Cobbett, the political journalist, exhumed the bones and took them to England, where he hoped to give Paine a funeral worthy of his great contributions to humanity. But the plan backfired, and the bones were lost, never to be recovered.

Legacy of Thomas Paine

Thomas Paine

Thomas Paine, painting after a portrait by George Romney; in the collection of the American Antiquarian Society, Worcester, Massachusetts. 41.59 cm × 36.51 cm.[26]

Thomas Paine and Democracy

It would be hard to find a more strident, vocal supporter of popular government during America's founding period than Thomas Paine. The proposals put forth in his January 1776 pamphlet *Common Sense* for an "unmixed" and unchecked democratic scheme for America, designed to replace the British arrangement of balanced

---

[26] https://collections.americanantiquarian.org/portraits/bios/92.pdf

and mixed powers of King, Lords, and Commons, were radical. Remarkably, the pamphlet appeared just over a year after Paine had immigrated to America from England. But while his ideas helped push the colonies toward separating from British rule, they rattled at least one leading voice for independence in the Second Continental Congress. John Adams asserted that Paine's ideas were too "democratical." A decade later, Paine agreed, at least on several important points.

Believing that the true source of legitimate power was to be found only in the sovereignty of the people and not in any governmental institutions or claims to higher authority, Paine set out in *Common Sense*—following forceful arguments urging Americans to separate themselves from Great Britain—to outline what kind of government the colonies should create: a new, more egalitarian, democratic scheme of representative government. "Let the assemblies be annual, with a president only. The representation is more equal, their business wholly domestic, and subject to the authority of a Continental Congress." Although many welcomed Paine's vigorous call for independence, his simple formula for "a government of our own" in *Common Sense must* have elicited a sardonic smile or two at the time. It still does.

At the heart of Paine's proposals was his advocacy of a unicameral legislative body with no independent executive, no mention of a judiciary, and no internal balanced powers or checks anywhere to be found. Instead, he envisioned separate roles for the colonial assemblies and the national Congress to play, divided along the lines of domestic and international duties. He hinted at a fundamental principle of a federal structure: any such a division of delegated powers between the states and national government should tilt in the direction of the latter.

But *Common Sense* found no room for royalty, aristocracy, or clerical absolutism. These were relics of the Old World, Paine advised. There was no place in Paine's recommendations for America for the venerated "balanced" powers in the British constitution that French thinker Montesquieu so admired in the British model. For there was nothing left to balance. The only institution that Paine found useful in the British system of government was the Commons. But it was corrupted by the allegiance-owing king's ministers. So, Paine did away with the foundations of British authority and representation and grounded both instead in the people.

One who did not find Paine's ideas so attractive was Adams, a kindred rebellious spirit and powerful voice for independence in Congress. Alarmed by Paine's radical recommendations for government in *Common Sense* (though supportive of the pamphlet's call for independence and envious of its popular appeal), he rushed to counter Paine's proposals for forming a government by publishing a pamphlet of his own later that spring: *Thoughts on Government: Applicable to the Present State of the American Colonies.*[5] Holding that the only valuable thing about the British constitution was its republican features (a republic is an "empire of laws, and not of men"), Adams set out in his pamphlet to build a better republican model than Paine's democratic prescriptions offered.

Adams made no bones about his skepticism of Paine's single-chamber, all-powerful legislature, wondering whether all powers of government, legislative, executive, and judicial, should be contained in a single legislative body. He answered no because such an assembly would be "liable to all the vices, follies, and frailties of an individual." Paine did not possess this insight at the time.

The Second Continental Congress meeting in Philadelphia that spring and summer had two competing, widely read pamphlets informing delegates of what sort of republican government ought to replace British rule should independence be declared. Many colonies were already in the process of building their own new governments, drawing on ideas from these and other sources.

After the Declaration of Independence was promulgated in July, Congress moved to create America's first national constitution by proposing the Articles of Confederation. Paine's recommendations for a single-house legislative body, devoid of separation of powers and checks and balances, contrary to Adams' proposals, prevailed and was formally put into place at the successful conclusion of America's War for Independence. Adams paid little attention to the structure of the national government when writing down his proposals in *Thoughts on Government* for New Colonial Constitutions.

Differing from Paine's thinking, the new states' powers remained superior over those meager few delegated by the Articles to Congress. However, many of Adams' recommendations, though he supported the creation and ratification of the Articles, informed several of the new state governments being created at the time and eventually were incorporated in the proposals for a new Constitution in 1787.

Pennsylvania's first constitution had more similarities to Paine's democratic proposals found in *Common Sense*. Though he worked for a while as a clerk to the Pennsylvania Assembly, he was never a delegate, just as he never was to the Continental Congress. However, his influence was certainly apparent in the structure of both the Articles and Pennsylvania models from the start. Notably, however, both constitutions were short-lived. Both were flawed, but for different reasons: A lack of power for national government and unbridled legislative powers in a single-chamber assembly in Pennsylvania where the powers of a partisan majority could be wielded unchecked. The Articles were replaced by the ratification of the Constitution, the Pennsylvania constitution, soon after.

At least one Paine scholar has questioned the notion that Pennsylvania's constitution of 1776 was the most democratic of all the states. Pointing out that a vote of the people never approved the constitution, that representation was not based on "per head" but on counties (giving the western "back-country" counties an advantage over the Assembly from the beginning), and that it disenfranchised most of the eligible electorate in the state, J.C.D. Clark argued that the idea was a myth. He also pointed out that Paine had no objections to the constitution's arrangements.

In his last published pamphlet prior to heading off to Europe on the eve of the Constitutional Convention (both Paine and Adams were in Europe during the Convention), Paine confronted the stresses and cracks in the functioning of the Pennsylvania model: the problem of an overbearing majority. His *Dissertations on Government: The Affairs of the Bank: And Paper Money*, 1786, came about because of actions taken by "back-country" Pennsylvania farmers and the Constitutionalist Party they controlled in the Pennsylvania Assembly beginning in 1785.

The most important problem that Paine addressed in his pamphlet, as well as in letters and articles in the local papers at the time, was that the state assembly revoked the Pennsylvania charter of Robert Morris's Bank of North America, chiefly over its preference for paper money. Rural debtors feared that the value of paper money, which the state had attempted to regulate to help, among other things, keep the farmers afloat, would not be accepted on par with money, based on specie, issued by the national bank. They believed the bank unfairly favored the urban, mercantilist class. The conflict began about the same time as Shays's Rebellion, a similar battle, though one much more threatening and violent, between debtors and creditors, that broke out in Massachusetts.

The Pennsylvania dispute tested Paine's majoritarian principles, for he also favored the national bank. Originally aligned with the Constitutionalist Party, he broke with it over the issue. Paine was an early nationalist: he believed that a national bank was necessary to tie the colonies (and then states following Independence) together in order to fund and win the war and then to establish an independent nation. A national debt, he declared in *Common Sense*, is a national bond. Conflicts over national and state monetary policies, such as those arising in Pennsylvania and Massachusetts, amounted to existential threats to the new nation.

He also earlier had worked for a time for Robert Morris, a point not lost on the farmers who accused Paine, after publishing his articles and *Dissertations on Government*, of abandoning the common man by defending the bank. They accused him of being a hired pen.

But Paine's pamphlet revealed that he was beginning to explore limits to the principles of majority rule. His solution to limiting an overbearing majority was found in the idea of fundamental law. An enabling charter, such as that of the national bank, was the kind of law, like a constitution, that could not, he argued, be overridden by routine legislation.

For admitting a question of law to arise, whether the charter, which that act attempts to repeal, is a law of the land in the manner in which laws of universal operations are or of the nature of a contract made between the public and the bank . . . the repealing act does not and cannot decide the question, because it is the repealing act that makes the question, and its own fate is involved in the decision. It is a question of law and not a question of legislation and must be decided on in a court of justice and not by a House of Assembly.

In a rudimentary way, Paine anticipated Alexander Hamilton's *Federalist 78* essay on the necessity for judicial review. Though he had not mentioned an independent judiciary in *Common Sense* (assuming, following the English model, that it would reside in the legislative body), Paine began to understand that courts might have to step in to mediate disputes between a charter and a politically motivated legislative majority. Fundamental law was superior to ordinary law, as he and many others understood it. As Pennsylvania had granted a perpetual charter to Morris' bank, mere legislation could not repeal it. A founding charter constituted a "higher law," a doctrine echoed thirty years later by Chief Justice John Marshall in *Dartmouth College v. Woodward*, 17 U.S. 518 (1819).[13]

Paine also took Adams' concern about a majority in the legislature, capable of acting just as ruthlessly as an individual could, to a new level: "Despotism may be more effectually acted by many over the few, than by one man over many."[14] In short, the potential tyranny of the majority, especially a party majority, was worse. That forced him to rethink his position on bicameralism:

My idea of a single legislature was always founded on the hope that whatever personal parties there might be in the state, they would all unite and agree on the general principles of good government—that these party differences would be dropped at the threshold of the state house, and that the public good, or the good of the whole, would be the governing principle of the legislature. . . . But when a party operates to produce party laws, a single house is a single person and subject to the haste, rashness, and passion of individual sovereignty. At least, it is an aristocracy.

Adams, if he read the piece (he was in Europe), must have grinned. Perhaps Paine rethought the advice offered in Adams' *Thoughts on Government*. Furthermore, James Madison had yet to pen his famous *Federalist 10*, a piece that directly confronted this problem of popular government: the problem of a majority faction acting in its own self-interest against the common good, a potential problem of the era that bore serious consideration.

One Paine scholar and historian, Eric Foner, remarked that "Paine on popular sovereignty did not get along easily with Paine on charter contracts." But at the very least, Paine's *Dissertations on Government* demonstrated the evolution and the necessity for an accommodation in the political philosophy of one of early America's most radical voices for popular government.[27]

The Albany Plan

While not utilized, it was instrumental in eventually drawing the 13 colonies and the Iroquois Confederacy together. The colonial governments were to select members of a "Grand Council," while the British Government would appoint a "president General." Together, these two branches of the unified government would regulate colonial-Indian relations to protect British interests.

---

[27] https://allthingsliberty.com/2022/11/thomas-paine-on-popular-government-in-america-evolution-of-a-radicals-thinking/

Albany Plan of Union, 1754

The Albany Plan of Union was a plan to place the British North American colonies under a more centralized government. On July 10, 1754, representatives from seven of the British North American colonies adopted the plan. Although never carried out, the Albany Plan was the first important proposal to conceive of the colonies as a collective whole united under one government.

Cartoon originally appearing in Benjamin Franklin's Pennsylvania Gazette in 1754

Representatives of the colonial governments adopted the Albany Plan during a larger meeting known as the Albany Congress. The British Government in London had ordered the colonial governments to meet in 1754, initially because of a breakdown in negotiations between the colony of New York and the Mohawk nation, which was part of the Iroquois Confederation. More generally, imperial officials wanted a treaty between the colonies and the Iroquois that would articulate a clear colonial-Indian relations policy. The colonial governments of Maryland, Pennsylvania, New York, Connecticut, Rhode Island, Massachusetts, and New Hampshire all sent commissioners to the Congress. Although the treaty with the Iroquois was the main purpose of the Congress, the delegates also met to discuss intercolonial cooperation on other matters. With the

French and Indian War looming, the need for cooperation was urgent, especially for colonies likely to come under attack or invasion.

Prior to the Albany Congress, a number of intellectuals and government officials had formulated and published several tentative plans for centralizing the colonial governments of North America. Imperial officials saw the advantages of bringing the colonies under closer authority and supervision, while colonists saw the need to organize and defend common interests. One figure of emerging prominence among this group of intellectuals was Pennsylvanian Benjamin Franklin. Earlier, Franklin had written to friends and colleagues proposing a plan of voluntary union for the colonies. Upon hearing of the Albany Congress, his newspaper, *The Pennsylvania Gazette*, published the political cartoon "Join or Die," which illustrated the importance of union by comparing the colonies to pieces of a snake's body. The Pennsylvania government appointed Franklin as a commissioner to the Congress, and on his way, Franklin wrote to several New York commissioners outlining 'short hints towards a scheme for uniting the Northern Colonies' by means of an act of the British Parliament.

The Albany Congress began on June 19, 1754, and the commissioners voted unanimously to discuss the possibility of union on June 24. The union committee submitted a draft of the plan on June 28, and commissioners debated aspects of it until they adopted a final version on July 10.

Although only seven colonies sent commissioners, the plan proposed the union of all the British colonies except for Georgia and Delaware. The colonial governments were to select members of a "Grand Council," while the British Government would appoint a "president General." Together, these two branches of the unified government would regulate colonial-Indian relations and also resolve territorial disputes between the colonies. Acknowledging the tendency of royal colonial governors to override colonial legislatures and pursue unpopular policies, the Albany Plan gave the Grand Council greater

293

relative authority. The plan also allowed the new government to levy taxes for its own support.

Despite the support of many colonial leaders, the plan, as formulated at Albany, did not become a reality. Colonial governments, sensing that it would curb their own authority and territorial rights, either rejected the plan or chose not to act on it at all. The British Government had already dispatched General Edward Braddock as military commander in chief along with two commissioners to handle Indian relations and believed that directives from London would suffice in the management of colonial affairs.

The Albany Plan was not conceived out of a desire to secure independence from Great Britain. Many colonial commissioners actually wished to increase imperial authority in the colonies. Its framers saw it instead as a means to reform colonial-imperial relations and to recognize that the colonies collectively shared certain common interests. However, the colonial governments' own fears of losing power, territory, and commerce, both to other colonies and to the British Parliament, ensured the Albany Plan's failure.

Despite the failure of the Albany Plan, it served as a model for future attempts at union: it attempted to establish the division between the executive and legislative branches of government while establishing a common governmental authority to deal with external relations. More importantly, it conceived of the colonies of mainland North America as a collective unit, separate not only from the mother country but also from the other British colonies in the West Indies and elsewhere.

Articles of Confederation, 1777–1781

The Articles of Confederation served as the written document that established the functions of the national government of the United States after it declared independence from Great Britain. It established a weak central government that mostly, but not entirely, prevented the individual states from conducting their own foreign diplomacy.

The Articles of Confederation

The Albany Plan , an earlier pre-independence attempt at joining the colonies into a larger union, had failed in part because the individual colonies were concerned about losing power to another central institution. As the American Revolution gained momentum, however, many political leaders saw the advantages of a centralized government that could coordinate the Revolutionary War. In June of 1775, the New York Provincial Congress sent a plan of union to the Continental Congress, which, like the Albany Plan, continued to recognize the authority of the British Crown.

Some Continental Congress delegates had also informally discussed plans for a more permanent union than the Continental Congress, whose status was temporary. Benjamin Franklin had drawn up a plan for "Articles of Confederation and Perpetual Union." While some delegates, such as Thomas Jefferson, supported Franklin's proposal, many others were strongly opposed. Franklin introduced his plan before Congress on July 21 but stated that it should be viewed as a draft for when Congress was interested in reaching a more formal proposal. Congress tabled the plan.

Following the Declaration of Independence, the members of the Continental Congress realized it would be necessary to set up a national government. Congress began to discuss the form this government would take on July 22, disagreeing on a number of issues, including whether representation and voting would be proportional or state-by-state. The disagreements delayed final discussions of confederation until October of 1777. By then, the British capture of Philadelphia had made the issue more urgent. Delegates finally formulated the Articles of Confederation, in which they agreed to state-by-state voting and proportional state tax burdens based on land values, though they left the issue of state claims to western lands unresolved. Congress sent the Articles to the states for ratification at the end of November. Most delegates realized that the Articles were a flawed compromise but believed that it was better than the absence of a formal national government.

On December 16, 1777, Virginia was the first state to ratify. Other states ratified during the early months of 1778. When Congress reconvened in June of 1778, the delegates learned that Maryland, Delaware, and New Jersey refused to ratify the Articles. The Articles required unanimous approval from the states. These smaller states wanted other states to relinquish their western land claims before they would ratify the Articles. New Jersey and Delaware eventually agreed to the conditions of the Articles, with New Jersey ratifying on Nov 20, 1778, and Delaware on Feb 1, 1779. This left Maryland as the last remaining holdout.

Irked by Maryland's recalcitrance, several other state governments passed resolutions endorsing the formation of a national government without the state of Maryland, but other politicians, such as Congressman Thomas Burke of North Carolina, persuaded their governments to refrain from doing so, arguing that without unanimous approval of the new Confederation, the new country would remain weak, divided, and open to future foreign intervention and manipulation.

Meanwhile, in 1780, British forces began to conduct raids on Maryland communities in the Chesapeake Bay. Alarmed, the state government wrote to the French minister Anne-César De la Luzerne asking for French naval assistance. Luzerne wrote back, urging the government of Maryland to ratify the Articles of Confederation. Marylanders were given further incentive to ratify when Virginia agreed to relinquish its western land claims, and so the Maryland legislature ratified the Articles of Confederation on March 1, 1781.

French minister Anne-César De la Luzerne

The Continental Congress voted on Jan 10, 1781, to establish a Department of Foreign Affairs; on Aug 10 of that year, it elected Robert R. Livingston as Secretary of Foreign Affairs. The Secretary's duties involved corresponding with U.S. representatives abroad and with ministers of foreign powers. The Secretary was also charged with transmitting Congress' instructions to U.S. agents abroad and was authorized to attend sessions of Congress. A further Act of Feb 22, 1782, allowed the Secretary to ask and respond to questions during sessions of the Continental Congress.

The Articles created a sovereign national government and, as such, limited the rights of the states to conduct their own diplomacy and foreign policy. However, this proved difficult to enforce, as the national government could not prevent the state of Georgia from pursuing its own independent policy regarding Spanish Florida, attempting to occupy disputed territories and threatening war if Spanish officials did not work to curb Indian attacks or refrain from harboring escaped slaves. Nor could the Confederation government prevent the landing of convicts that the British Government continued to export to its former colonies. In addition, the Articles did not allow Congress sufficient authority to enforce provisions of the 1783 <u>Treaty of Paris</u> that allowed British creditors to sue debtors for pre-Revolutionary debts, an unpopular clause that many state governments chose to ignore. Consequently, British forces continued to occupy forts in the Great Lakes region. These problems, combined with the Confederation government's ineffectual response to the Shays' Rebellion in Massachusetts, convinced national leaders that a more powerful central government was necessary. This led to the Constitutional Convention that formulated the current Constitution of the United States.

Benjamin Franklin – A larger-than-life colonial patriot who had Native Influence.

Those who support the theory that the First Peoples influenced the drafting of the founding documents point to the words of founders such as Benjamin Franklin, who in 1751 wrote to his printer colleague James Parker that "It would be a strange thing if Six Nations of ignorant savages should be capable of forming a scheme for such a union, and be able to execute it in such a manner as that it has subsisted ages and appears indissoluble; and yet that a like union should be impracticable for ten or a dozen English colonies." Native American Studies Professor Bruce Johansen and American Studies Professor Donald Grinde, among others, argue that American colonists, in Johansen's words, "drew freely on the image of the American Indian as an exemplar of the spirit of liberty they so cherished." These scholars argue that the framers of American governments understood and admired Native American government structures, and they borrowed certain indigenous concepts for their own governments.

Was the Iroquois Great Law of Peace the Source of the U.S. Constitution?

By: Patrick J. Kiger—I have made many attempts to contact this person that I want to give excerpt credit. No response.

Representatives from various Native American tribes: from left to right, an Iroquois, an Assiniboine, a Crow, a Pawnee, an Assiniboine in gala dress, a Dakota or Sioux warrior, and a Dakota or Sioux woman. (Original artwork engraved by JJ Crew after a drawing by A Huttula.) HULTON ARCHIVE/GETTY IMAGES

In 1744, colonial leaders from Pennsylvania, Virginia, and Maryland met with a delegation from what, at the time, was one of the great powers on the North American continent. It was a confederation of Native American nations who called themselves the Haudenosaunee, though we're more familiar with them by their French name, the Iroquois. As recounted in **James Wilson's** book "The Earth Shall Weep: A History of Native America," the native leader Canassatego expressed frustration at the colonists' quarreling with one another.

"We heartily recommend Union and a good agreement between you, our brethren," he admonished the colonists. He advised that they follow the example of the Iroquois, who had established a well-organized system of self-government, codified in the Great Law of Peace, with both a central council and checks and balances that protected individual freedoms. "We are a powerful confederacy, and by observing the same methods our wise forefathers have taken, you will acquire fresh strength and power."

Among those in attendance was **Benjamin Franklin**, who, in Wilson's account, took careful notes and later used some of the Iroquois' ideas about government a decade later in a proposal for a confederation of the American colonies. If "ignorant savages" could form such an effective union, Franklin wrote in a 1751 letter, the "English colonies" should be able to do the same. The Albany Plan championed by Franklin never came to fruition, but the notion of the colonies cooperating and governing themselves was a big step toward what eventually became the United States of America.

Over the years, some have argued that we ought to give the Iroquois credit for inspiring the birth of American democracy and even have suggested that the U.S. Constitution and the system of self-government that it created actually was based upon the Iroquois Great Law.

Author comment: While very similar, the Iroquois Constitution differed quite a bit from the finished Constitution of the United Colonies, especially in the treatment of women. I do agree that a good bit of suggestive materials was used. I particularly refer to the tree example and the arrow suggestion, which we incorporated, and the eagle representing the directions of the tree. Another that I like is having thick skin.

If you poke around the internet or social media long enough, you may even find the meme depicted in this 2014 PolitiFact article, which claims that the U.S. Constitution "owes its notion of democracy to the Iroquois Tribes, including freedom of religion, freedom of speech, and separation of powers in government." The big difference, the meme notes, is that, unlike the Founding Fathers, the Iroquois didn't disenfranchise nonwhites and women.

The point about women is clearly true. Women are mentioned throughout the Great Law, and in the Iroquois system of government, they had the power to select chiefs and veto wars. In this 2016 Washington Post essay, journalist Jessica Nordell writes that 19th-century American feminists such as Elizabeth Cady Stanton, who had Iroquois neighbors in upstate New York, were inspired by their notion of gender equality.

Congress even passed a resolution in 1988, acknowledging the Iroquois contribution to American democracy and noting that "the original framers of the Constitution, including, most notably, **George Washington** and **Benjamin Franklin**, are known to have greatly admired the concepts of the Six Nations of the Iroquois Confederacy." The resolution also noted that "the confederation of the original Thirteen Colonies into one republic was influenced by the political system developed by the Iroquois Confederacy as were many of the democratic principles which were incorporated into the Constitution itself."

Nevertheless, the consensus among historians seems to be that there's no compelling evidence that the Founding Fathers directly imitated the Iroquois Great Law when they wrote the U.S. Constitution. As PolitiFact details, the Iroquois system had some significant differences from the political system that the former colonists created. For one, the Iroquois had hereditary officeholders, something that more resembled the English system that the Americans were rebelling against.

"There are lots of significant and fascinating ways in which one can trace the interactions between indigenous and settler populations," Stanford University history and political science professor **Jack Rakove**, author of the 2017 book "A Politician Thinking: The Creative Mind of James Madison," writes in an email. "But the transmission of political ideas — including ideas about democracy — is not one of them. The basic fact is that the colonists were direct heirs to an extremely rich body of political practices and ideas derived from English history, and especially from the great controversies of the 17th-century Stuart era. There just is not much, if anything, that native forms of political organization could have added to that."

Charles C. Mann, author of the 2006 book "1491: New Revelations of the Americas Before Columbus," contends that even if the

Constitution wasn't actually modeled on the Great Law, the Iroquois still exerted an influence upon the development of American democracy.

"The Great Law codified something pretty fundamental to Haudenosaunee culture, which was that people are autonomous individuals with the right to decide their own lives and that the authority of the ruler over them was limited," Mann emails. "This is a really important part of U.S. political culture to this day."

"I suspect that the Great Law did not inspire the Constitution, but that Haudenosaunee culture, of which the Great Law is one example, was influential to what became U.S. culture in the same way that, say, African-American teenagers in Queens are influenced by Asian-American teenagers (viz, the Wu-Tang Clan). The colonial Americas were a much more mixed place than we are often taught in school, so this influence is, to me, not surprising."

Learn more about the Iroquois Great Law of Peace in "The Great Law and the Longhouse: A Political History of the Iroquois Confederacy" by William N. Fenton. HowStuffWorks picks related titles based on books we think you'll like. Should you choose to buy one, we'll receive a portion of the sale.

Now That's Interesting

The Great Law of Peace, which originally was an oral document, is still recited aloud at a Six Nations ceremony held every year.

The Native American Government That Helped Inspire the US Constitution

The constitutional framers may have viewed Indigenous people of the Iroquois Confederacy as inferior, but that didn't stop them from admiring their federalist principles.

BECKY LITTLE

UPDATED: JULY 12, 2023 | ORIGINAL: NOVEMBER 10, 2020

History Shorts: Who Wrote the U.S. Constitution?

"You had the Cherokee chiefs having dinner with [Thomas] Jefferson's father in Williamsburg, and then in the northern area, of course, you had this Philadelphia interaction with the Delaware and the Iroquois," says Kirke Kickingbird, a lawyer, member of the Kiowa Tribe and coauthor with Lynn Kickingbird of *Indians and the United States Constitution: A Forgotten Legacy*.

Since the U.S. had trade and diplomatic relationships with Native governments, Kickingbird says, thinking the constitutional framers weren't familiar with them is like saying, "Gosh, I didn't know the Germans and the French knew each other."

Similarities and Differences Between the Iroquois Confederacy and the US Constitution

The Iroquois Confederacy was in no way an exact model for the U.S. Constitution. However, it provided something that Locke and Montesquieu couldn't: a real-life example of some of the political concepts the framers were interested in adopting in the U.S.

The Iroquois Confederacy dates back several centuries to when the Great Peacemaker founded it by uniting five nations: the Mohawks, the Onondaga, the Cayuga, the Oneida, and the Seneca. In around 1722, the Tuscarora nation joined the Iroquois, also known as the

Haudenosaunee. Together, these six nations formed a multi-state government while maintaining their own individual governance.

HIAWATHA IS CREDITED IN NATIVE AMERICAN TRADI-TION AS THE FOUNDER OF THE IROQUOIS CONFEDER-ACY.

This stacked-government model influenced constitutional framers' thinking, says <u>Donald A. Grinde, Jr.</u>, a professor of transnational studies at the University of Buffalo, member of the Yamasee nation and co-author with Bruce E. Johansen of <u>*Exemplar of Liberty: Native America and the Evolution of Democracy*</u>.

The constitutional framers "cite the Iroquois and other Native governments as examples of [federalism]," he says. "Marriage and divorce are taken care of right in the village; it's not a thing that the national government or the chiefs have to do with. Each tribe might have its own issues, but the Iroquois Confederacy is about…unification through mutual defense, and it conducts foreign affairs."

The chiefs of the six nations were hereditary rulers, something the framers wanted to avoid, given their grievances with Britain's <u>King George III</u>. Still, the framers "did seek to borrow aspects of Iroquois government that enabled them to assert the people's sovereignty over vast geographic expanses since they found no governments in Europe with these characteristics," <u>Grinde and Johansen write</u> in *Exemplar of Liberty.*

Congress Formally Recognizes Iroquois Influence

The fact that many of the framers looked to Native governments for inspiration didn't stop them from viewing Native people as inferior. This disconnect is evident in a <u>1751 letter</u> from <u>Benjamin Franklin</u> describing the need for the 13 colonies to form a "voluntary Union" similar to that of the Iroquois Confederacy:

Savages should not be capable of forming a Scheme for such a document: "It would be a very strange thing if six Nations of ignorant Union, and be able to execute it in such a manner, as that it has subsisted Ages, and appears indissoluble; and yet that a like Union should be impracticable for ten or a Dozen English Colonies, to whom it is more necessary, and must be more advantageous; and who cannot be supposed to want an equal Understanding of their Interests."

The United States' bias and violence against Native Americans may have helped obscure the framers' interest in their governments. However, public awareness of this connection increased around the 1987 bicentennial, marking the 200th anniversary of the Constitution.

"Oren Lyons, who was a Faith keeper for the Iroquois Confederacy, went to the Senate Select Committee on Indian Affairs and broached this subject," Grinde says. "And then I went down to Washington and testified before the Senate Select Committee on Indian Affairs."

This motivated the committee's chair, Daniel Inouye of Hawaii, to help Congress pass a <u>1988 resolution</u> formally acknowledging the influence of the Iroquois Confederacy on the U.S. Constitution. In addition to this recognition, the resolution reaffirmed "the continuing government-to-government relationship between Indian tribes and the United States established in the Constitution"—an acknowledgment of the legitimacy and sovereignty of Native nations and their governments.

Benjamin Franklin was a critical "bigger than life" character in the formation of our country. I sit and read his tumultuous history in wonderment but feel compelled to write about a man who gave us a "foot in the door" in the construct of our government, whether it be in England, France, in the colonies, with the Iroquois and his pulling together whatever needed to be done to push/pull the colonies to a constitution. Of all the players in our early colonial existence, I do not believe there is another whom I could eulogize personally, in this writing, in early history, for his credentials and accomplishments.

Benjamin Franklin

Benjamin Franklin was an American founding father, consummate statesperson, diplomat, inventor, writer, and newspaperman who pioneered many civic institutions in the American colonies, such as the postal service, volunteer fire department, and libraries. Franklin believed in the virtues of contributing to the community and being a model of an upstanding citizen through one's actions. He's famous for having edited Thomas Jefferson's first draft of the "Declaration of Independence," and his kite experiment that proved lightning is electricity. He was mostly self-educated and received many honorary degrees throughout his lifetime.[28]

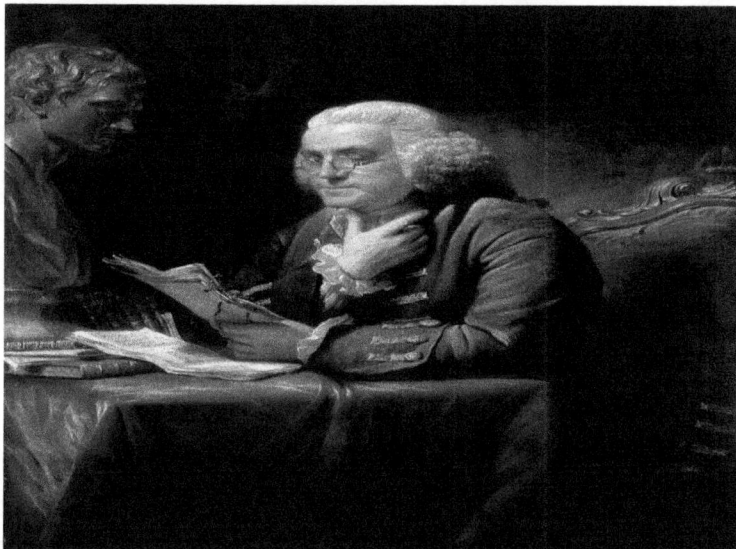

Benjamin Franklin was a learned man of papers. Wikimedia Commons.

Benjamin Franklin: Biography

On January 17, 1706, Benjamin Franklin was born in Boston, Massachusetts, to Josiah Franklin and Abiah Folger. Benjamin Franklin was their tenth child and last son to Josiah, who fathered over a dozen children. As a child, he worked at his father's soap shop and finished his formal schooling at age ten. Young Franklin was an avid reader and writer. From an early age, Benjamin Franklin proved himself a resourceful and capable learner.

At his father Josiah Franklin's urging, he apprenticed at his older brother James' print shop. Franklin wanted to submit writing for his

---

[28] https://www.studysmarter.co.uk/explanations/english-literature/essayists/benjamin-franklin/#:~:text=Despite%20the%20informative%20premise%2C%20Benjamin,of%20satirical%20and%20serious%20information.

brother's newspaper but James declined, feeling the young Benjamin Franklin was too young to work as a columnist. Franklin persisted anyway and wrote a series of letters under the pseudonym Mrs. Silence Dogood. The letters were popular in his brother's latest paper, the *New England Courant,* and were openly discussed in town. When his brother learned the truth, their relationship soured, and Franklin ran away to Philadelphia at age seventeen.

In Philadelphia, Benjamin Franklin met Governor Sir William Keith, who offered to send him to England to buy printing equipment. Keith ultimately didn't follow through on his offer, and the teenage Franklin found work as a typesetter in London. After a couple of years of working and saving money, he returned to Philadelphia in 1726. In 1729, Franklin started a printing business with a friend and bought the paper *The Pennsylvania Gazette.* Franklin regularly submitted his own column, establishing his reputation as a witty and knowledgeable intellectual, frequently commenting wryly on local social movements and events. It became one of the most popular newspapers in the British American colonies.

On September 1, 1730, Franklin married Deborah Read. They had two children, and additionally, Franklin recognized his **illegitimate** son William, and he raised him with the rest of his family.

Illegitimate child - a child born to parents who are not married.

Franklin continued to publish under different pseudonyms. His most popular effort was *Poor Richard's Almanac* (1732-1758) under his pseudonym Richard Saunders.

An almanac is a yearly publication that focuses on weather, astronomy statistics, and data, along with important dates and a variety of information like maps, forecasts, and proverbs. Despite the informative premise, Benjamin Franklin understood that most people read Almanacs for entertainment. His character and created author, Richard Saunders, antagonized almanac authorship while providing a mix of satirical and serious information.

Famous adages of Franklin's are still in use today, such as "A fish and a visitor stink in three days." Almanac authors usually had a local following and no competition. As Saunders, he jokingly predicted the death of **Titan** Lead, an established almanac author, concluding that he was now justified in filling the void left behind. Titan Leeds took the bait and publicly commented on the shenanigans of Franklin's alter ego, only to help propel the popularity of *Poor Richard's Almanac,* selling over 10,000 copies a year.

The rivalry would continue posthumously for Leeds. In the following edition, Saunders included a letter from Leeds's ghost affirming his correct prediction.

Benjamin Franklin had a prolific career and was heavily invested in his community. His status as a newspaperman gave him far-reaching access and influence. He was a proponent of public services and was known for the founding of the first of many organizations that are now commonplace. Franklin started the Library company in 1731, which became the colonies' first library. Investors bought books, and customers could subscribe to borrow books at a fraction of the cost to buy one. In 1736, he assisted with the Union Fire Company, the first volunteer fire department in Philadelphia. In 1743, he organized the American Philosophical Society, which promoted scientific research and public education. In 1740, he founded the University of Pennsylvania.

Benjamin Franklin was recognized for his civic engagement and public intellectualism, earning several honorary degrees. In 1753, Harvard and Yale separately awarded him a Master of Arts degree. In 1756, he received a Master of Arts degree from the College of William and Mary. In 1762, Oxford University of England awarded him an honorary doctorate.

Facts About Benjamin Franklin's Death and Legacy

On April 17, 1790, Benjamin Franklin died from complications of **pleurisy** at his home in Philadelphia.

Pleurisy - inflammation of the lungs

Despite not going to church, Franklin was a major proponent of the Puritan virtues of good character and hard work. Throughout his books, newspapers, and columns, Franklin emphasized the importance of these virtues. So much so that they are now very much considered American traits. Many adages from his *Poor Richard's Almanac* are still in use today.

While Benjamin Franklin did own a few slaves throughout his lifetime, he ultimately freed them, renounced slavery, and became an early abolitionist.

Benjamin Franklin is the only person to have signed four crucial American documents: the "Declaration of Independence" in 1776, the Treaty of Alliance with France in 1778, the Treaty of Paris in 1783, and the U.S. Constitution in 1787. Franklin is considered one of the Founding Fathers, along with George Washington. Franklin's likeness, since 1928, has adorned American $100 bills, among other issued money.

"It's All About the Benjamins" is a famous rap song by Puff Daddy because of the iconic image of Benjamin Franklin. Wikimedia Commons.

Benjamin Franklin: Political Career

Benjamin Franklin's success as a newspaper editor and printer built his reputation in the Philadelphia community. As his wealth grew, so did his interest in confronting local power. Pennsylvania was a **proprietary colony**. The Penn family were the sole proprietors and selected their government officials. The Pennsylvania Assembly, a body of elected officials, could be easily overturned by the Penn family's influence. The assembly elected Benjamin Franklin as a representative and sent him to England. He ultimately failed to reduce the power of the Penn family but built his reputation as a champion of American interests. He was sent back to England to protest the Stamp Act. The Stamp Act sought to pay for Britain's wars by forcing colonists to pay higher stamp prices on various documents. He testified before the House of Commons, where the British parliament scrutinizes the government. While he was unable to prevent the passage of the Stamp Act initially, his testimony, among others, later persuaded the British parliament to repeal the act

Proprietary colony - indirect, undemocratic rule through partition and charters granted by another authority.

In 1773, Benjamin Franklin wrote a series of pro-American satirical essays. His most famous was "Rules by Which a Great Empire May Be Reduced to a Small One," in which he created a fictional address to the ruler. The rules were thinly disguised grievances of the American colonies to the British Crown. In short, the British Empire would lose its American colonies if it persisted in taxes and regulations without the colonists' consent. It was well-received and further propelled Franklin into national politics. His contemporaries noted he would be an ideal example to represent American colonies' interests.

In July 1775, Benjamin Franklin was elected to draft the "Declaration of Independence" barely a month after having returned to America from England. While Thomas Jefferson wrote the first draft, Benjamin Franklin, with his decades of editorial experience, made key changes to the document.

On July 26, 1775, the Second Continental Congress established the United States Post Office and elected Benjamin Franklin as the first United States postmaster general. Franklin had served as postmaster in Philadelphia for decades. He instituted reforms and raised more funding to increase the network and reliability of the post office, resulting in unprecedented weekly mail delivery.

While abroad, Benjamin Franklin used London as a base to travel around Europe. He took trips to Scotland, Ireland, Germany, and France. His reputation preceded him, so he was easily introduced into influential social circles of power. As an ambassador to France, he secured a military alliance in 1778. In 1783, he helped form the terms for ending the American War for Independence from Great Britain in the Treaty of Paris.

When he returned to America, he was celebrated as a champion of American independence.

Benjamin Franklin: Inventions Benjamín

Franklin is known for creating many inventions. In accordance with his philosophy of civic duty and providing public goods, he did not patent any of his inventions. Many are still in use today and remain relatively unchanged.

Lightning Rod

Benjamin Franklin had previously done experiments with electricity and theorized that lightning was electricity. He proved his theory right with his famed kite experiment to catch an ambient electrical charge. Lightning was an unmitigated threat in Franklin's time, frequently destroying buildings, with townspeople at a complete loss in fighting the hazard. Franklin learned one could use a rod of iron positioned on the highest point of a building to attract lightning, grounded by a copper wire leading to the ground, to avoid catching fire.

In colonial America, a person heavily relied on wood to build their home and a fireplace to heat them. Fireplaces are not very energy efficient or effective, as most of the heat is lost through the chimney. The Franklin stove is essentially an iron container that can radiate heat from all directions, can be placed within the home for more effective heating, and safely keeps the fire from spreading. Furthermore, one can control the rate of burning by controlling the airflow.

Franklin stoves are still common today. Wikimedia Commons. Bifocals

To see off into the distance and up close, one had to have a pair of glasses for each view. Benjamin Franklin was the first to merge the two glasses into one pair—then called "double spectacles." Bifocal glasses have lenses with two parts. The upper portion allows the user to see farther distances, while the lower part is for objects close up, such as reading, when one typically glances downward.

Franklin literally merged two sets of lenses, as seen by the line. Nowadays, the line on bifocals is invisible to the naked eye. Wikimedia Commons.

Pro & Con List

While it's possible that such a decision-making tool existed before Franklin, he was the first known published example.[3] He divided a piece of paper into two columns. One considers the possible positive and negative impacts of a particular decision on each side.

Urinary Catheter

Previously, catheters were inflexible, rigid metal tubes that were painful to insert into the urethra. His brother frequently had to use one, and Franklin wanted to lessen his discomfort. Franklin had the insertion tube modified by a silversmith for more flexibility and comfort.

Benjamin Franklin's Famous Quotes

Guests, like fish, begin to smell after three days."

(Poor Richard's Almanack)

In Benjamin Franklin's time, proverbs and adages were sources of wisdom. People felt that if someone had a saying for every situation, they were wise. While Franklin toyed with the notion of an Almanac as a source of wisdom, he also delighted in using them as a source of humor.

Well done is better than well said."

Poor Richard's Almanack speaks for itself

Benjamin Franklin liked to take action and believed in civic duty. Even though he spent much of his career expressing his thoughts through his newspaper and books, he was quite active in his civic duty. The founder of many institutions, community service, was a virtue and value he sought to propagate through his words and actions.

We must, indeed, all hang together or, most assuredly, we shall all hang separately."

(Franklin comment at the signing of the "Declaration of Independence")

Later in life, Benjamin Franklin became very involved in the national politics of the British American colonies. He understood the direction that momentum was moving, and believed it almost inevitable for the colonies to break away from British rule. He figured it was better that they all "hang" together instead of separately. Hanging was the punishment for treason under the British Crown, and technically, the signing of the "Declaration of Independence" was an act of treason under British rule.

Sunday, January 17, 1706, Benjamin Franklin was born in the City of Boston. His parents were Josiah Franklin and Abiah Folger.

In 1718, he started his career in printing, starting as an apprentice at age 12. In 1722, he published his first letter in the New England Courant under the pen name of "Silence Dogood," a person of strong opinions. He took over the paper in 1723. He moved to Philadelphia in 1724 and common law, married Deborah Reed, and became a printer with Samuel Keimer.

Pennsylvania Governor William Keith encouraged Franklin to go to England to purchase printing equipment, but they could not get a loan and were stranded in London. He got a job with Samuel Palmer and John Watts and printed his first pamphlet, "A Dissertation on Liberty and Necessity, Pleasure and Pain; he returned to the colonies and worked as a shopkeeper and printer with Samuel Keimer.

In Philadelphia, Franklin founded the Junto Club, a group of young men who met on Friday evenings to discuss intellectual, personal, business, and community topics. The Junto Club lasted until 1765. Established the first library through donated books.

1728-1730 Franklin and Hugh Meredith opened their own printing shop and purchased the Pennsylvania Gazette from former employer Samuel Keimer. The Gazette became one of the most prominent publications in Colonial America. In 1730 they were elected the official government printer for Pennsylvania. Also, in 1730, Franklin bought Meredith's share in the printing shop and became the sole owner. In 1731, he published "Apology for Printers," defending freedom of the press. He also became a Freemason this year. Also entered a partnership with Thomas Whitmarsh in South Carolina. Franklin provided printing equipment in return for one-third of the profits over six years, creating the first commercial franchise.

1732 - Benjamin Franklin and Deborah Read have their first child, Francis Folger Franklin. Also in this year, he published the first edition of Poor Richard's Almanack under the pseudonym "Richard Saunders." It became an instant bestseller in the colonies.

1736 - Franklin was appointed clerk of the Pennsylvania Assembly.

Helped organize the Union Fire Company of Philadelphia, which trained and organized firemen.

1737 - Appointed Postmaster of Philadelphia, his service continued until 1753.

1740 - Became the official printer for New Jersey.

1741 - Advertised his first model of the Pennsylvania fireplace for sale, also known as the Franklin Stove. He declined on principle to take a patent for the sole right to sell it. Started electrical experiments after receiving an electric tube from Peter Collision.

1747 - Helped organize a volunteer militia.

1749 - Wrote and published pamphlet "Proposals Relating to the Education of Youth in Pennsylvania." He also helped organize the Academy of Philadelphia, which later became the University of Pennsylvania. Franklin, along with Dr. Thomas Bond, founded Pennsylvania Hospital, the nation's first hospital, to care for the "sick poor and insane of Philadelphia."

1752 - Conducted kite experiments by flying a kite in a thunderstorm, proving that lightning is electrical. He published how to conduct the experiment in the Pennsylvania Gazette.

1753 - Appointed joint Deputy Postmaster General of the Colonies. Eventually, postal routes for the colonies. 1775 - Elected as Postmaster General of the Colonies

1754 - To make a point about their own defense and colonial unity with the British against the French and Indians, Franklin printed his famous cartoon "Join, or Die" in the Pennsylvania Gazette. A decade later, the cartoon would mean colonial unity against the British. Attended the Albany Congress as a representative of Pennsylvania

1757

Franklin was elected to go to England as a colonial agent.

1762

Awarded an honorary degree of Doctor of Law from Oxford University.

Invented the glass armonica. Mozart and Beethoven later composed for it. The **armonica** made quite a hit, particularly in Germany. Mozart was introduced to it by Franz Mesmer, who used his to 'mesmerize' his patients, and later Mozart wrote two works for it (a solo **armonica** piece and a larger quintet for **armonica**...

1764

Franklin lost his seat in the <u>Pennsylvania Assembly</u>.

Returned to London as a colonial agent.

1765

<u>The Stamp Act</u> was passed by the House of Commons.

<u>Charted the Gulf Stream</u>.

1769

The American Philosophical Society elected Franklin as its president. He was elected every year until his death.

1775

Elected as Pennsylvania delegate to the Second Continental Congress.

King George III declared the American colonies in rebellion.

1776

Franklin was appointed as part of the committee of 5 who drafted the <u>Declaration of Independence</u>.

Appointed to the French Court as one of the commissioners of the Continental Congress.

1778

Negotiated <u>Treaty of Alliance with France</u>. France declared war on Great Britain.

1783

<u>John Adams</u>, John Jay, and Benjamin Franklin signed the Treaty of Paris, which put an end to the war between the colonies and Great Britain.

1784

Franklin wrote the essay "An Economical Project for Diminishing the Cost of Light," proposing the innovative concept of Daylight Savings Time.

1785

Franklin described his invention of <u>bifocal glasses</u>.

Returned to the United States after 18 of years of service in Europe.

Elected <u>President of the Pennsylvania Executive Council.</u>

1786

Invented instrument for taking books down from a library shelf.

1787

Signed the <u>United States Constitution.</u>

1788

Franklin wrote his will, leaving most of his estate to his daughter Sarah.

1789

Elected president of the Pennsylvania Society for Promoting the Abolition of Slavery.

Submitted the first antislavery petition before the U.S. Congress.

1790

April 17 – Franklin <u>died at age 84</u>. He is buried in <u>Christ Church burial ground in Philadelphia</u>.

How the Iroquois Great Law of Peace Shaped U.S. Democracy

This revelation of the Iroquois Confederation and its history will lead us to an amazing series of events that eventually lead us to our infant nation. Please bear with the history lesson my revealing; it actually goes along with my honoring the indigenous natives of our land and their freely given contributions in many critical areas.

Authors note: Before you read the passages below, it might be interesting to know with a fully function "Great Law" society, the Iroquois today see themselves as a sovereign nation, not just an ethnic group within our nation. Further recognition of their status is forefront of their sovereign status. As examples can attest, they also, with the United States, declared war on Germany in 1917. Another instance they attended the groundbreaking for the United Nations in 1949. They have inserted themselves in land issues, the Keneza Dam project, the St. Lawrence Seaway, the Niagara Power Plant, land rights, toxic waste issues, air pollution of nearby plants, and gambling corruption of their people seeking personal gain. All within their Constitution as a sovereign nation.

Iroquois athletes use Iroquois passports as they travel around the world.

Terri Hanson's honorarium statement

The author of the excerpted materials I will be presenting is wholly from Terri Hanson. Terri is deceased as of 2018. Terri was a native independent journalist writing for the Indian Country Today, Yes! Magazine, The Revelator, Pacific Standard, VICE, Earth Island Journal, and others. She is missed by her people.

Overview of the Iroquois Confederacy

The Iroquois Confederacy is an association of related tribes, a society of approximately 5,500 people when found by white explorers at the beginning of the seventeenth century. Currently, its census is over 49,000 living in the United States. Additionally, 5,000 live in Canada. They are a people who will embrace technology but maintain their traditional identity. They have been honored by the US government which insured their identity. This fact will be revealed later in this chapter and will surprise you.

Its history started with five tribes forming the Iroquois Confederacy, or League as they define it. The tribes were the Mohawk, Oneida,

Onondaga, Cayuga, and Seneca. They called themselves Haudeno-saunee {pronounced "Hoo-dee-noh-SHAW-nee" or people of the longhouse, their living quarters housing up to 50 people. The bark covered; wooden frame houses were 50-150 feet long. They envisioned a longhouse some 300 miles long, with the Mohawk guarding the eastern door and the Seneca guarding the western end.

The Mohawk called themselves "people of the Flint country" and were known to be overpowering. The enemies of the Mohawk called them meaning "man-eaters." The Oneida name means "people of the standing stone," gained from the legend that when they moved, a large rock appeared to give them directions. The Onondaga, "people of the hills." The Cayuga is "where they land the boats." The Seneca are "the people of the big hill."

Not to be forgotten are the Algonquin living on both sides of the Iroquois corridor, but there is no evidence where they came from but continually warred with the Iroquois, in almost continual warfare. The other major tribe was the Cherokee, who shared linguistic commonality. The range in relation to the Iroquois is uncertain. **Author note**: I live in Tennessee, and I do know the Cherokee were in the Carolinas, Kentucky, Tennessee, Georgia, and Alabama. The Cherokee may have occupied other close states.

They found a functioning government in their own backyard. A well-constructed governing system most would not recognize as being viable but, in actuality, proved to be very valuable to the original framers in ways they never imagined. It was the *Iroquois Nation and its Constitution.*

Excerpts are from the original Kevin Wandrei article taken to extract the Constitution and key historical references relating to inter-governmental cooperation with the *Iroquois Nation.* My belief is that this is one of the most important sources of input towards our framers needs. It provided critical stability to the colonies that needed cohesion and a clear definition of the rule of law towards the concept of *"we the people."* I would say that this was truly "a Hands Across the Waters Event" totally unanticipated, save for good ole Ben

Franklins' efforts. Let's take a look at this remarkable example of "Who would have thought this was possible?

By Terri Hansen: Much has been said about the inspiration of the ancient Iroquois *"Great League of Peace"* in planting the seeds that led to the formation of the United States of America and its representative democracy.

Author Note: The colonies, prior to any confederation of the thirteen colonies, each acted independently, conducting trade with anyone they wanted. Trade was conducted with England, France, the Caribbean Island nations, the Dutch, and many others, including Native Americans. When it became time to combine the colonies/states into the 13 colonies, it became, as they say, "a sticky wicket," with each colony not wanting to give up what they had as income. In fact, there developed two groups of 6 colonies and one reluctant colony, Maryland, that had some sweet deals they did not want to lose, and getting them all together was becoming difficult. So difficult that the colonies actually wanted to split into two separate nations rather than melding together as 13 united colonies. Good ole Ben rose to the occasion and rang up the Iroquois Nation, and as far as I am concerned, the phenomenal magic occurred. Read below for the amazing actions that made them the thirteen colonies; it will amaze you to no end and make you think about what we did to the Native Americans later.

Iroquois Native American Confederation of The League of Nations

Last Updated by Terri Hansen on Dec 17, 2018 at 10:48 am

(A Tweet has been sent to Terri on 1/19/2020 for permission to excerpt her article) (She is Indigenous and lives in the backcountry, and is difficult to reach)

"The Great Peacemaker[4] brought peace to the five nations," explains Oren Lyons in a 1991 interview with Bill Moyers. Lyons is the faith

keeper of the Turtle Clan of the Seneca Nations and a member of both the Onondaga and Seneca nations of the Iroquois Confederacy.

At that time, the nations of the Iroquois had been enmeshed in continuous inter-tribal conflicts. The cost of the war was high and had weakened their societies. The Great Peacemaker and the wise *Hiawatha, chief of the Onondaga tribe*, contemplated how best to bring peace between the nations. They traveled to each of the five nations to share their ideas for peace.

The forming of the Iroquois government occurred after a council meeting was called for with the original five nations. An extremely important effort of the Great Peacemaker and Hiawatha, who visited each tribal council earlier to convince each of them to gather together in a joint council.

When in the tribal council, Hiawatha presented the Great Law of Peace. Eventually, this served to unite the five nations into a League of Nations, the Iroquois Confederacy and became the basis for the Iroquois Confederacy Constitution consisting of the Mohawks, Onondaga, Cayuga, Oneida, Seneca, and later the Tuscarora nation added in 1722.

Each nation was to maintain its own leadership, but all agreed that common causes would be decided in a Grand Council of Chiefs. "The concept was based on peace and consensus rather than fighting."

The Founding Fathers actually very closely studied *The Native American Iroquois Confederation*, known as the *Six Nations*, or Haudenosaunee, meaning *"peoples of the longhouse,"* actually founded in the year 1142 by the *Great Peace Master,* **Deganawida,** and acknowledged as the oldest participatory democracy on earth.

Much has been said about the inspiration of the ancient Iroquois "Great League of Peace" in planting the seeds that led to the formation of the United States of America and its representative democracy. Originally the Iroquois first met the European explorers encountering them in the early seventeenth century. This, obviously looking forward, would be an efficacious meeting for all.

Benjamin Franklin did not need to travel far afield in search of a durable and successfully practiced government. He actually met with delegates of the Six Nations in 1744, where he became inspired to copy the Iroquois and implement a federalist confederacy in the U.S. Constitution. When the Constitution was being drafted, delegates to the Constitutional Convention met with Iroquois representatives where they learned about how power comes from "we, the people" and how effective a union of the 13 American colonies could be.

In 1744, the *Onondaga leader Canassatego* gave a speech urging the contentious 13 colonies to unite, as the Iroquois had at the signing of the Treaty of Lancaster. This cultural exchange inspired the English colonist Benjamin Franklin to print Canassatego's speech.

"We heartily recommend Union and a good Agreement between you, our Brethren," Canassatego had said. "Never disagree, but preserve a strict Friendship for one another, and thereby you, as well as we, will become the stronger. Our wise Forefathers established Union and Amity between the Five Nations; this has made us formidable this has given us great Weight and Authority with our neighboring Nations. We are a powerful Confederacy, and by your observing the same Methods our wise Forefathers have taken, you will acquire fresh Strength and Power; therefore, whatever befalls you, never fall out one with another."

NOTE: Actually, in 1988, hundreds of years later, the U.S. Senate paid tribute with a resolution that said, "The confederation of the original 13 colonies into one republic was influenced by the political system developed by the *Iroquois Confederacy,* as were many of the democratic principles which were incorporated into the constitution itself."

The Great Seal of the United States ca. 1917 - 1919

Canassatego used a metaphor that many arrows cannot be broken as easily as one. This inspired the bundle of 13 arrows, representing the 13 colonies, held by an eagle in the Great Seal of the United States. This metaphor actually influences our Great Seal.

Great Seal of the United States

Attribute to American Heritage Education Foundation Inc. for the Seal to include the original wording and the arrows.

The Great Seal of the United States is used to authenticate certain documents issued by the federal government of the United States. The phrase is used both for the physical seal itself, which is kept by the United States Secretary of State, and more generally for the design impressed upon it. The Great Seal was first used in 1782.

Actual Comparisons of Iroquois and US Constitution Laws

Iroquois Confederacy and the Great Law of Peace	United States Constitution
Restricts members from holding more than one office in	Article I, Section 6, Clause 2, also known as the Ineligibility Clause or the Emoluments Clause, bars members of serving members of Congress from holding offices established by the federal government while also baring

Iroquois Confederacy and the Great Law of Peace	United States Constitution
the Confederacy.	members of the executive branch or judicial branch from serving in the U.S. House or Senate.
Outlines processes to remove leaders within the Confederacy	**Article II, Section 4** reads, "The President, Vice President, and all civil Officers of the United States shall be removed from Office on Impeachment for, and the conviction of, Treason, Bribery, or other High Crimes and Misdemeanors."
Designates two branches of the legislature with procedures for passing laws	**Article I, Section 1**, or the **Vesting Clauses**, read, "All legislative Powers herein granted shall be vested in a Congress of the United States, which shall consist of a Senate and House of Representatives." It goes on to outline their legislative powers.
Delineates, who has the power to declare war	**Article I, Section 8, Clause 11**, also known as the **War Powers Clause**, gives Congress the power "To declare War, grant Letters of Marque and Reprisal, and make Rules concerning Captures on Land and Water;"
Creates a balance of power between the Iroquois Confederacy and individual tribes	The differing duties assigned to the three branches of the U.S. Government: Legislative (Congress), Executive (President), and Judicial (Supreme Court) act to balance and separate power in government.

Franklin referenced the Iroquois model as he presented his Plan of Union[8] at the Albany Congress in 1754, attended by representatives of the Iroquois and the seven colonies. *He invited the Great Council members of the Iroquois to address the Continental Congress in 1776.*

The Native American model of governance was taken from the Iroquois Confederacy. Dictates that decisions that are made today should lead to sustainability and are, for the most part, organized by democratic principles that focus on the creation of strong kinship bonds that promote leadership in which honor is not earned by material gain but by service to others.

In my humble opinion, this alliance of the Iroquois and the 13 Colonies and further meetings at the Plan of Union at the Albany Congress in 1754 were attended by representatives of the Iroquois and the seven colonies. Then, his invitation of the Great Council members of the Iroquois to address the Continental Congress and our Constitution gave our country feet and a life.

Not mentioned in the above narrative is the important Treaty of Lancaster, which gave the colonists protection and solidified the alliance between the Iroquois League of Nations, and some of it appears to be sage advice.

Two weeks that changed the nation

Known as the Lancaster Treaty of 1744, the two-week meeting shaped our nation's history. Discussions in the courthouse were lively and included much rum drinking. In exchange for Indian land claims in Maryland and Virginia, the Indians bargained for gunpowder, shot, guns, blankets, clothing, and rum. Indian leaders made lengthy speeches, exchanged belts of wampum, applauded, and shouted, "Jo-Ha!" The treaty also created a strong alliance between the settlers and Indians, protecting Pennsylvania during the French and Indian War. In the spirit of cooperation, the Indians advised colonial leaders on how to create a better form of government modeled after the Iroquois League of Nations.

Visit –

lancasterhistory.org

Historic mural displayed at Lancaster County Convention Center

Albany Plan of Union

The *Albany Plan of Union* was a proposal made at the Albany Congress back in 1754 aimed at the formation of a strong union of the colonies under one single government and direction. The need was justified because of the necessity for defense against the threats and consequences posed by the infamous French and Indian War. The Franklin Plan was among the many plans presented by the different delegates who took part in the Albany Congress.

- Benjamin Franklin

The Albany Congress formed a committee tasked to carefully consider the different plans and proposals, finally settling on Franklin's proposal with modifications. The committee included Chief Justice Benjamin Chew, Isaac Norris, and Richard Peters. The general government will be administered by a President General fully supported by the Crown.

The proposal called for a Grand Council with members chosen by representatives coming from the colonial assemblies. As anticipated, there were many objections debated by the different sides. Difficulties presented were addressed, resolved, and were unanimous; Albany Congress delegates adopted the proposal. The approved plans were sent to the Colonial Assemblies and the British Board of Trade in London.

Looking to the Future

The Albany Plan had all the makings of remarkable things to come; it was noteworthy in most aspects. Franklin had anticipated many of the serious problems that would pose risks to a post-independence government. The issues that could derail national development would be finance, control of commerce activities, national defense, and dealing with the different Indian tribes. The plan had the perfect ingredients for a true union. Great ideas would be adopted in Philadelphia. It is worth noting that the plan was rejected by both sides. It was never acceptable. Most of the people, and the colonial assemblies in general, were thought to think backward and were suspicious of the idea of a central taxing authority. The British government was never in favor of a consolidation of added power. They were already aware of these strong-willed colonial assemblies and their absolute resolutions. The British government instead preferred that colonists should focus more on the French/Indian military campaign.

The Board of Trade never sought any official approval from the Crown. They instead proposed that the colonial governors and their councils should raise armies and build forts. They said money for these activities would come from the Treasury of Great Britain to be reimbursed through an Act of Parliament that would tax America, which would never happen. The plans' real implementation would not happen until American settlements finally declared their independence.

The Virginia Declaration of Rights June 12, 1776, adopted

July 1776

This declaration was incorporated into the Virginia State Constitution in 1830 as Article 1. It was "the basis and foundation of government" in Virginia and is legally in effect today. It was developed around May 20-26, 1776 was written by George Mason. Other articles were added to the committee by Thomas Ludwell Lee. James Madison proposed liberalizing the article on religious freedom. Patrick Henery persuaded the Convention to delete the section that would have prohibited "bill of attainder" arguing ordinary laws could be ineffective.

George Mason based his initial draft on the rights of citizens, as found in the English Bill of Rights of 1689 and the writings of John Locke. This Declaration can be considered the first Constitutional protection of individual civil rights in North America. It rejected the notion of privileged political classes or heredity offices found in the Parliament, and House of Lords found in the English Bill of Rights. The Declaration describes the separation of powers and the government as a servant of the people. It is unusual because it prescribes legal rights and moral principles on the operation of government.

By articles contained in the Declaration:

Authors note: You will find that these articles eventually made their way into our Federal Constitution.

- ➤ **Articles 1-3** address the subject of rights: "All men are by nature equally free and independent. This means acquiring and possessing property and obtaining happiness and safety. This can actually be found in the U.S. Declaration of Independence: "We hold these truths to be self-evident that all men are created equal, and are endowed by their creator with certain unalienable rights of Life, liberty and the pursuit of happiness."
- ➤ **Specifically, articles 2 & 3 engender that** "all power is vested in and consequently derived from the people and that whenever any government shall be found inadequate (abbreviated) has an indefeasible right to reform, or abolish it.

- ➤ **Article 4** relates to privileged political or heredity offices such as the House of Lords and those of peerage. From the community Or privileges Also addressed serves entitlement either exclusive or separate emoluments.
- ➤ **Articles 5 & 6** address the separation of powers of government pertaining to legislative, executive, and judicial. They actually have and clearly state once again that no public offices should be heredity-based, have fixed periods of office, and then return them to the populace
- ➤ Articles 7 through 16 proposed restrictions on the powers of government, declaring the government should not have the power of suspending or executing laws "without the consent of the representatives of the people".

  These articles deal with rights as they pertain to the accused and accuser and a speedy trial, baseless search and seizure, a trial by jury, freedom of religion, defense of a free state and a militia of the people, and against a standing army as avoided as dangerous to liberty. **Article 8** protects a person from "being deprived of his liberty, except by the Law of the Land." This article becomes a due process clause in our federal Bill of Rights. **Article 12** addresses the right to a free press and is actually a precursor to our First Amendment in the U.S. Constitution.

Author note: I view the Virginia Declaration as a strong document written by key members within the move to the freedom of our country. Many "rights" within the declaration found their way into our U.S. Constitution. I, a bit late, applaud their foresight and hard work in obviously referring to the ancient documents to develop a working document to support their populace through responsible government.

Authors note: I have taken the liberty of placing into this book the full unabridged texts of the <u>Articles of Confederation</u> and <u>The Declaration of Independence</u> as they exist in the Archives of our Nation. These documents do not deserve my interpretation.

Articles of Confederation

U.S. Department of State Archive January 20, 2009

Constitution of the United States.

Articles of Confederation, 1777-1781

The Articles of Confederation served as the written document that established the functions of the national government of the United States after it declared independence from Great Britain. It established a weak central government that mostly, but not entirely, prevented the individual states from conducting their own foreign diplomacy.

The Albany Plan, an earlier pre-independence attempt at joining the colonies into a larger union, had failed in part because the individual colonies were concerned about losing power to another central institution. However, as the American Revolution gained momentum, many political leaders saw the advantages of a centralized government that could coordinate the Revolutionary War. In June of 1775, the New York Provincial Congress sent a plan of union to the Continental Congress, which, like the Albany Plan, continued to recognize the authority of the British Crown.

Some Continental Congress delegates had also informally discussed plans for a more permanent union than the Continental Congress, whose status was temporary. Benjamin Franklin had drawn up a plan for "Articles of Confederation and Perpetual Union." While some delegates, such as Thomas Jefferson, supported Franklin's proposal, many others were strongly opposed. Franklin introduced his plan before Congress on July 21 but stated that it should be viewed as a draft for when Congress was interested in reaching a more formal proposal. Congress tabled the plan.

Following the Declaration of Independence, the members of the Continental Congress realized that it would be necessary to set up a national government. Congress began to discuss the form this would take on July 22, and disagreed on a number of issues, including whether representation and voting would be proportional or state-by-state. The disagreements delayed final discussions of confederation until October of 1777. By then, the British capture of Philadelphia had made the issue more urgent. Delegates finally formulated the Articles of Confederation, in which they agreed to state-by-state voting and proportional state tax burdens based on land values, though they left the issue of state claims to western lands unresolved. Congress sent the Articles to the states for ratification at the end of November. Most delegates realized that the Articles were a flawed compromise, but believed that it was better than an absence of formal national government.[29]

Virginia was the first state to ratify on December 16, 1777, while other states ratified in 1778. When Congress reconvened in June of 1778, the delegates learned that Maryland, Delaware, and New Jersey refused to ratify the Articles. The Articles required unanimous approval from the states. These smaller states wanted other states to relinquish their western land claims before they would ratify the Articles; New Jersey and Delaware eventually agreed to the conditions of the Articles, with New Jersey ratifying them on Nov 20, 1778, and Delaware on Feb 1, 1779. This left Maryland as the last remaining holdout.

Irked by Maryland's recalcitrance, several other state governments passed resolutions endorsing the formation of a national government without the state of Maryland, but other politicians, such as Congressman Thomas Burke of North Carolina, persuaded their governments to refrain from doing so, arguing that without unanimous approval of the new Confederation, the new country would remain weak, divided, and open to future foreign intervention and manipulation.

Meanwhile, in 1780, British forces began to conduct raids on Maryland communities in the Chesapeake Bay. Alarmed, the state

---

[29] The Declaration of Independence, 1776 (state.gov)

government wrote to the French minister Anne-César de La Luzerne asking for French naval assistance. Luzerne wrote back, urging the government of Maryland to ratify the Articles of Confederation. Marylanders were given further incentive to ratify when Virginia agreed to relinquish its western land claims, and so the Maryland legislature ratified the Articles of Confederation on March 1, 1781.

The Continental Congress voted on Jan 10, 1781, to establish a Department of Foreign Affairs; on Aug 10 of that year, it elected Robert R. Livingston as Secretary of Foreign Affairs. The Secretary's duties involved corresponding with U.S. representatives abroad and with ministers of foreign powers. The Secretary was also charged with transmitting Congress' instructions to U.S. agents abroad and was authorized to attend sessions of Congress. A further Act of Feb 22, 1782, allowed the Secretary to ask and respond to questions during sessions of the Continental Congress.

The Articles created a sovereign, national government, and as such limited the rights of the states to conduct their own diplomacy and foreign policy. However, in practice, this proved difficult to enforce, and the state of Georgia pursued its own independent policy regarding Spanish Florida, attempting to occupy disputed territories and threatening war if Spanish officials did not curb Indian attacks or refrain from harboring escaped slaves. Nor could the Confederation government prevent the landing of convicts that the British Government continued to export to its former colonies. The Articles also did not allow Congress sufficient authority to compel the states to enforce provisions of the 1783 Treaty of Paris that allowed British creditors to sue debtors for pre-Revolutionary debts, an unpopular clause that many state governments chose to ignore. Consequently, British forces continued to occupy forts in the Great Lakes region. These problems, combined with the Confederation government's ineffectual response to Shays' Rebellion in Massachusetts, convinced colonial leaders that a more powerful central government was necessary. This led to the Constitutional Convention that formulated the current Constitution of the United States.

The Constitution of the United States: A Transcription U.S. National Archives

Note: The following text is a transcription of the Constitution as it was inscribed by Jacob Shallus on parchment (the document on display in <u>the Rotunda at the National Archives Museum</u>.) *The spelling and punctuation reflect the original.*[30]

Authors note #1: During the Revolutionary war the government of the colonial colonies had to move several times to avoid being captured by the British troops. If you recall they were in Philadelphia for 14 years, Lancaster, Pa in 1729 and again in 1777, New York in September 13, 1788 and again on 4/30/1789, Baltimore , Md. Dec 1766, York, Pa 9/30/1777 Princeton , NJ 1781,Annapolis, MD 11/24/1783 and Trenton, NJ 11/1/1784. And finally in Washington, DC.

Authors note #2: Somedays are better then others but this one has NO EQUAL! One day I was working outside of my home in Epping, NH and the phone rang, I answered and an excited voice said get here quickly I have something extraordinary you need to see, I asked him what and he said just come now! This friend of mine in Exeter, NH greeted me and confided in me that they were renovating the building and had come across something. "This is an official post on the

Exeter, NH Town page. Exeter a community with an amazing history. Exeter served as New Hampshire's Revolutionary War Capital. The American Independence Museum on Water Street is caretaker of one of the **rare original versions of the Declaration of Independence**, which was found in the wall during a renovation in 1983! Why am I posting this note? well I will tell you I got to see and touch this document before it was secured.

If you question why I am writing this book, if you have been closely following my ancient history connections there are not many of us

---

[30] <u>The National Archives in Washington, DC | National Archives Museum</u>

that can honestly reveal connections to ancient history as a living descendant of virtual history of the ages.

Thanks for reading my journey.

James Boynton.

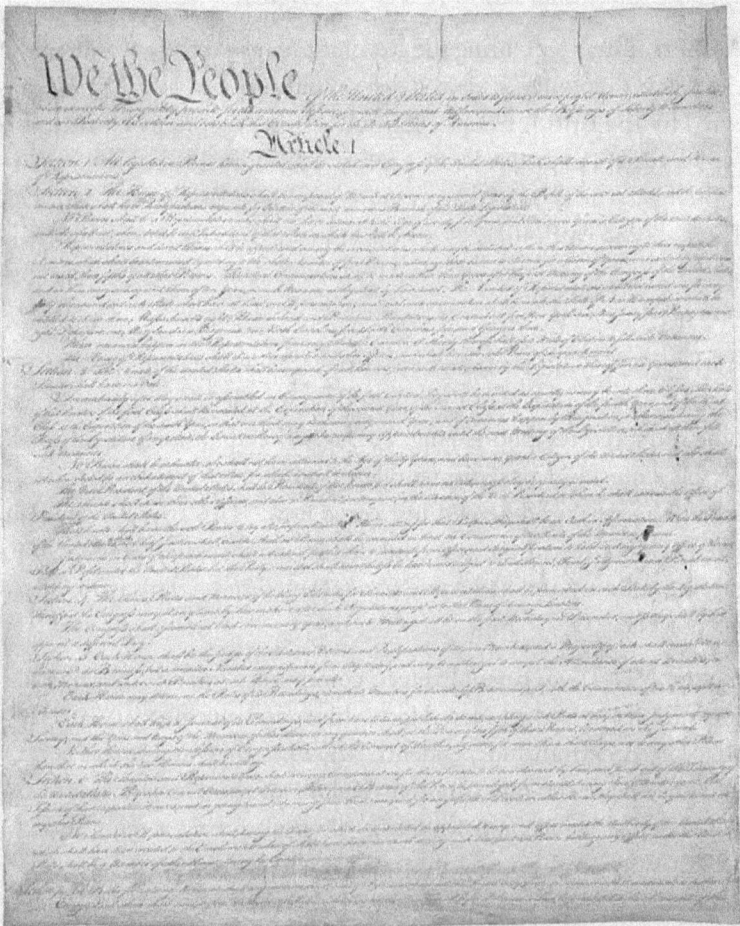

We, the People of the United States, in Order to form a more perfect Union, establish Justice, ensure domestic Tranquility, provide for the common defense, promote the general Welfare, and secure the Blessings of Liberty to ourselves and our Posterity, do ordain and establish this Constitution for the United States of America.

Article. I.

Section. 1.

All legislative Powers herein granted shall be vested in a Congress of the United States, which shall consist of a Senate and House of Representatives.

Section. 2.

The House of Representatives shall be composed of Members chosen every second Year by the People of the several States, and the Electors in each State shall have the Qualifications requisite for Electors of the most numerous Branch of the State Legislature.

No Person shall be a Representative who shall not have attained to the Age of twenty-five Years, and been seven Years a Citizen of the United States, and who shall not, when elected, be an Inhabitant of that State in which he shall be chosen.

Representatives and direct Taxes shall be apportioned among the several States which may be included within this Union, according to their respective Numbers, which shall be determined by adding to the whole Number of free Persons, including those bound to Service for a Term of Years, and excluding Indians not taxed, three fifths of all other Persons. The actual Enumeration shall be made within three Years after the first Meeting of the Congress of the United States, and within every subsequent Term of ten Years, in such Manner as they shall by Law direct. The Number of Representatives shall not exceed one for every thirty Thousand, but each State shall have at Least one Representative; and until such enumeration shall be made, the State of New Hampshire shall be entitled to choose three, Massachusetts eight, Rhode-Island and Providence Plantations one,

Connecticut five, New-York six, New Jersey four, Pennsylvania eight, Delaware one, Maryland six, Virginia ten, North Carolina five, South Carolina five, and Georgia three.

When vacancies happen in the Representation from any State, the Executive Authority thereof shall issue Writs of Election to fill such Vacancies.

The House of Representatives shall choose their Speaker and other Officers; and shall have the sole Power of Impeachment.

Section. 3.

The Senate of the United States shall be composed of two Senators from each State, chosen by the Legislature thereof, for six Years; and each Senator shall have one Vote.

Immediately after they shall be assembled in Consequence of the first Election, they shall be divided as equally as may be into three Classes. The Seats of the Senators of the first Class shall be vacated at the Expiration of the second Year, of the second Class at the Expiration of the fourth Year, and of the third Class at the Expiration of the sixth Year, so that one third may be chosen every second Year; and if Vacancies happen by Resignation, or otherwise, during the Recess of the Legislature of any State, the Executive thereof may make temporary Appointments until the next Meeting of the Legislature, which shall then fill such Vacancies.

No Person shall be a Senator who shall not have attained to the Age of thirty Years and been nine Years a Citizen of the United States, and who shall not, when elected, be an Inhabitant of that State for which he shall be chosen.

The Vice President of the United States shall be President of the Senate, but shall have no Vote, unless they be equally divided.

The Senate shall choose their other Officers, and also a President pro tempore, in the Absence of the Vice President, or when he shall exercise the Office of President of the United States.

The Senate shall have the sole Power to try all Impeachments. When sitting for that Purpose, they shall be on Oath or Affirmation. When the President of the United States is tried, the Chief Justice shall preside: And no Person shall be convicted without the Concurrence of two thirds of the Members present.

Judgment in Cases of Impeachment shall not extend further than to removal from Office, and disqualification to hold and enjoy any Office of honor, Trust or Profit under the United States: but the Party convicted shall nevertheless be liable and subject to Indictment, Trial, Judgment and Punishment, according to Law.

Section. 4.

The Times, Places and Manner of holding Elections for Senators and Representatives, shall be prescribed in each State by the Legislature thereof; but the Congress may at any time by Law make or alter such Regulations, except as to the Places of choosing Senators.

The Congress shall assemble at least once in every Year, and such Meeting shall be on the first Monday in December, unless they shall by Law appoint a different Day.

Section. 5.

Each House shall be the Judge of the Elections, Returns and Qualifications of its own Members, and a Majority of each shall constitute a Quorum to do Business; but a smaller Number may adjourn from day to day, and may be authorized to compel the Attendance of absent Members, in such Manner, and under such Penalties as each House may provide.

Each House may determine the Rules of its Proceedings, punish its members for disorderly Behavior, and, with the Concurrence of two thirds, expel a Member.

Each House shall keep a Journal of its Proceedings, and from time to time publish the same, excepting such Parts as may in their

Judgment require Secrecy; and the Yeas and Nays of the Members of either House on any question shall, at the Desire of one fifth of those Present, be entered on the Journal.

Neither House, during the Session of Congress, shall, without the Consent of the other, adjourn for more than three days, nor to any other Place than that in which the two Houses shall be sitting.

Section. 6.

The Senators and Representatives shall receive a Compensation for their Services, to be ascertained by Law, and paid out of the Treasury of the United States. They shall in all Cases, except Treason, Felony and Breach of the Peace, be privileged from Arrest during their Attendance at the Session of their respective Houses, and in going to and returning from the same; and for any Speech or Debate in either House, they shall not be questioned in any other Place.

No Senator or Representative shall, during the Time for which he was elected, be appointed to any civil Office under the Authority of the United States, which shall have been created, or the Emoluments whereof shall have been increased during such time; and no Person holding any Office under the United States, shall be a Member of either House during his Continuance in Office.

Section. 7.

All Bills for raising Revenue shall originate in the House of Representatives; but the Senate may propose or concur with Amendments as on other Bills.

Every Bill which shall have passed the House of Representatives and the Senate, shall, before it become a Law, be presented to the President of the United States; If he approve he shall sign it, but if not he shall return it, with his Objections to that House in which it shall have originated, who shall enter the Objections at large on their Journal, and proceed to reconsider it. If after such Reconsideration two thirds of that House shall agree to pass the Bill, it shall be sent, together with the Objections, to the other House, by which it shall likewise be reconsidered, and if approved by two thirds of that House, it shall become a Law. But in all such Cases the Votes of both Houses shall be determined by yeas and Nays, and the Names of the Persons voting for and against the Bill shall be entered on the Journal of each House respectively. If any Bill shall not be returned by the President within ten Days (Sundays excepted) after it shall have been presented to him, the Same shall be a Law, in like Manner as if he had signed it, unless the Congress by their Adjournment prevent its Return, in which Case it shall not be a Law.

Every Order, Resolution, or Vote to which the Concurrence of the Senate and House of Representatives may be necessary (except on a question of Adjournment) shall be presented to the President of the United States; and before the Same shall take Effect, shall be approved by him, or being disapproved by him, shall be repassed by two thirds of the Senate and House of Representatives, according to the Rules and Limitations prescribed in the Case of a Bill.

Section. 8.

The Congress shall have Power To lay and collect Taxes, Duties, Imposts and Excises, to pay the Debts and provide for the common Defense and general Welfare of the United States; but all Duties, Imposts and Excises shall be uniform throughout the United States.

To borrow Money on the credit of the United States.

To regulate Commerce with foreign Nations, and among the several States, and with the Indian Tribes.

To establish a uniform Rule of Naturalization, and uniform Laws on the subject of Bankruptcies throughout the United States;

To coin Money, regulate the Value thereof, and of foreign Coin, and fix the Standard of Weights and Measures.

To provide for the Punishment of counterfeiting the Securities and current Coin of the United States.

To establish Post Offices and post Roads.

To promote the Progress of Science and useful Arts, by securing for limited Times to Authors and Inventors the exclusive Right to their respective Writings and Discoveries.

To constitute Tribunals inferior to the supreme Court.

To define and punish Piracies and Felonies committed on the high Seas, and Offences against the Law of Nations.

To declare War, grant Letters of Marque and Reprisal, and make Rules concerning Captures on Land and Water.

To raise and support Armies, but no Appropriation of Money to that Use shall be for a longer Term than two Years.

To provide and maintain a Navy.

To make Rules for the Government and Regulation of the land and naval Forces.

To provide for calling forth the Militia to execute the Laws of the Union, suppress Insurrections and repel Invasions.

To provide for organizing, arming, and disciplining, the Militia, and for governing such Part of them as may be employed in the Service of the United States, reserving to the States respectively, the Appointment of the Officers, and the Authority of training the Militia according to the discipline prescribed by Congress.

To exercise exclusive Legislation in all Cases whatsoever, over such District (not exceeding ten Miles square) as may, by Cession of particular States, and the Acceptance of Congress, become the Seat of the Government of the United States, and to exercise like Authority over all Places purchased by the Consent of the Legislature of the State in which the Same shall be, for the Erection of Forts, Magazines, Arsenals, dock-Yards, and other needful Buildings;—And

To make all Laws which shall be necessary and proper for carrying into Execution the foregoing Powers, and all other Powers vested by this Constitution in the Government of the United States, or in any Department or Officer thereof.

Section. 9.

The Migration or Importation of such Persons as any of the States now existing shall think proper to admit, shall not be prohibited by the Congress prior to the Year one thousand eight hundred and eight, but a Tax or duty may be imposed on such Importation, not exceeding ten dollars for each Person.

The Privilege of the Writ of Habeas Corpus shall not be suspended, unless in Cases of Rebellion or Invasion the public Safety may require it.

No Bill of Attainder or ex post facto Law shall be passed.

No Capitation, or other direct, Tax shall be laid, <u>unless in Proportion to the Census or enumeration herein before directed to be taken.</u>

No Tax or Duty shall be laid on Articles exported from any State.

No Preference shall be given by any Regulation of Commerce or Revenue to the Ports of one State over those of another: nor shall Vessels bound to, or from, one State, be obliged to enter, clear, or pay Duties in another.

No Money shall be drawn from the Treasury, but in Consequence of Appropriations made by Law; and a regular Statement and Account of the Receipts and Expenditures of all public Money shall be published from time to time.

No Title of Nobility shall be granted by the United States: And no Person holding any Office of Profit or Trust under them, shall, without the Consent of the Congress, accept of any present, Emolument, Office, or Title, of any kind whatever, from any King, Prince, or foreign State.

Section. 10.

No State shall enter into any Treaty, Alliance, or Confederation; grant Letters of Marque and Reprisal; coin Money; emit Bills of Credit; make any Thing but gold and silver Coin a Tender in Payment of Debts; pass any Bill of Attainder, ex post facto Law, or Law impairing the Obligation of Contracts, or grant any Title of Nobility.

No State shall, without the Consent of the Congress, lay any Imposts or Duties on Imports or Exports, except what may be absolutely necessary for executing it's inspection Laws: and the net Produce of all Duties and Imposts, laid by any State on Imports or Exports, shall be for the Use of the Treasury of the United States; and all such Laws shall be subject to the Revision and Control of the Congress.

No State shall, without the Consent of Congress, lay any Duty of Tonnage, keep Troops, or Ships of War in time of Peace, enter into any Agreement or Compact with another State, or with a foreign Power, or engage in War, unless actually invaded, or in such imminent Danger as will not admit of delay.

Article. II.

Section. 1.

The executive Power shall be vested in a President of the United States of America. He shall hold his Office during the Term of four Years, and, together with the Vice President, chosen for the same Term, be elected, as follows.

Each State shall appoint, in such Manner as the Legislature thereof may direct, a Number of Electors, equal to the whole Number of Senators and Representatives to which the State may be entitled in the Congress: but no Senator or Representative, or Person holding an Office of Trust or Profit under the United States, shall be appointed an Elector.

The Electors shall meet in their respective States, and vote by Ballot for two Persons, of whom one at least shall not be an Inhabitant of the same State with themselves. And they shall make a List of all the Persons voted for, and of the Number of Votes for each, which List they shall sign and certify, and transmit sealed to the Seat of the Government of the United States, directed to the President of the Senate. The President of the Senate shall, in the Presence of the Senate and House of Representatives, open all the Certificates, and the Votes shall then be counted. The Person having the greatest Number of Votes shall be the President, if such Number be a Majority of the whole Number of Electors appointed; and if there be more than one who have such Majority, and have an equal Number of Votes, then the House of Representatives shall immediately choose by Ballot one of them for President; and if no Person have a Majority, then from the five highest on the List the said House shall in like Manner chuse the President. But in chusing the President, the Votes shall be taken by States, the Representation from each State having one Vote; A quorum for this Purpose shall consist of a Member or Members from two thirds of the States, and a Majority of all the States shall be necessary to a Choice. In every Case, after the Choice of the President, the Person having the greatest Number of Votes of the Electors shall be the Vice President. But if there should remain two or more who have equal Votes, the Senate shall chuse from them by Ballot the Vice President.

The Congress may determine the Time of chusing the Electors, and the Day on which they shall give their Votes, which Day shall be the same throughout the United States.

No Person except a natural born Citizen, or a Citizen of the United States, at the time of the Adoption of this Constitution, shall be eligible to the Office of President; neither shall any Person be eligible to that Office who shall not have attained to the Age of thirty five Years, and been fourteen Years a Resident within the United States.

In Case of the Removal of the President from Office, or of his Death, Resignation, or Inability to discharge the Powers and Duties of the said Office, the Same shall devolve on the Vice President, and the Congress may by Law provide for the Case of Removal, Death,

Resignation or Inability, both of the President and Vice President, declaring what Officer shall then act as President, and such Officer shall act accordingly, until the Disability be removed, or a President shall be elected.

The President shall, at stated Times, receive for his Services, a Compensation, which shall neither be encreased nor diminished during the Period for which he shall have been elected, and he shall not receive within that Period any other Emolument from the United States, or any of them.

Before he enter on the Execution of his Office, he shall take the following Oath or Affirmation:—"I do solemnly swear (or affirm) that I will faithfully execute the Office of President of the United States, and will to the best of my Ability, preserve, protect and defend the Constitution of the United States."

Section. 2.

The President shall be Commander in Chief of the Army and Navy of the United States, and of the Militia of the several States, when called into the actual Service of the United States; he may require the Opinion, in writing, of the principal Officer in each of the executive Departments, upon any Subject relating to the Duties of their respective Offices, and he shall have Power to grant Reprieves and Pardons for Offences against the United States, except in Cases of Impeachment.

He shall have Power, by and with the Advice and Consent of the Senate, to make Treaties, provided two thirds of the Senators present concur; and he shall nominate, and by and with the Advice and Consent of the Senate, shall appoint Ambassadors, other public Ministers and Consuls, Judges of the supreme Court, and all other Officers of the United States, whose Appointments are not herein otherwise provided for, and which shall be established by Law: but the Congress may by Law vest the Appointment of such inferior Officers, as they think proper, in the President alone, in the Courts of Law, or in the Heads of Departments.

The President shall have Power to fill up all Vacancies that may happen during the Recess of the Senate, by granting Commissions which shall expire at the End of their next Session.

Section. 3.

He shall from time to time give to the Congress Information of the State of the Union, and recommend to their Consideration such Measures as he shall judge necessary and expedient; he may, on extraordinary Occasions, convene both Houses, or either of them, and in Case of Disagreement between them, with Respect to the Time of Adjournment, he may adjourn them to such Time as he shall think proper; he shall receive Ambassadors and other public Ministers; he shall take Care that the Laws be faithfully executed, and shall Commission all the Officers of the United States.

Section. 4.

The President, Vice President and all civil Officers of the United States, shall be removed from Office on Impeachment for, and Conviction of, Treason, Bribery, or other high Crimes and Misdemeanors.

Article. III.

Section. 1.

The judicial Power of the United States shall be vested in one supreme Court, and in such inferior Courts as the Congress may from time to time ordain and establish. The Judges, both of the supreme and inferior Courts, shall hold their Offices during good Behaviour, and shall, at stated Times, receive for their Services, a Compensation, which shall not be diminished during their Continuance in Office.

Section. 2.

The judicial Power shall extend to all Cases, in Law and Equity, arising under this Constitution, the Laws of the United States, and Treaties made, or which shall be made, under their Authority;—to all Cases affecting Ambassadors, other public Ministers and Consuls;—to all Cases of admiralty and maritime Jurisdiction;—to Controversies to which the United States shall be a Party;—to Controversies between two or more States;— between a State and Citizens of another State,—between Citizens of different States,—between Citizens of the same State claiming Lands under Grants of different States, and between a State, or the Citizens thereof, and foreign States, Citizens or Subjects.

In all Cases affecting Ambassadors, other public Ministers and Consuls, and those in which a State shall be Party, the supreme Court shall have original Jurisdiction. In all the other Cases before mentioned, the supreme Court shall have appellate Jurisdiction, both as to Law and Fact, with such Exceptions, and under such Regulations as the Congress shall make.

The Trial of all Crimes, except in Cases of Impeachment, shall be by Jury; and such Trial shall be held in the State where the said Crimes shall have been committed; but when not committed within any State, the Trial shall be at such Place or Places as the Congress may by Law have directed.

Section. 3.

Treason against the United States shall consist only in levying War against them, or in adhering to their Enemies, giving them Aid and Comfort. No Person shall be convicted of Treason unless on the Testimony of two Witnesses to the same overt Act, or on Confession in open Court.

The Congress shall have Power to declare the Punishment of Treason, but no Attainder of Treason shall work Corruption of Blood, or Forfeiture except during the Life of the Person attainted.

Article. IV.

Section. 1.

Full Faith and Credit shall be given in each State to the public Acts, Records, and judicial Proceedings of every other State. And the Congress may by general Laws prescribe the Manner in which such Acts, Records and Proceedings shall be proved, and the Effect thereof.

Section. 2.

The Citizens of each State shall be entitled to all Privileges and Immunities of Citizens in the several States.

A Person charged in any State with Treason, Felony, or other Crime, who shall flee from Justice, and be found in another State, shall on Demand of the executive Authority of the State from which he fled, be delivered up, to be removed to the State having Jurisdiction of the Crime.

No Person held to Service or Labour in one State, under the Laws thereof, escaping into another, shall, in Consequence of any Law or Regulation therein, be discharged from such Service or Labour, but shall be delivered up on Claim of the Party to whom such Service or Labour may be due.

Section. 3.

New States may be admitted by the Congress into this Union; but no new State shall be formed or erected within the Jurisdiction of any other State; nor any State be formed by the Junction of two or more States, or Parts of States, without the Consent of the Legislatures of the States concerned as well as of the Congress.

The Congress shall have Power to dispose of and make all needful Rules and Regulations respecting the Territory or other Property belonging to the United States; and nothing in this Constitution shall be so construed as to Prejudice any Claims of the United States, or of any particular State.

Section. 4.

The United States shall guarantee to every State in this Union a Republican Form of Government and shall protect each of them against Invasion; and on Application of the Legislature, or of the Executive (when the Legislature cannot be convened) against domestic Violence.

Article. V.

The Congress, whenever two thirds of both Houses shall deem it necessary, shall propose Amendments to this Constitution, or, on the Application of the Legislatures of two thirds of the several States, shall call a Convention for proposing Amendments, which, in either Case, shall be valid to all Intents and Purposes, as Part of this Constitution, when ratified by the Legislatures of three fourths of the several States, or by Conventions in three fourths thereof, as the one or the other Mode of Ratification may be proposed by the Congress; Provided that no Amendment which may be made prior to the Year One thousand eight hundred and eight shall in any Manner affect the first and fourth Clauses in the Ninth Section of the first Article; and that no State, without its Consent, shall be deprived of its equal Suffrage in the Senate.

Article. VI.

All Debts contracted and Engagements entered into, before the Adoption of this Constitution, shall be as valid against the United States under this Constitution, as under the Confederation.

This Constitution, and the Laws of the United States which shall be made in Pursuance thereof; and all Treaties made, or which shall be made, under the Authority of the United States, shall be the supreme Law of the Land; and the Judges in every State shall be bound thereby, any Thing in the Constitution or Laws of any State to the Contrary notwithstanding.

The Senators and Representatives before mentioned, and the Members of the several State Legislatures, and all executive and judicial Officers, both of the United States and of the several States, shall be bound by Oath or Affirmation, to support this Constitution; but no religious Test shall ever be required as a Qualification to any Office or public Trust under the United States.

Article. VII.

The Ratification of the Conventions of nine States shall be sufficient for the Establishment of this Constitution between the States so ratifying the Same.

The Word, "the," being interlined between the seventh and eighth Lines of the first Page, The Word "Thirty" being partly written on an Erazure in the fifteenth Line of the first Page, The Words "is tried" being interlined between the thirty second and thirty third Lines of the first Page and the Word "the" being interlined between the forty third and forty fourth Lines of the second Page.[31]

Attest William Jackson Secretary

Done in Convention by the Unanimous Consent of the States present the Seventeenth Day of September in the Year of our Lord one thousand seven hundred and eighty seven and of the Independence of the United States of America the Twelfth In witness whereof We have hereunto subscribed our Names,

G. Washington

President and Deputy from Virginia

Delaware

Geo: Read

---

[31] The Constitution: Amendments 11-27 | National Archives

Gunning Bedford Jr.

John Dickinson

Richard Bassett

Jaco: Broom

Maryland

James McHenry

Dan of St Thos. Jenifer

Danl. Carroll

Virginia

John Blair

James Madison Jr.

North Carolina

Wm. Blount

Richd. Dobbs Spaight

Hu Williamson

South Carolina

J. Rutledge

Charles Cotesworth Pinckney

Charles Pinckney

Pierce Butler

Georgia

William Few

Abr Baldwin

New Hampshire

John Langdon

Nicholas Gilman

Massachusetts

Nathaniel Gorham

Rufus King

Connecticut

Wm. Saml. Johnson

Roger Sherman

New York

Alexander Hamilton

New Jersey

Wil: Livingston

David Brearley

Wm. Paterson

Jona: Dayton

Pennsylvania

B. Franklin

Thomas Mifflin

Robt. Morris

Geo. Clymer

Thos. FitzSimons

Jared Ingersoll

James Wilson

Gouv Morris

Chief Justice Pennsylvania - Benjamin Chew

Photo by:

Chrisfromcali Creative Commons

A prominent and successful Philadelphia lawyer, head of the Pennsylvania Judiciary System under both Colony and Commonwealth, and <u>Chief Justice</u> of the <u>Supreme Court</u> of the <u>Province of Pennsylvania</u>. Chew was well known for his precision and brevity in making legal arguments as well as his excellent memory, judgment, and knowledge of <u>statutory law</u>. His primary allegiance was to the supremacy of law and constitution. Chew lived and practiced law in <u>Philadelphia</u> four blocks from <u>Independence Hall</u>, and provided *<u>pro bono</u>* his knowledge of <u>substantive law</u> to America's <u>Founding Fathers</u> during the creation of the <u>United States Constitution</u> and <u>Bill of Rights</u>. Chew was strongly influenced by

Hamilton's ideas about a free press, and also the reading materials which his mentor provided him, especially Sir Francis Bacon's *Law tracts*.[3] His understanding of English legal history, and especially the Charter of Liberties, enhanced by his later studies at London's Middle Temple, fostered Chew's enduring commitment to the civil liberties that are guaranteed by the First Amendment to the United States Constitution, especially the right to free speech.

The Bible's Influence A Not So Surprising Revelation

The Foundation of Rule of Law has been set, but an important ingredient, The Bible, is usually missing in most all research efforts about the formation of the government and the role of the framers, people, and religion.

The Constitution and Human Nature were profound but often not appreciated by secular historians and political theorists. Two decades ago, Constitutional scholars and political historians assembled 15,000 writings from the Founding Era (1760-1805). They counted 3154 citations in these writings and found that the book most frequently cited in that literature was the Bible. The writers from the Foundering Era quoted from the Bible 34 percent of the time. Even more interesting was that about three-fourths of all references to the Bible came from reprinted sermons from that era. Fifty of the fifty-five men who signed the Constitution were church members who endorsed the Christian faith.

The Bible and biblical principles were important in the framing of the Constitution. In particular, the framers started with a biblical view of human nature. James Madison argued in *Federalist #51* that government must be based upon a realistic view of human nature. (Examine God and Federalist Papers Below by John E. Appleseed, American Patriot, 12 July 2002.)

Government itself is the greatest reflection of human nature. If men were angels, no government would be necessary. If angels were to govern men, neither external nor internal controls on government would be necessary. In framing a government which is to be administered by men over men, the great difficulty is that you first need to enable the government to control the governed and, in the next place, oblige it to control itself to serve the people it wishes to govern.

Framing a republic requires a balance of power that liberates human dignity and rationality and controls human sin and depravity.

As there is a degree of depravity in mankind that requires a certain degree of circumspection and distrust, so there are other qualities in human nature that justify a certain portion of esteem and confidence. Republican government presupposes the existence of these qualities to a higher degree than any other form.

A Christian view of government is based upon a balanced view of human nature. It recognizes both human dignity (we are created in God's image) and human depravity (we are sinful individuals). Because both grace and sin operate in government, we should neither be too optimistic nor too pessimistic. Instead, the framers constructed a government with a deep sense of biblical realism.

God, The Bible, Federalist Papers, and Government?

FEDERALIST PAPERS

EXAMPLES OF FAITH-BASED EXPRESSIONS

Founding Fathers Have Provided Significant Examples of Faith-Based Beliefs in Essays Arguing for Ratification of the Constitution
|||

It can be convincingly be argued that our US Constitution would not have been ratified had not the **Federalist Papers** convinced our country's founding fathers that it was in the interest of the thirteen individual states and of the United States, as a united whole, to do so.

Three of the founding fathers wrote jointly under the pen name of *Plubius*; Alexander Hamilton, **James Madison**, and **John Jay** published a series of 85 essays beginning immediately after the Constitutional Convention of September 1787. By the following spring, their effort had succeeded, and the Constitution had been ratified.

In light of the affront taken by a minority of law-makers, judges, and citizens to the inclusion of "One Nation under God" in our Pledge of Allegiance, a reading of the Federalist Papers can help dispel the fiction that our founding fathers envisioned a "fire-wall" between governance and theist or deist principles.

Knowing something of the factious temperament of people and the nature of people to divide with animosity over both frivolous and profound issues, our founding fathers did not shy away from initiating legislative measures in the Constitution that would work to minimize the power of any group or person, no matter their power, or numbers, or wealth.

Our founding fathers recognized that factions are elemental to the running of a government, and they sought ways to minimize political and religious tyranny, but in writing the Federalist Papers, they certainly expressed the country's clear connection with moral values and God.

Let us consider some of the ways in which the authors of the Federalist Papers display faith-based beliefs:

Essay 20, Topic 21, urges Americans to let their praise of gratitude for auspicious amity distinguishing political counsels rise to heaven.

Essay 37, Topic 14, tells us that any person of pious reflection must perceive that in drafting the Constitution, there is to be found in it a finger of that Almighty hand that has so frequently and signally extended to our relief in the critical stages of the revolution.

Essay 43, Topic 30, asserts that nothing is more repugnant than intolerance in political parties, stressing the importance of moderation; the essay concludes that one cannot avoid a belief that the great principle of self-preservation is a transcendent law of both nature and God...

Essay 1, Topic 4, concludes that in politics, as in religion, it's absurd to aim at making proselytes by fire and sword. Heresies in either can rarely be cured by persecution.

Essay 2, Topic 4, refers to God in three separate instances; referring to the country, they wrote that God blessed it with a variety of soils, watered with innumerable streams, for the delight and accommodation of its inhabitants. In other instance, the author makes note with equal pleasure that God gave this one connected country to one united people. And in a third instance wrote that it appears like this inheritance was designed by God for a band of brethren united by the strongest ties.

Essay 31, Topic 2, informs us that theorems may conflict with common sense. Mathematicians agree on the infinite divisibility of matter, the infinite divisibility of a finite thing, but that this is no more comprehensible to common sense than religious mysteries that nonbelievers have worked so hard to debunk.

Essay 37, Topic 10, addresses how difficult it is to express ideas and words clearly without ambiguity. The task of clear writing is limited, for when the Almighty himself condescends to address mankind in their own language, his meaning, luminous as it must be, is rendered dim and doubtful by the cloudy medium through which it is communicated.

Essay 44, Topic 24, sets forward the idea that there must be safeguards against the misuse of religion, in that no religious test shall ever be required as a qualification to any office or public trust under the United States.

Essay 51, lets us know that in a free government, the security for civil rights must be the same as that for religious rights.

Essay 57, Topic 6, briefly elaborates that no qualification of wealth, birth, religious faith, or civil profession is permitted to fetter the judgment or disappoint the inclination of the people.

The importance of the Federalist Papers in helping lay the foundation of the United States cannot be overestimated.

RELEGION/ORGANIZATIONS WERE HELD SEPARATE

FROM GOVERNMENT

On one hand, the authors expressed their faith-based beliefs, but on the other hand, they forged ahead in making certain that religion would not be permitted to divide the people or to otherwise tyrannize any individual or group.

"**Separation of church and state**" is a metaphor paraphrased from Thomas Jefferson and used by others in discussions regarding the Establishment Clause and Free Exercise Clause of the First Amendment to the United States Constitution which reads: "Congress shall make no law respecting an establishment of religion, or prohibiting the free exercise thereof..."

The principle is paraphrased from Thomas Jefferson's "separation between Church & State." It has been used to express the understandings of the intent and function of this amendment, which allows freedom of religion. It is generally traced to a January 1, 1802, letter by Jefferson, addressed to the Danbury Baptist Association in Connecticut, and published in a Massachusetts newspaper.

Jefferson wrote, Believing with you that religion is a matter which lies solely between Man & his God, that he owes account to none other for his faith or his worship, that the legitimate powers of government reach actions only, & not opinions, I contemplate with sovereign reverence that act of the whole American people which declared that their legislature should "make no law respecting an establishment of religion, or prohibiting the free exercise thereof," thus building a wall of separation between Church & State. Adhering to this expression of the supreme will of the nation in behalf of the rights of conscience, I shall see with sincere satisfaction the progress of those sentiments which tend to restore to man all his natural rights, convinced he has no natural right in opposition to his social duties."[1]

Jefferson reflects other thinkers, including Roger Williams, a Baptist Dissenter and founder of Providence, Rhode Island. He wrote:

When they [the Church] have opened a gap in the hedge or wall of separation between the garden of the church and the wilderness of the world, God hath ever broke down the wall itself, removed the Candlestick, etc., and made His Garden a wilderness as it is this day. And that, therefore, if He will ever please to restore His garden and paradise again, it must of necessity be walled in peculiarly unto Himself from the world, and all that be saved out of the world are to be transplanted out of the wilderness of the World.[2]

In keeping with the lack of an established state religion in the United States, unlike in many European nations at the time, Article Six of the United States Constitution specifies that "no religious Test shall ever be required as a Qualification to any Office or public Trust under the United States" meaning that there will be no official state religion lawfully established.

Jefferson's metaphor of a wall of separation has been cited repeatedly by the U.S. Supreme Court. In *Reynolds v. United States* (1879), the Court wrote that Jefferson's comments "may be accepted almost as an authoritative declaration of the scope and effect of the [First] Amendment.

However, by their very example in writing the Federalist Papers, its authors showed that while government may not make any law respecting an establishment of religion, expressions of faith-based beliefs are natural and wholesome whether in government or among the populace, the only criteria in government being to steadfastly remain within the expressed bounds of both the letter and spirit of the second amendment law.

And the Iroquois? They continue to live under their own constitution and government. We too, since this meeting of two nations, until today live under the principles fundamentally established at this critical juncture of the establishment of our nation.

The Iroquois see themselves as a sovereign nation.

REVOLUTIONARY WAR

Authors note: While doing research for this manuscript, I found something that I had never known (many of these revelations came from my research), and for this segment, General George Washington and Native relations come to bear. The natives of the Oneida Tribe were an ally in the Revolutionary War and very supportive of General Washington. They respected him enough to honor him with a special name, a distinction they had given to Washington's grandfather.

Conotocarious

The name Conotocarious was given to George Washington, which showed the communication and memory of the various eastern Native American tribes. This name, meaning "town destroyer," was first given to George Washington's grandfather in the 17th century, but his grandson had the name bestowed upon him with his first contact with Native Americans in 1753. The name stayed with Washington through the American Revolution and into his presidency.

Author notes: During my research, I found profound examples of heroic women who were, for many reasons, drawn into the pitch of battle and are now heroes of the revolution. Their stories are truly inspiring, and I have included them as their due.

Heroic Women in the American Revolution

On the homefront and on the battlefield

Painting of Molly Pitcher firing a cannon at the Battle of Monmouth in June 1778 by E. Percy Moran

Library of Congress, Prints and Photographs Division

Women played critical roles in the American Revolution and subsequent War for Independence. Historian Cokie Roberts considers these women our Founding Mothers.

Women like Abigail Adams, the wife of Massachusetts Congressional Delegate John Adams, influenced politics, as did Mercy Otis Warren. It was Abigail Adams who famously and voluminously corresponded with her husband while he was in Philadelphia, reminding him that in the new form of government that was being established, he should "remember the ladies," or they, too, would foment a revolution of their own. Warren, just as politically astute as Adams, was a prolific writer, not only recording her thoughts about the confluence of events swirling around Boston but also dabbling in playwriting. She was a fierce devotee to the patriot cause, writing in December 1774, four months before the war broke out at Lexington and Concord, "America stands armed with resolution and virtue, but she still recoils at the idea of drawing the sword against the nation from whence she derived her origin." In 1805 she published *History of the Rise, Progress, and Termination of the American Revolution.*

Mercy Otis Warren Wikimedia Commons

Women often followed their husbands in the Continental Army. These women, known as camp followers, often tended to the domestic side of army organization, washing, cooking, mending clothes, and providing medical help when necessary. Sometimes they were flung into the vortex of battle.

Phillis Wheatley, The Poet who read to General Washington

Phillis Wheatley, an enslaved African American living in Boston, took up the pen and wrote poetry, becoming one of the first published female authors in America and the first African American woman to be published. Her 1773 collection *Poems on Various Subjects, Religious and Moral,* was popular on both sides of the Atlantic. Her poems focused on patriotism and human virtues. She even wrote a poem about George Washington, "To His Excellency, George Washington," in 1775, which she personally read to him at his Cambridge headquarters in 1776 while he was with the Continental Army in Massachusetts besieging the British. Her visit was the result of an invitation from Washington. Wheatley obtained her freedom upon the death of her master in 1778.

Illustration, Karen B. Winnick, Sybil's Night Ride

Sybil Ludington

The 16-Year-Old Revolutionary Hero Who Rode Twice as Far as Paul Revere?

Author notes: This post of Sybil is being made while some call it apocryphal. Apocryphal implies "*an unknown or dubious source or origin*" or may imply that the thing itself is dubious or inaccurate. (of a story or statement) of doubtful authenticity, although widely circulated as being true.

So why did her neighbors and even General George Washington personally thank her? Read, you decide.

On the night of April 26, 1777, 16-year-old Sybil Ludington climbed onto her horse Star and set off on a mission: a 40-mile ride to muster local militia troops in response to a British attack on the town of Danbury, Connecticut. Riding all night through the rain — and traveling twice the distance that Paul Revere rode during his famous midnight ride — Sybil returned home at dawn having given nearly the entire regiment of 400 Colonial troops the order to assemble. Following the battle, General George Washington personally thanked Sybil for her service and bravery. Although every American school child knows the story of Paul Revere — largely thanks to the famous poem by Henry Wadsworth Longfellow — unfortunately, few are taught about Sybil Ludington's courageous feat.

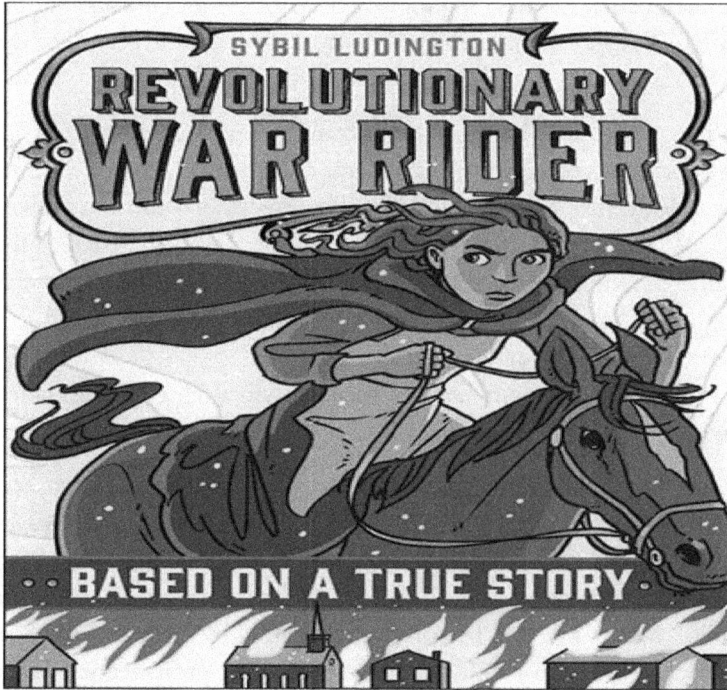

Born on April 5, 1760, in Fredericksburg, New York, Sybil Ludington was the oldest of Colonel Ludington's twelve children. His militia troops had disbanded for the planting season when word came that British troops were marching towards Danbury, Connecticut, where the Continental Army had a supply depot. While her father planned their response, Sybil volunteered to rally the militia following her father's instruction to "ride to the men and tell them to be at his house by daybreak."

It was 9 pm, already dark and raining heavily, when she mounted her horse, Star, and set off through Putnam County, New York. She rode from her family's farm in Kent, south to the village of Carmel, down to Mahopac, then west to Mahopac Falls, north to Kent Cliffs and Farmers Mills; from there, she rode further north to Stormville before returning south to the farm. As she rode 40 miles through the night mustering the militia, she used a stick to bang on the shutters of neighbors' homes, yelling, "The British are burning Danbury!" By the time she returned home, exhausted and soaked to the skin, most of the four hundred soldiers were on their way.

While Colonel Ludington's troops could not save Danbury from being burned, they joined forces with the Continental Army at the Battle of Ridgefield the following day. The American forces drove General William Tryon, the British governor of New York, back to the British fleet at Long Island Sound, halting their advance and protecting more American cities from attack. The British raid also led to a surge of support for the Patriot cause, and 3,000 local residents joined the Connecticut Army of Reserve soon after the British sailed away.

Following her daring nighttime ride, Sybil was thanked for her heroism and service by grateful neighbors and by General George Washington, then Commander of the Continental Army. Unlike Paul Revere, whose name became universally known thanks to Longfellow's poem, Sybil's ride had been mostly forgotten by her death in 1839 at the age of 77. In 1907, however, Ludington's great-nephew Louis S. Patrick wrote an account of her ride, which piqued interest in this unsung Revolutionary War figure.

Sybil Ludington was the female equivalent of Paul Revere, though she rode twice as far as Revere and in a driving rainstorm in April 1777. Her ride took her through Putnam and Dutchess Counties, New York, where she roused local militia to fight a British force that had attacked nearby Danbury, Connecticut. The Daughters of the American Revolution erected a heroic equestrian statue to Ludington in Carmel, New York along the forty-mile route she traveled.

Origin of our First American Flag Musings to Consider

Author note: I post a section of a report from the Heritage Foundation in a recent 6/29/24 report in a possible clarification of the issue of whom, where and what actually may have been the origin of our

American Flag. I thank the Heritage Foundation, a premier organization whose interest is the United States.

THE SECOND CONTINENTAL CONGRESS ADOPTS A RESOLUTION PRESCRIBING A GENERAL AMERICAN FLAG TO SUPERSEDE THE AD HOC COLLECTION OF FLAGS used by the Continental Army and Navy (and displaying various mottoes: "Don't Tread on Me," "An Appeal to Heaven," "Liberty and Union," and "Liberty or Death") during the two years since the beginning of the American Revolution. In January 1776, George Washington introduced the use of a red-and-white striped flag (similar to one employed by the East India Company) with the British Union Jack in the upper-left corner and known as the Grand Union Flag. The Continental Congress's resolution set the standard for "the flag of the United States" as a field (or fly) of "thirteen stripes, alternate red and white," with a blue upper-left corner (or union) displaying "thirteen stars" in white, "representing a new constellation." The flag remained unaltered until 1794, when Congress passed legislation to add two stars and two stripes to the flag in recognition of the admission of Vermont and Kentucky to the Union. A third statute in 1818 permanently fixed the number of stripes at 13. Because no pattern for the stars in the union was specified in the June 14 resolution, Revolutionary flags alternately displayed the stars as a circlet or a pattern of June 14, 1777, five columns (with alternating three and two stars). In fact, no overall flag code was adopted until 1942. In 1780, Francis Hopkinson claimed to have been the original designer of the flag, and in 1870, the descendants of Betsy Ross advanced the claim that she had sewn the first flag at the behest of George Washington in 1776. Both claims are dubious. Although an early version of the flag may have been used at the Battle of the Brandywine on September 11, 1777

See the below posts for Betsey Ross and Francis Hopkinson; both were consummate patriots.

Betsey Ross

The story of one of the most famous revolutionary women, Betsy Ross, is likely just that - a story. Ross is often credited with sewing the first American flag, thirteen red and white stripes with thirteen stars in a field of blue in the corner. Subsequent research, however, shows that the story only surfaced around the Centennial in 1876 and was promoted by Ross's grandson William Canby. Given that Congress passed the Flag Act in June of 1777, nearly a year after Ross is purported to have made the flag, the story is likely apocryphal. (?)

"The Birth of Old Glory" depicts the supposed creation of the first American flag by Betsy Ross. Wikimedia Commons

Ross did run a successful upholstery shop, but evidence suggests founding Father Francis Betsy Ross Probably Didn't Design the First American Flag. Francis Hopkinson actually created stars and stripes. Betsey probably sewed it with a friend.

Famed seamstress, **Betsy Ross** receives much of the glory for creating the American flag. However, many experts believe the person actually responsible for designing the first version of "Old Glory" was a **founding father** named Francis Hopkinson.

Hopkinson, who signed the Declaration of Independence in 1776 and served as a delegate in the Continental Congress, was a lawyer, poet, satirist, musician, and an artist. **He designed** seals for the U.S. Treasury and the state of New Jersey, as well as U.S. currency predating the dollar bill. And there's evidence that he was the creator of the American flag—not Ross, as her descendants and many history books have suggested.

With Friday marking Flag Day—which was celebrated as early as the late 1880s and which President **Harry Truman** made into **a national day of observance** in August 1949—let's take a look at Hopkinson's life and surprising connections to the flag.

Who Was Francis Hopkinson?

Francis Hopkinson signed the Declaration of Independence and played a role in the creation of the U.S. Constitution.

Hopkinson **was born** in the fall of 1737 in Philadelphia. His parents were Thomas Hopkinson, the founder of the Academy of Philadelphia (now the University of Pennsylvania), and Mary Johnson Hopkinson.

Francis attended his father's academy and the College of Philadelphia, where he proved to be a gifted musician who could play the organ and harpsichord, as well as sing. He loved music, and according to the Mount Vernon estate, **he composed** odes, instrumental works, psalms, sacred music, and even operatic pieces throughout his life.

In addition to honing his musical abilities, Hopkinson studied law and passed the Pennsylvania bar in 1761. From 1779 until his death on May 9, 1791, he served as a federal judge. One proposal is that he also designed the Stars and Stripes flag.

However, some of Hopkinson's most important contributions were as a statesman. He **was elected** to represent New Jersey in the

Continental Congress in 1778 and became an active member of the Constitutional Convention of 1787. This group convened to address the weak central government existing under the Articles of Confederation. From their meetings, the U.S. Constitution took shape and became law in 1789.

Famous so-called camp followers during the Revolution

As wives of the common soldier often followed the Continental Army so, too, did the wives of general officers. General Henry Knox, the Continental Army's Artillery Commander married the vivacious and popular Bostonian Lucy Flucker, the daughter of Bostonian Loyalists. Once she and Henry were married, all ties between her and her family were cut. Henry and Lucy were devoted to one another, and she would join him whenever she could while he was on campaign.

She endured the bitter encampment at Valley Forge and became fast friends with the wife of General Nathanael Greene, the equally popular Kitty. George Washington's wife, Martha Custis, spent every winter with her husband wherever the army was camped. In fact, once George Washington left his beloved Mount Vernon estate in 1775 to attend the 2nd Continental Congress in Philadelphia, he did not return to his home until 1781, as the combined American and French Army maneuvered south from the city of New York to Yorktown, Virginia, where the war was eventually won.

The wives of generals were as equally helpful in matters of caring and providing compassion to sick and wounded soldiers, as were the wives of the common soldiers.

Ordinary women also endured the horrors of the battlefield when those fights came to their doorstep.

Sally Kellogg of Vermont and her family escaped the gods of War in 1776 when the War for Independence found its way into the northern reaches of upstate New York and Benedict Arnold's makeshift fleet and the British Navy clashed on Lake Champlain during the Battle of Valcour Island. As the Kellogg family made good its escape by water, Sally's family "fell in between Arnold's fleet and the British fleet," she later recalled. As the family rowed to safety at Fort Ticonderoga, the exchange of gunfire between ships could be seen and heard Sally recalled, "but happy for us the balls went over us. We heard them whis, (wiz)." Nevertheless, the war continued to follow the Kellogg family. A year later, after having relocated to Bennington, Vermont the Kellogg's were once more forced to be witnesses to carnage and once again upon recollection Sally claimed the results were, "a sight to behold. There was not a house [in Bennington's vicinity] but was stowed full of wounded.

Not unlike women eighty years later who disguised themselves as men to serve in the armies of the Civil War, women of the Revolutionary Era also itched to get into the fight, do their part for the cause, and be engaged in a historical moment.

Molly Pitcher

American patriot

Also known as: Mary Ludwig, Mary Ludwig Hays, Mary Ludwig Hays McCauly, Mary McCauly

Written by

Dennis E. Showalter

Fact-checked by

The Editors of Encyclopaedia Britannica

Molly Pitcher

Mary Ludwig Hays McCauly

Born:

1754, near Trenton, New Jersey [U.S.]

Died:

January 22, 1832, Carlisle, Pennsylvania, U.S. (aged 78)

Role In:

American Revolution

Battle of Monmouth

Molly Pitcher (born 1754, near <u>Trenton</u>, <u>New Jersey</u> [U.S.]—died January 22, 1832, <u>Carlisle</u>, <u>Pennsylvania</u>, U.S.) was a heroine of the <u>Battle of Monmouth</u> during the <u>American Revolution</u>.

According to <u>legend</u>, at the Battle of Monmouth (June 28, 1778), Mary Hays, wife of artilleryman William Hays, carried water to cool both the <u>cannon</u> and the soldiers in her husband's battery—hence the <u>nickname</u> "Molly Pitcher." Legend also asserts that when William Hays collapsed or was wounded, she took her husband's place in the gun crew for the rest of the battle.

Molly Pitcher

Molly Pitcher firing a cannon during the Battle of Monmouth during the American Revolution. (more)

Molly Pitcher: grave

Grave of Mary Hays—who, according to legend, was Molly Pitcher—in Carlisle, Pennsylvania. (more)

Patriotic prints and literature depicting the <u>alleged</u> event initially referred to "Captain Molly." The less martial and more nurturing "Molly Pitcher" did not appear as a cognomen until the mid-19th century. Neither image was identified with a specific person until 1876, when the citizens of Carlisle claimed a woman buried there was the literal heroine of Monmouth. Military records indicate that a William Hays did enlist in the artillery in 1776 and died about 1789. His wife Mary remarried and eventually applied for a pension as a soldier's widow. Instead, on February 21, 1822, Pennsylvania awarded her an annual grant of $40 "for services she rendered." The services were unspecified, though the wording of the pension bill suggests that she may have played some kind of direct role in the Revolution. Whether she was this particular woman or not, monuments near the Monmouth battle site and at Mary Hays's grave recognize Molly Pitcher's contribution to American independence.

Dennis E. Showalter

American Revolution [1778] Deborah Sampson

Deborah Sampson (1760-1827) was an American Revolutionary War hero and the first woman to serve in combat for the U.S. military. She was born into poverty in Plympton, Massachusetts, on December 17, 1760, and grew up working as an indentured servant and weaver to support herself. In 1782, at the age of 21, she disguised herself as a man named Robert Shurtleff and enlisted in the Continental Army's Fourth Massachusetts Regiment.

Biography of Deborah Sampson

Born into poverty in Plympton, Massachusetts, Deborah Sampson (1760-1827) learned how to p...

Sampson fought in several skirmishes and battles, including one outside of Terrytown, New York, where she was shot in the thigh and cut on the forehead with a saber. She removed the bullet herself to avoid revealing her identity during medical care. Sampson also contracted a fever while serving in Philadelphia in the summer of 1783, which led to her identity being discovered by her doctor. Despite this, he kept her secret and cared for her until she was well enough to return to West Point, where she was honorably discharged in October 1783:

- May 20, 1782: Enlists in the Light Infantry Company of the Fourth Massachusetts Regiment under the name Robert Shurtleff
- Summer 1782: Shot in the thigh during a skirmish.
- Summer 1783: Contracts a fever in Philadelphia, where her identity is discovered by her doctor.
- October 25, 1783: Honorably discharged from the army at West Point

Sampson was one of the first women to receive a military pension for her service and went on to become an early female lecturer in the United States. She died in Sharon, Massachusetts, on April 29, 1827, at the age of 66.

One of the best examples of a woman who disguised herself as a man to fight in the Continental Army was Deborah Sampson from Uxbridge, Massachusetts. Amazingly, she also has a paper trail concerning her combat service in the army, where she fought under the alias of Robert Shurtliff, the name of her deceased brother, in the light infantry company of the Fourth Massachusetts Regiment. She mustered into service in the spring of 1782 and saw action in Westchester County, New York, just north of the City of New York, where she was wounded in her thigh and forehead. Not wanting her identity to be revealed during medical care, she permitted physicians to treat her head wound and then slipped out of the field hospital unnoticed, where she extracted one of the bullets from her thigh with a penknife and sewing needle. The other bullet was lodged too deep, and her leg never fully healed. Her identity was finally revealed during the summer of 1783 when she contracted a fever while on duty in Philadelphia. The physician who treated her kept her secret and cared for her. After the Treaty of Paris, she was given an honorable discharge from the army by Henry Knox. Like other veterans of the Continental Army, she was continually petitioning the state and federal government for her service pension. She later married and had three children, settling down in Sharon, Massachusetts. To help make ends meet, she often gave public lectures about her wartime service. By the time she died in 1827, she was collecting minimal pensions for her service from Massachusetts and the federal government. In her memory, a statue stands today outside the public library in Sharon, honoring her Revolutionary War service and sacrifices.

Many women of all stripes and from all backgrounds recognized the value of the American cause and stepped up to serve the cause of the new nation as best they could.

REV WAR | ARTICLE

10 Facts: Native Americans

Native American Involvement in the American Revolution.

Many Native Americans played an important role in the American Revolution. Here are 10 facts that outline some of the contributions of the Native Americans in the 18th-century War for American Independence.

Fact #1: The American Revolution split the Iroquois Confederacy of Native Americans, with the Oneidas and Tuscarora siding with the Americans and the other five tribes aligning themselves with the British.

The Oneida occupied land in central New York and were closest geographically to the eastern seaboard. They became the staunchest allies of the Patriot cause among the Iroquois Confederacy. The Tuscarora, who was accepted into the six nations with the help of the

Oneida, had factions that supported both sides in the war and shared reservation land after the conflict with Oneidas before getting their own allotted spot.

Fact #2: Catawba Native Americans assisted militia and Patriot partisans in actions in North and South Carolina.

Although the Catawbas sided with the British during the French and Indian War, on the eve of the American Revolution, a reservation in South Carolina was formed for them. With the British presence in the area during 1780-1781, the Catawba saw many of their homesteads torched. This propelled them more into the American camp, where they served at places like Guilford Courthouse in March 1781, and with the famed militia commander General Thomas Sumter in South Carolina.

Fact #3: Stockbridge Native Americans assisted in the defining American victory at Saratoga and the last major engagement in the Northern Theater at Monmouth in June 1778.

The first of many Native American tribes to side with the Americans, the Mohican, Wappinger, and Munsee Native Americans, all in the general area of Stockbridge, Massachusetts, cast their lot with the revolutionaries. In 1774, meeting in Stockbridge, the tribe issued the following statement:

> "Wherever your armies go, there we will go; you shall always find us by your side; and if providence calls us to sacrifice our Lives in the field of battle, we will fall where you fall, and lay our bones by yours. Nor shall peace ever be made between our nation and the Red-Coats until our brothers -the white people- lead the way."

Author note: I will highlight Polly Cooper with a separate posting due to her incredible service during the Valley Forge encampment, along with the native Oneida Tribal members.

Fact #4: Polly Cooper, an Oneida, traveled with male warriors to Valley Forge during the Continental Army winter encampment.

While there, she showed the Army how to make soup from corn husks, which helped ease some of the hunger of the soldiery. This trek, through winter, covered hundreds of miles from New York to Pennsylvania and was part of the relief mission. Her companions, including her husband, brought hundreds of bushels of white corn to feed the Continental army. After the war, she refused any payment except a token of appreciation from Martha Washington.

Library of Congress

Fact #5: At the Battle of Barren Hill, fought on May 20, 1778, Oneida warriors acted as scouts for the American forces.

Serving alongside Daniel Morgan's Virginia riflemen to scout and fight as skirmishers, the Oneidas provided early warning of the advancing British forces. This allowed the Marquis de Lafayette's force to execute a fighting withdrawal in good order. Six Oneidas fell in the combat and are honored with a plaque in the St. Peter's Lutheran Church in Lafayette Hill, Pennsylvania.

Fact #6: Guy Johnson, British Superintendent of Indian Affairs, and Joseph Brant were crucial to influencing Native Americans in the north to be pro-British.

Guy Johnson took over for his uncle as Superintendent of Indian Affairs in 1774 and was instrumental in rallying the majority of the tribes of the Iroquois Confederacy to the British cause. Joseph

Brant rose to prominence as a Mohawk military and political leader and waged a partisan war in New York for the British.

Fact #7: Massacre at Gnadenhutten.

On March 8, 1782, peaceful Delaware or Lenape Native Americans were massacred at the Moravian missionary village at Gnadenhutten by Pennsylvania militiamen. Altogether, 96 Native Americans were killed in what future United States President Theodore Roosevelt called "a stain on frontier character that the lapse of time cannot wash away."

Fact #8: Native American Civil War.

Much like the overall war itself between former British colonists and Mother Country, the American Revolution tore Native American tribes apart as well. At the Battle of Oriskany in 1777, for example, tribes of the Six Nations fought on opposing sides. The Oneida with the New York militia and Senecas and Mohawks with their British allies. In the Ohio Valley country, Shawnees and Delaware Indians were courted by both the British and American military commanders. Within the Cherokee Nation, younger warriors defied the directives of elder tribal leaders and raided frontier settlements.

Library of Congress

Fact #9: Cherokee Tribe and the American Revolution.

One of the largest Native American tribes in the south, the Cherokees were mostly aligned with the British, seeing the colonials as encroaching on their land. Andrew Pickens, a South Carolina militia commander, led a devastating raid against the Cherokee in the latter stages of the war, which forced the tribe to cede land in Georgia.

Fact #10: Conotocarious.

The name Conotocarious was given to George Washington, which showed the communication and memory of the various eastern Native American tribes. This name, meaning "town destroyer" was first given to George Washington's grandfather in the 17th century, but his grandson had the name bestowed upon him with his first contact with Native Americans in 1753. The name stayed with Washington through the American Revolution and into his presidency.

Polly Cooper

American Battlefield Trust

TITLE Civilian

WAR & AFFILIATION Revolutionary War / Patriot

DATE OF BIRTH – DEATH unknown

Polly Cooper of the Oneida Indian Nation helped save Continental soldiers' lives after they suffered through the harsh winter of 1777-78 at Valley Forge. Yet, we know little about this Revolutionary War heroine. Historians have uncovered few details about her life in the archival record.

Thanks to the Oneida Indian Nation, Cooper's dedication to caring for General George Washington's army through illness and hunger endures in our memory and Oneida tribal legend.

The Oneida Indian Nation was an ally of the American cause during the Revolutionary War. Many Oneidas supported the war effort as warriors and scouts, playing critical roles in several engagements such as the Battle of Oriskany. But the Oneidas' bravery and generosity off the battlefield also proved pivotal to the fight for American independence.

In December of 1777, Washington moved the Continental Army to their winter quarters at Valley Forge. His exhausted troops struggled to survive the harsh conditions. Disease was rampant. Thousands of soldiers lacked proper clothing and food supplies.

So, when Oneida Chief Oskanondonha, or Skenandoah, sent a group of warriors to join the army at Valley Forge, he also sent a gift of surplus corn with the expedition. Cooper – skilled in cooking and medicine – joined roughly 50 warriors in their mission to provide much needed relief to Washington's men.

Cooper's party began its journey from New York in April 1778, traveling hundreds of miles by foot to Pennsylvania. They arrived in Valley Forge with hundreds of baskets of white corn. Since white corn takes careful preparation before it can be eaten, Cooper taught soldiers and their families how to properly cook it. She also cared for sick soldiers, refusing to accept any pay for her services.

According to oral tradition, some of the soldiers' wives – or even Martha Washington herself – presented Cooper with a black shawl to show their immense gratitude for her aid.

Cooper's descendants and the Oneida Indian Nation ensure her selfless acts are not forgotten. Her descendants recorded her story and have cared for her shawl for generations.

Recently, the Oneida Indian Nation donated a statue of Cooper standing alongside Washington and Oskanandonha to the Smithsonian's National Museum of the American Indian to commemorate the alliance between the Oneida Indian Nation and the United States.

Chapter 28

Washington D.C. Our Shining City
Shrouded in Mystery?

We know the architect of Washington, D.C. it is Pierre L'Enfant. It is also known that many writers have written about him and the city of Washington, D.C., and have varied opinions on how this so-called city of mystery evolved and of the work this architect did. It is commonly regarded as a city with a unique and complex design, one that represented unity for the colonies in a symbolic statement.

Pierre L'Enfant

We should define who Pierre L'Enfant was. He was French and he came to the colonies to fight in the Revolution and actually ended up as a close companion to General George Washington. He was a Freemason like Washington inducted into Lodge #8 in New York in 1789. He was the son of an architect at Versalles and familiar with ancient mathematical co and Phincepts such as Pi, the Fabonacci Sequence, and how they were used in ancient Rome, Greece, the ancient pyramids and the Temple of Solomon. This is not just mathematics this has spiritual connotations and I consider them Universal Truths. Work started on the capitol project in 1790.

The Phi or Golden Mean, the ratio of 1 to 1.618 found throughout nature find it seminal. Examples are the ratio of male to female honeybees, the pattern of pinecone bristles, the arrangement of petals on flowers and even in the structure of DNA.

There is a highly recommended text I would like to mention "The Sacred Geometry of Washington, D.C. by Nicholas Mann due to its coverage of American History and spiritual wisdom. I am not referring to it for any of my writing, but I am interested in the "spiritual" referred to since in previous chapters I address the mysterious organizations and one of these was the Freemasons.

Knowing L'Enfant was on board in an Act of Congress Washington, D.C. was born as a federal district located on the Potomac between the North and South colonies. His design was intended to signal the world that all citizens would have equal access the Nation's Capital.

Mystery, mystery. L'Enfant quickly resolved the issue with stated intent to make the city pattern to act as a physical ideal found in the Constitution, the Declaration of Independence "and the Heavens above", truly an idyllic and pleasantly simple. In his "as Above, so Below concept he mapped a celestial canopy above with over thirty different zodiacs matching the constellations in the sky. Today these can be seen as twelve zodiacs on the National Academy of Sciences in relief on the metal doors. Two more can be located at the Federal Reserve in glass. The Library of Congress displays five zodiacs, and the balance can be found on other important buildings throughout Washington, D.C.geography

The big question since the division between the colonies was made, L'Efant started by surveying the allotted land geography and analyzed its topography as to determine where to start. He noted wetlands and high points. From this he formed a 10-point plan:

> ➤ 1) Determine the central point. He chose Jenkin's Hill, the highest elevation This is now Capitol Hill and the center piece, (not the White House). Symbolically the "central point" in the new domocracy.

Seemingly while L'Efant's plans progressed, and the layouts of the various sectors were planned. Things concerning funding and failing other lot sales were not progressing to continue the project L'Efant quit the project and would not give the plans to anyone.

Benjamin Banneker

On the committee for the design and accomplishing the Washington D.C. project there was another architect who was highly recommended by Thomas Jefferson and hired by George Washington. His name is Benjamin Banneker, a black person who was able to save the project. He, by memory, was able to reproduce all the layout of the streets, parks and major buildings drawings. He did it in an amazing two days!

Now we think about the colonies and the ownership of slaves, an aberrant thought, and here comes Benjamin. There was a grandmother who migrated from England and married a black man named Bannaky. Their daughter also married one of their slaves and gave birth to Benjamin in 1731. Benjamin was not considered a slave because the law at that time, if the mother was a free person, it mattered not if she was bi-racial.

In fact, he was able to attend an elementary school run by Quakers and later adopted quaker habits and ideas. His brilliance began to shine when he was self-inspired to build a clock, a clock wholly made from wood. He was admired because of his invention, and he gained a reputation for perfection. In fact, it was said the clock kept perfect time for forty years. His genius was revealed by his early and later accomplishments, that propelled him to become a reputable architect, mathematician, engineer and an astronomer.

Due to his notoriety, he was able to promote social change for slavery and war.

Interestingly Benjamin published the annual Farmer's Almanac for which he did all the calculations himself. His almanac won him accords all over the planet.

He died in 1806 but left an inspirational life, remembered for his accomplishments, especially the development of the City of Washington D.C.

Documents published in 2003 and 2005 supporting the establishment of the Smithsonian Institution's National Museum of African American History and Culture in Washington, D.C. (including a report that a presidential commission planning the museum sent to the president and the Congress), also connected Banneker with L'Enfant's plan of the city of Washington.[26] When the museum opened on the National Mall in September 2016, an exhibit entitled "The Founding of America" displayed a statue of Banneker holding a small telescope while standing in front of a plan of that city.

Trivia facts about Washington, D.C. for the casual visitor I bet you didn't know.

Georgetown, the oldest part of Washington. D.C. existed in 1751 around 40 years before George Washington created our capitol.

> George Washington designated 100 acres in Virginia and Maryland The name of the central city fittingly became Washington.
> District of Columbia was named to honor Christopher Columbus
> President George Washington never slept in the White House, he actually passed away a year before the completion of construction.

- President John Adams was the first President to sleep in the White House
- A statue of Andrew Jackson on a horse is made from British cannons confiscated in the War of 1812 and is in Lafayette Square near the White House.
- If you need to use a restroom there are 35 bathrooms in the Presidents house
- The U.S. Capitol has a marble tub in the basement From 1859. Interestingly the area boarding houses had no running water and the workers had to bathe at work. It can be seen on a building tour.
- In 1878 the phone number for the White House was One (1) and the phone was not in the oval office until 1929.
- The Washington Monument completed in 1884 was the tallest building in the world at 555 feet 5-1/2" tall. writing
- The Lincoln Memorial has 36 columns each representing a state at the time on Lincoln's assassination. The architect, Henry Bacon used stone from Georgia, Tennessee, Colorado, Alabama, Indiania and Massachusetts as an example of the beauty created by unity wrought from the war.
- The U.S. Capital dome displays a 19 foot tall statue of a woman with an eagles head headdress. It weight is estimated to weigh 15,000 pounds. Its called the Statue of Freedom. It was designed by a Scottish architect William Thornton.
- The most extensive library in the world is the Library of Congress. 12,000 items are added daily and is estimated as having 157 million items as of this posting.

James Smithson, the founding donor of the Smithsonian, bequeathed his estate to establish the Smithsonian Institution in Washington, D.C., "for the increase and diffusion of knowledge." Smithson's gift inspired a unique public-private partnership that leverages an extraordinary commitment from Congress to activate additional private support to connect with more Americans. There are many other specially dedicated buildings holding many fantastic collections.

The Smithsonian, Institution holds 157 million specimens of art and objects

Smithsonian Institution, 600 Maryland Ave SW, Washington, DC

After the Civil War, 186 and legal-1865, Washington expanded is original boundaries. It remains a territory, not a state, and since 1974, has been governed by a duly elected mayor and has a city council, which Congress retains with veto power.

It has an interesting street layout originally designed in a mystical cosmic way and most have trouble initially navigating the streets.

EPILOGUE

As I look back over time spanning almost five years in just researching and then the mental work to assemble all my notes, actually a score of books read, learned papers, references from trusted sources, and my family's personal involvement reaching back to 850 AD in France to the seventeenth century, it was thought to be an almost impossible task.

I found that this would not properly fulfill or actually prove that people in societies who were conquerors had successes that drew their conquered peoples together by treating them with fairness, with fair rules, and placing like-minded, trusted people from the conquering entity or from within the population to advance and improve themselves with, and in some cases, to self-rule. I needed more concrete examples.

I knew of many conquerors like Alexander, the Romans, and the Greeks as famous examples—ones that built infrastructure like roads, buildings, aqueducts for water and bridges, armies and navies, and economic structures to sustain the populations, giving them security and structure to further their existence and growth. Examples of these infrastructure improvements are physically plentiful in a number of societies, but did they have sustained "right-minded" governments was the question.

What I looked for were ancient governments, or older than ours, with varying, sustained, long-term histories that were societal examples for a growing world. By now, you probably have read about the societies I exampled that actually blew through the 2,024 AD years and traveled back another 2,496 years into the BC era, totaling an amazing 4,520 years of history. I found many examples of governmental structures—about 24 of them—with different governmental structures, of which I studied for what I looked for. This research for the right examples that I wanted for our examples had some that had all, then some that had some of the qualities, and some that were not sustained for any long period of time. My education on societies definitely rose to a higher level of understanding of governmental structures.

What was I actually looking for?

The answer was simple: I was living in a model that has given us all that I articulated above. Our government provides us with a Constitution, a Bill of Rights, a legal rights structure, functional militaries, separate governmental agencies, layered law-making and control assemblies, a states' rights structure, nationwide infrastructure, internal tax, legal, and policing agencies, and there are more.

I was looking for a Rule of Law governmental example with checkmate control, and I found many that I did example in this manuscript that exemplified not a perfect societal structure but ones, including ours, that have the ability to handle and respond to societal issues and solve them without violating the Rule of Law guidelines protecting each and every one of us.

There was much that I wished to cover, but my goal was to give you, my reader, materials not commonly known. I tried not to be someone parroting well-worn subject matter but to give you something you probably did not know. How I tested the subject matter inclusion was to quiz others about things like the Iroquois involvement in actually providing their constitution as an example of Rule of Law where their spirit guided them to their form of governing that we actually included in our constitution. Another was the inclusion of Washington's spies. Another was my coverage of the ladies who supported our founding fathers. One I most personally enjoyed was including the ladies who fought in what was considered a man's job in the army.

I really enjoyed bringing this assemblage of what all coalesced into a country we love and cherish. I hope my work and the excerpted work of reference materials gleaned from what seemed like countless sources have pleased you.

Hon. James Robert Boynton